PUBLISHER
DAMIAN A. WASSEL

EDITOR-IN-CHIEF
ADRIAN F. WASSEL

ART DIRECTOR
NATHAN C. GOODEN

BRANDING & DESIGN
TIM DANIEL

DIRECTOR OF MARKETING
KIM McLEAN

PRINCIPAL
DAMIAN A. WASSEL, SR.

RICARDO MO
WRITER

TONY GREGORI
ILLUSTRATOR

CLAUDIA AGUIRRE
COLORIST

RYAN FERRIER & KIM McLEAN
LETTERERS

VAULT COMICS
PRESENTS

Deuce OF Hearts

CHAPTER

1

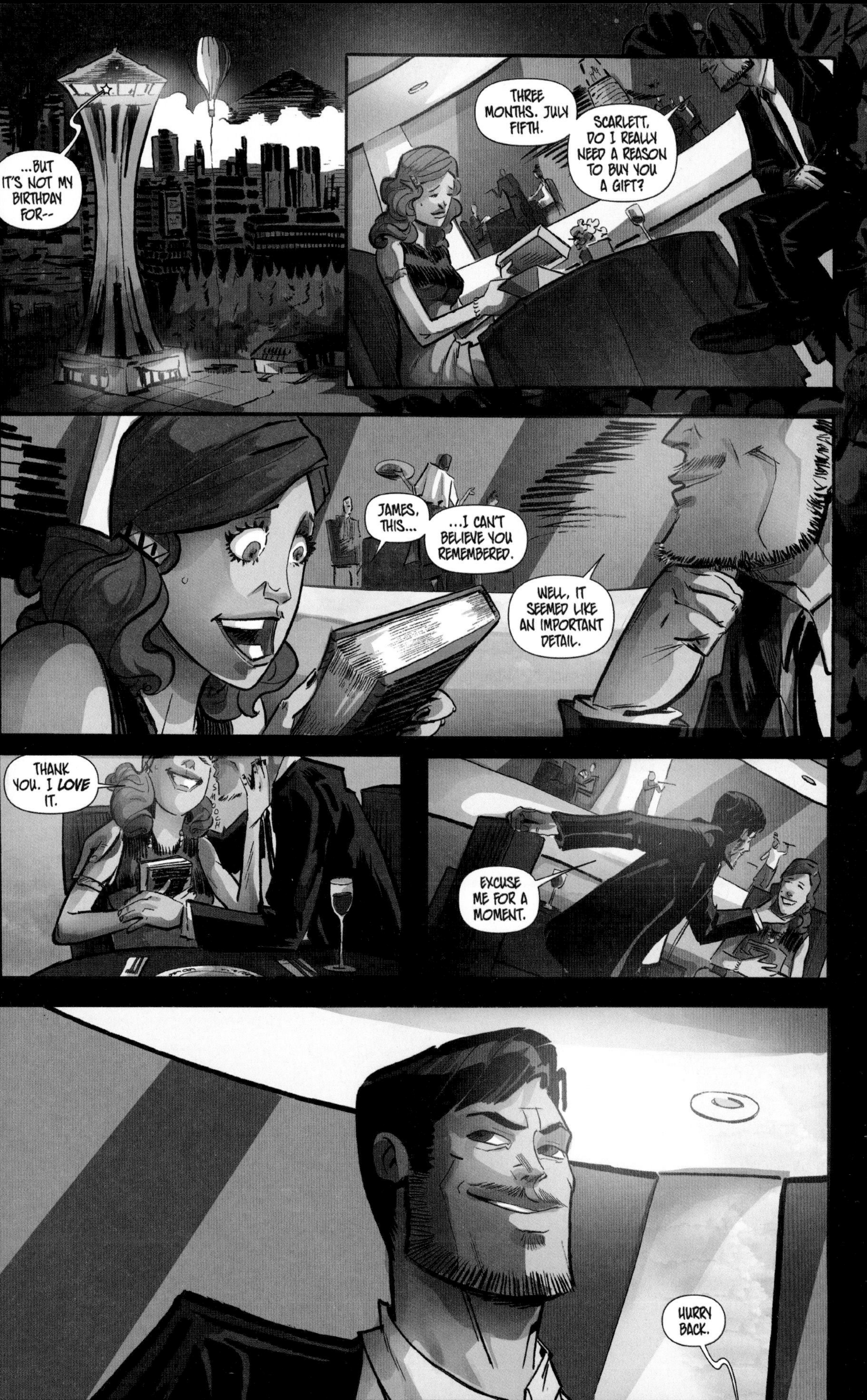
...BUT IT'S NOT MY BIRTHDAY FOR--
THREE MONTHS. JULY FIFTH.
SCARLETT, DO I REALLY NEED A REASON TO BUY YOU A GIFT?
JAMES, THIS...
...I CAN'T BELIEVE YOU REMEMBERED.
WELL, IT SEEMED LIKE AN IMPORTANT DETAIL.
THANK YOU. I LOVE IT.
SMOOCH
EXCUSE ME FOR A MOMENT.
HURRY BACK.

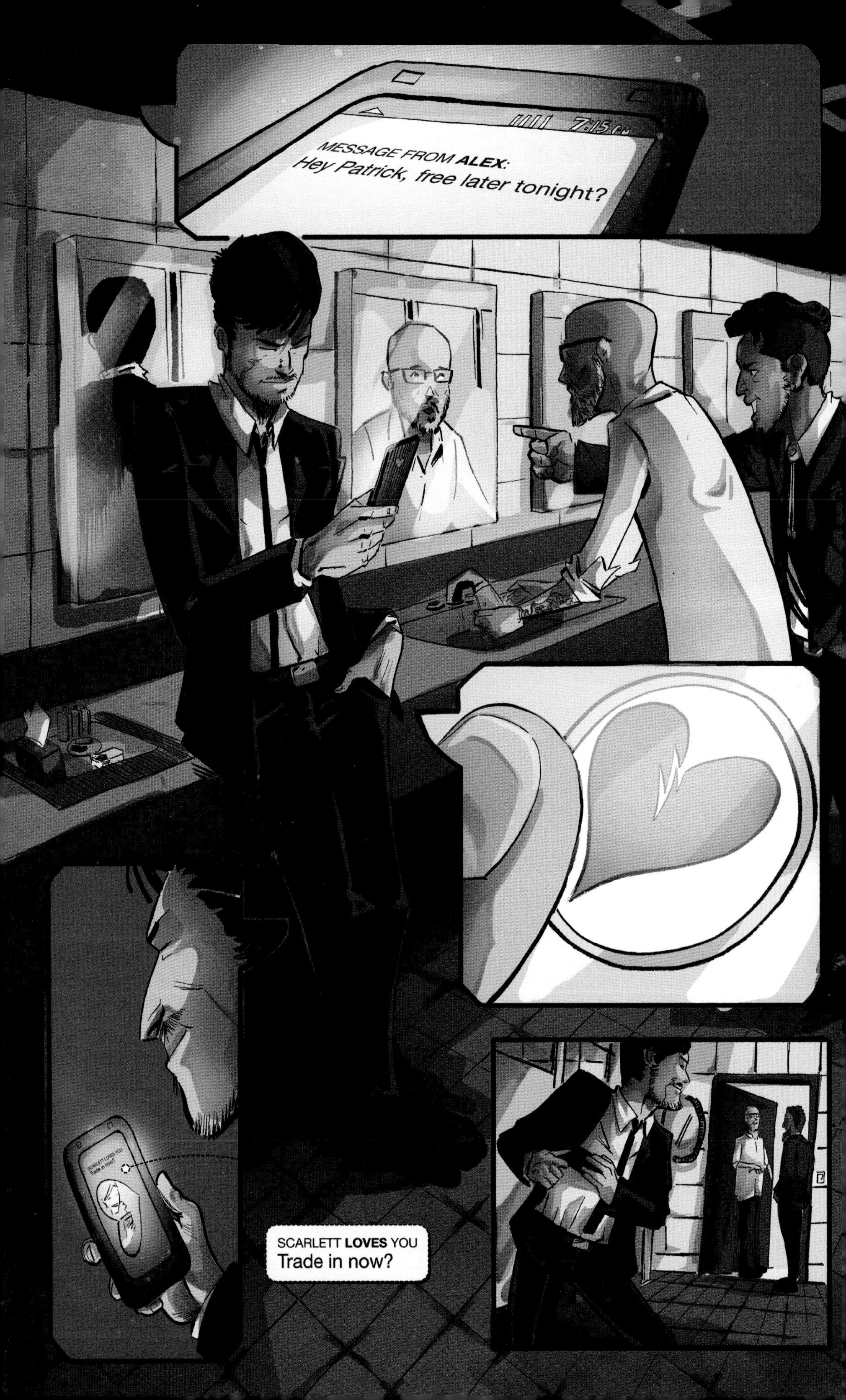
MESSAGE FROM **ALEX**:
Hey Patrick, free later tonight?
SCARLETT **LOVES** YOU
Trade in now?

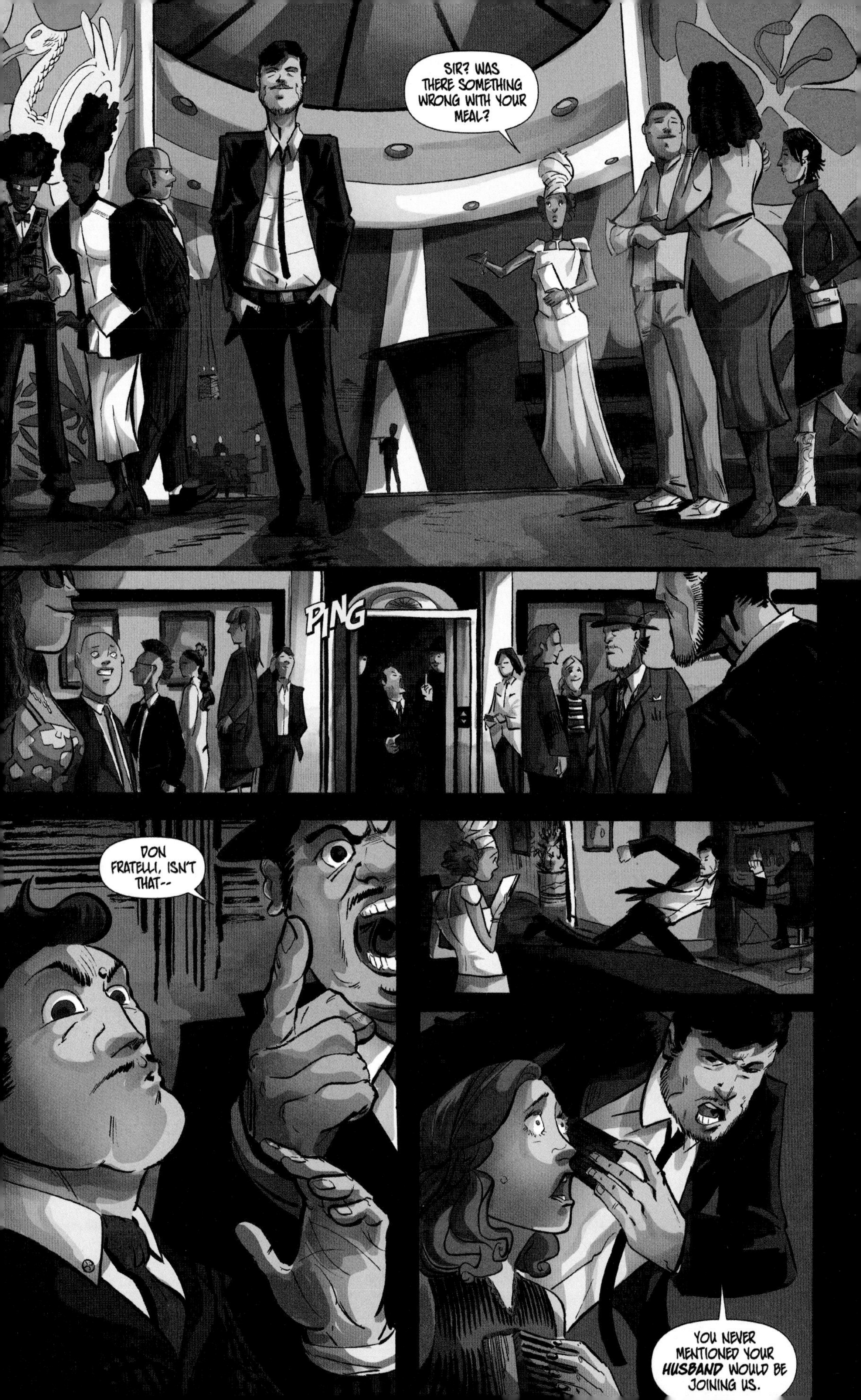
SIR? WAS THERE SOMETHING WRONG WITH YOUR MEAL?
PING
DON FRATELLI, ISN'T THAT--
YOU NEVER MENTIONED YOUR **HUSBAND** WOULD BE JOINING US.

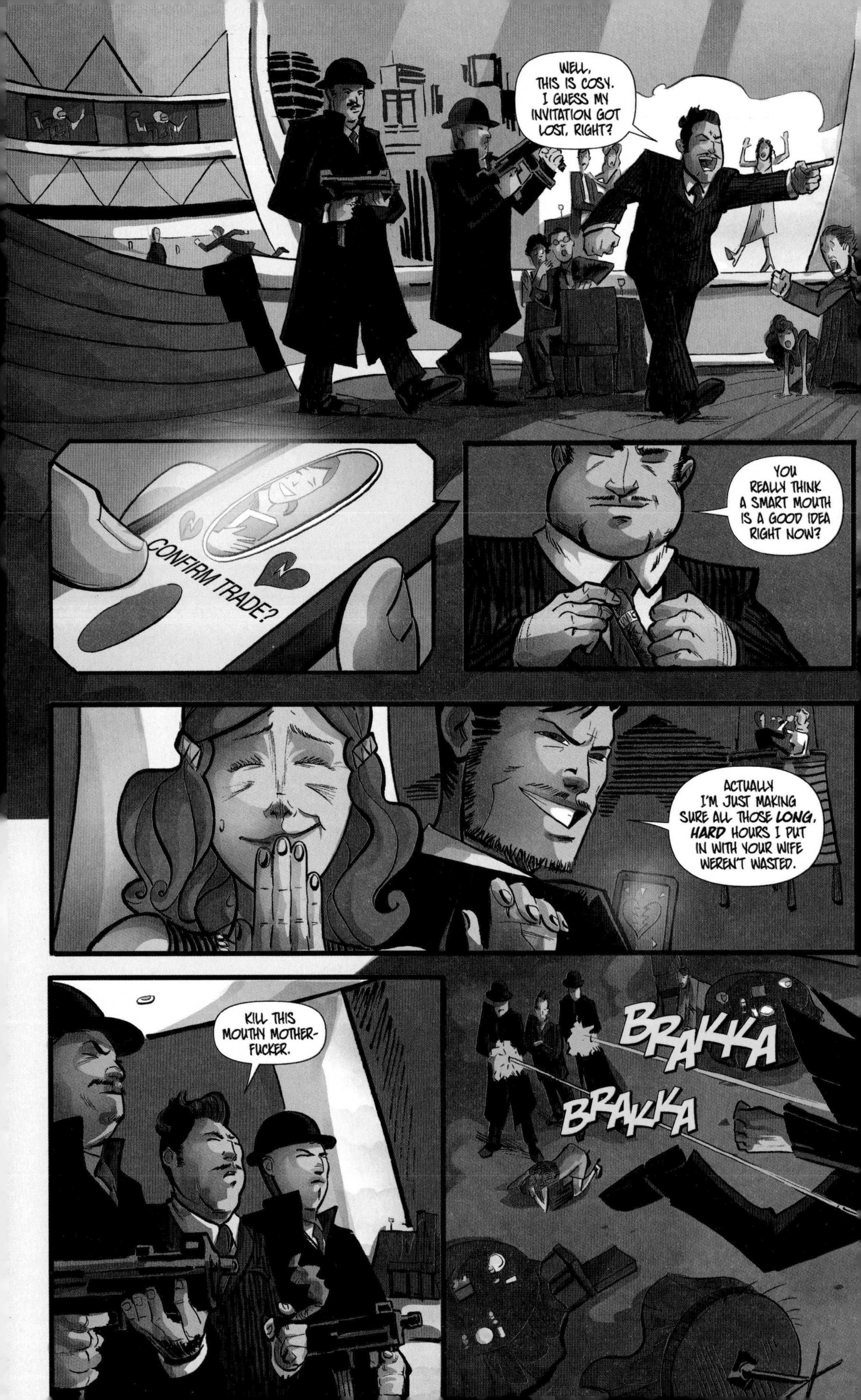
WELL, THIS IS COSY. I GUESS MY INVITATION GOT LOST, RIGHT?
CONFIRM TRADE?
YOU REALLY THINK A SMART MOUTH IS A GOOD IDEA RIGHT NOW?
ACTUALLY I'M JUST MAKING SURE ALL THOSE **LONG, HARD** HOURS I PUT IN WITH YOUR WIFE WEREN'T WASTED.
KILL THIS MOUTHY MOTHER-FUCKER.
BRAKKA
BRAKKA

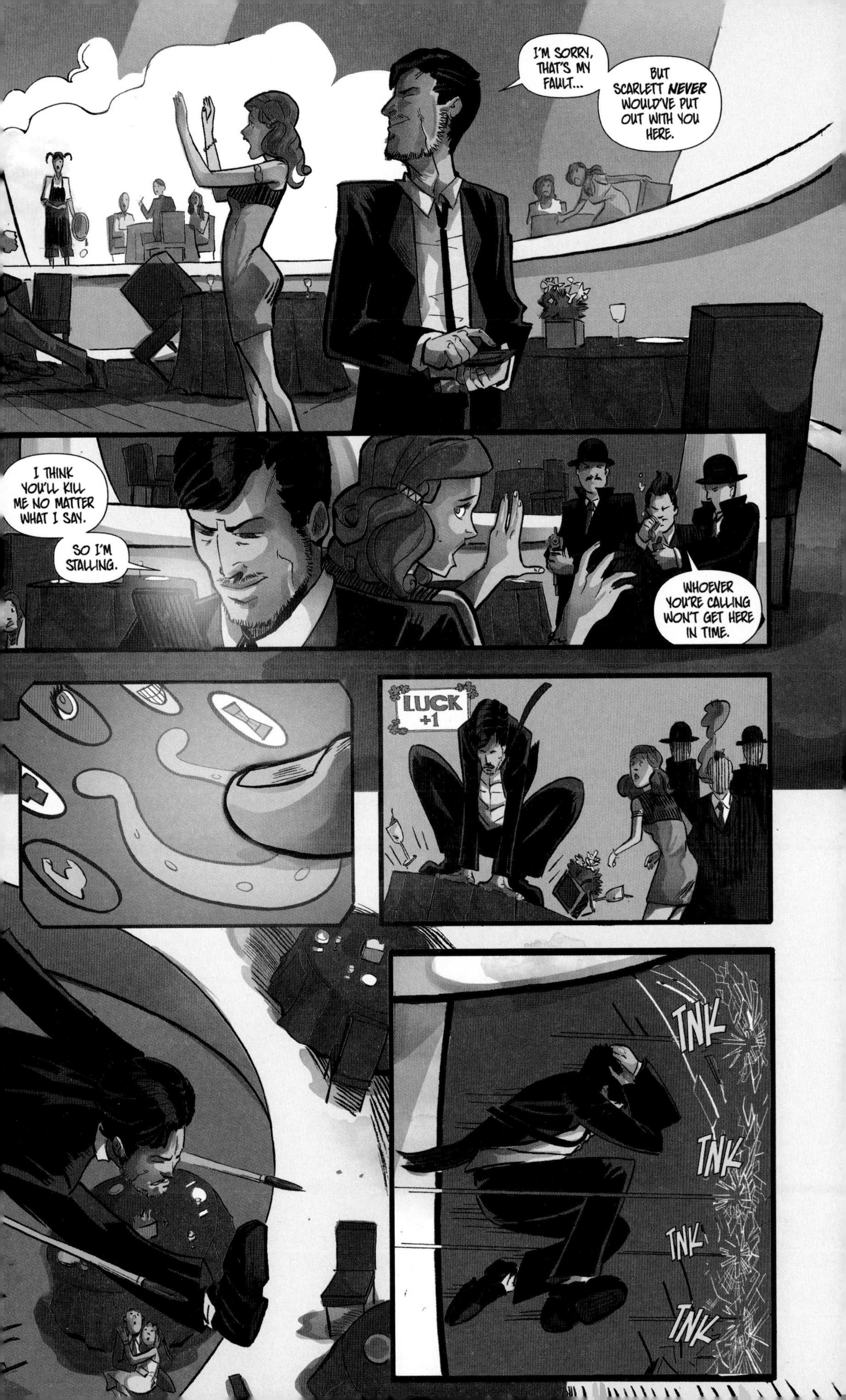
I'M SORRY, THAT'S MY FAULT...
BUT SCARLETT **NEVER** WOULD'VE PUT OUT WITH YOU HERE.
I THINK YOU'LL KILL ME NO MATTER WHAT I SAY.
SO I'M STALLING.
WHOEVER YOU'RE CALLING WON'T GET HERE IN TIME.
LUCK +1
TNK
TNK
TNK
TNK

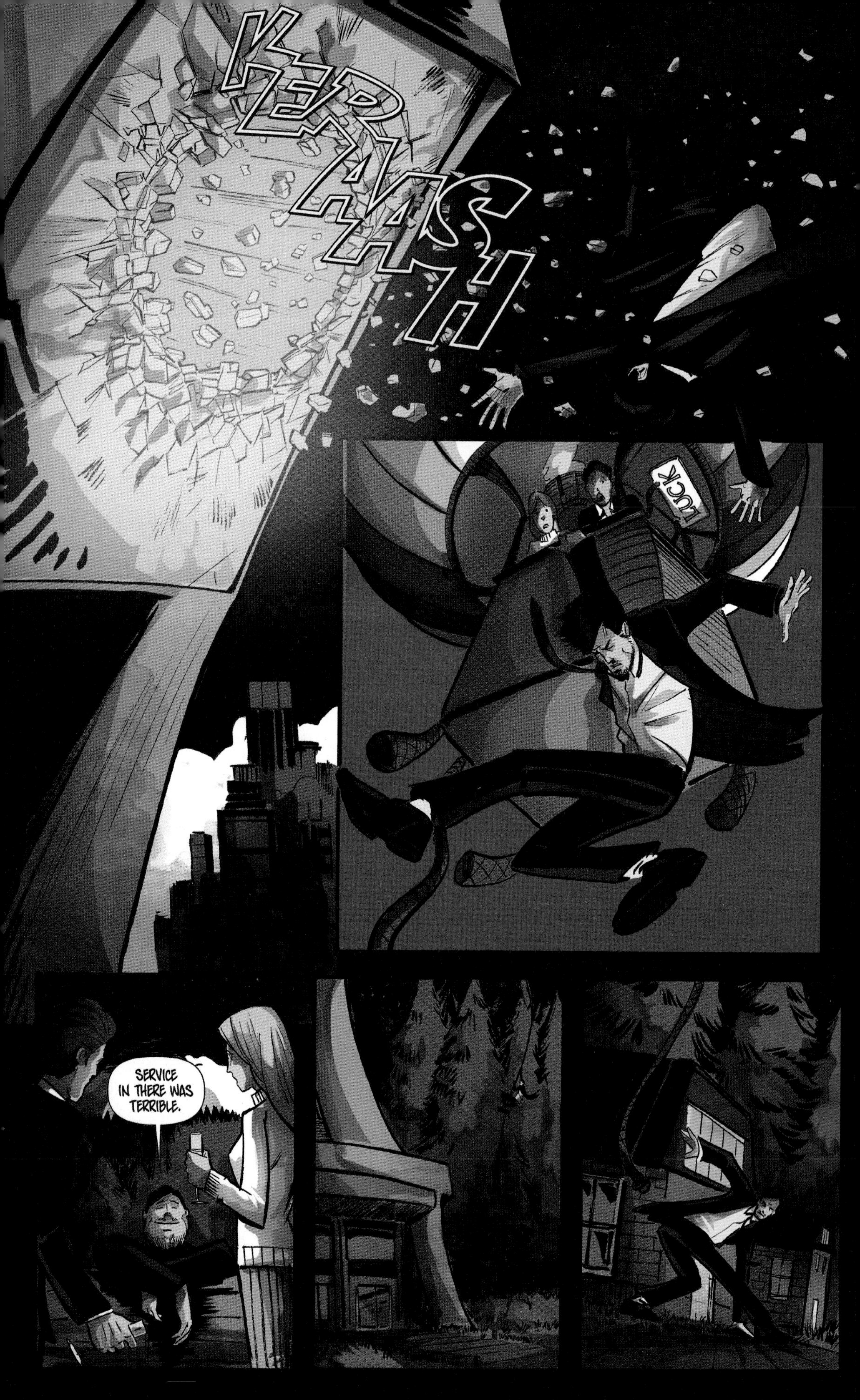
KERASH
LUCK
SERVICE IN THERE WAS TERRIBLE.

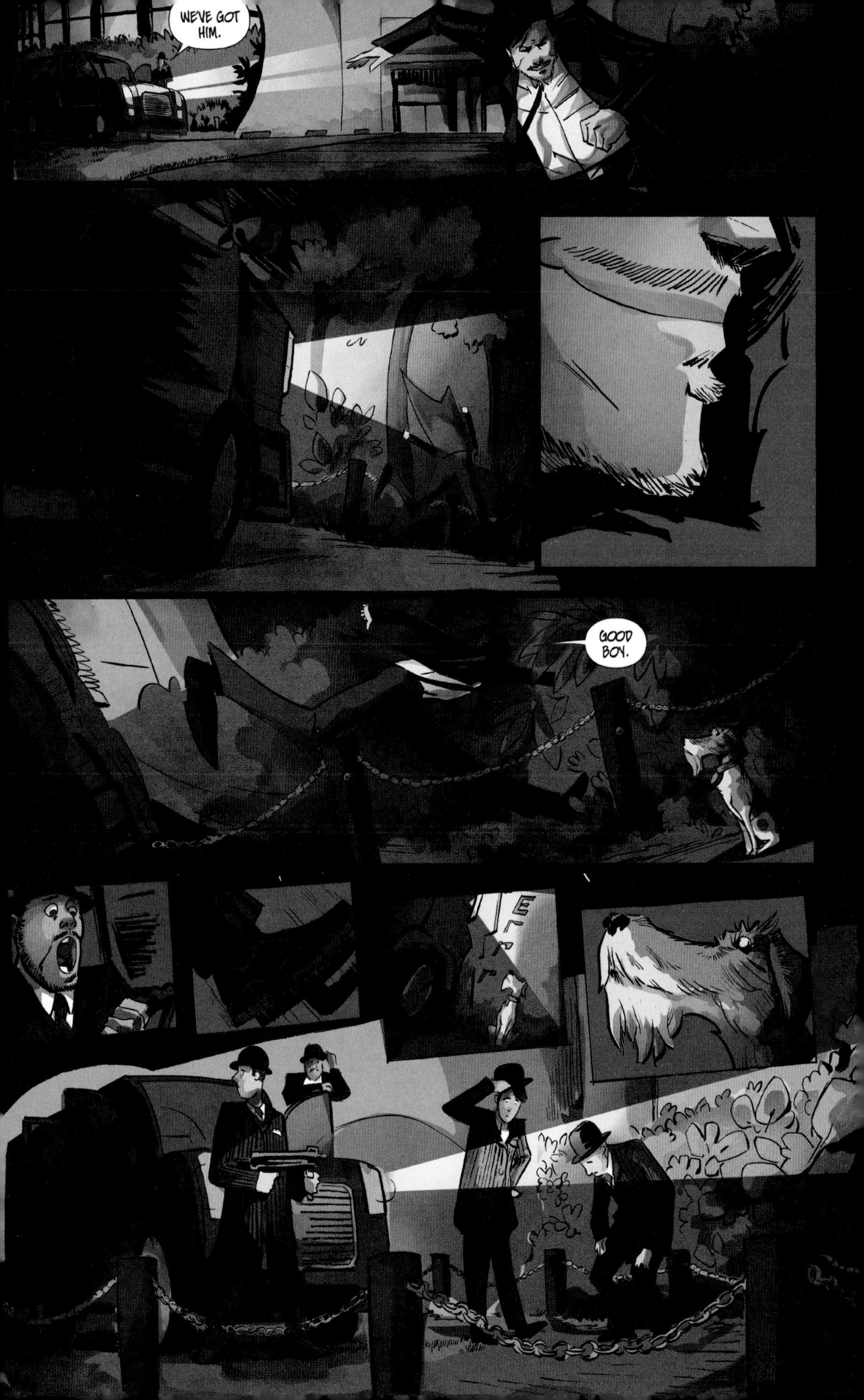
WE'VE GOT HIM.
GOOD BOY.

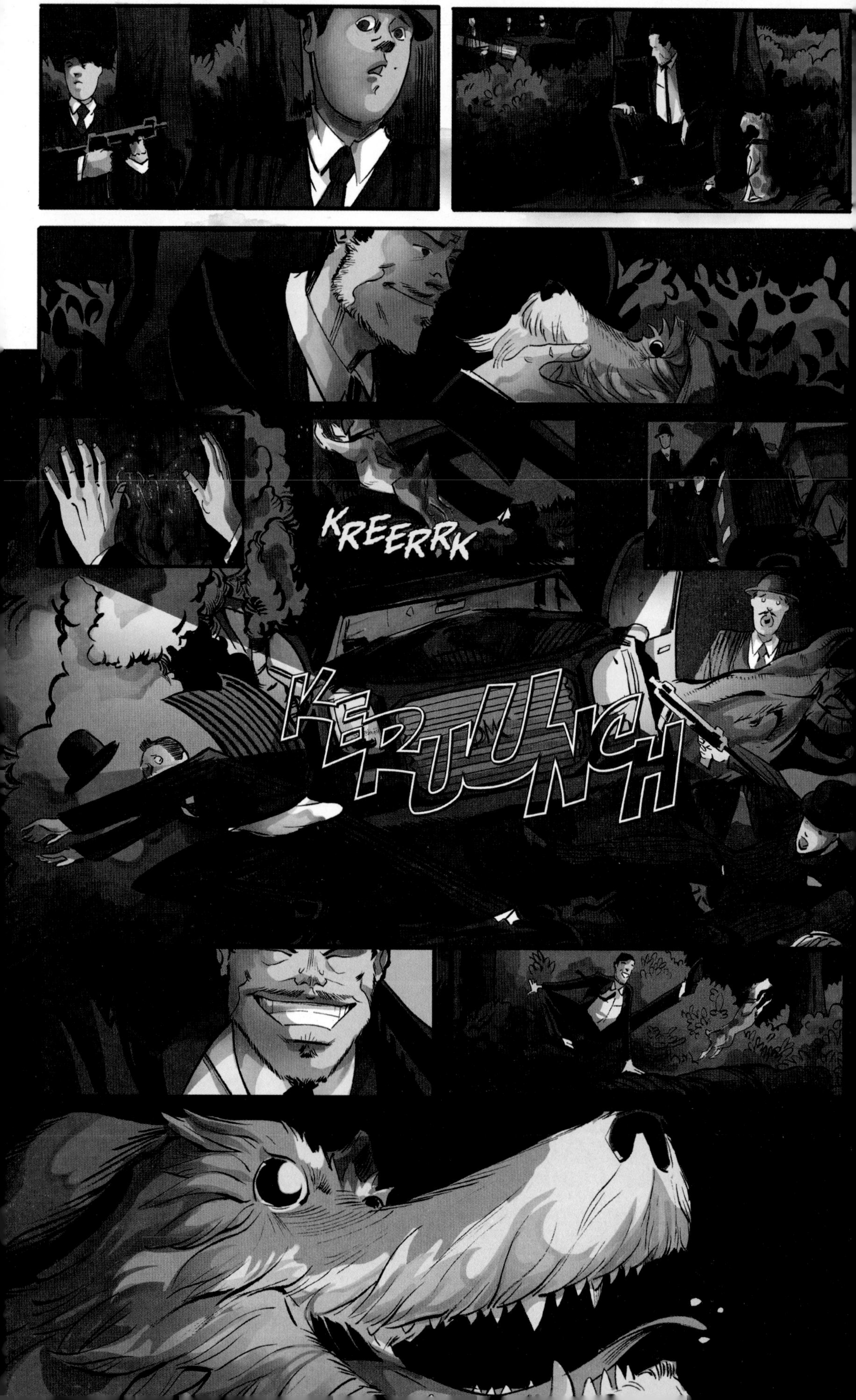
KREERRK
KERUUNCH

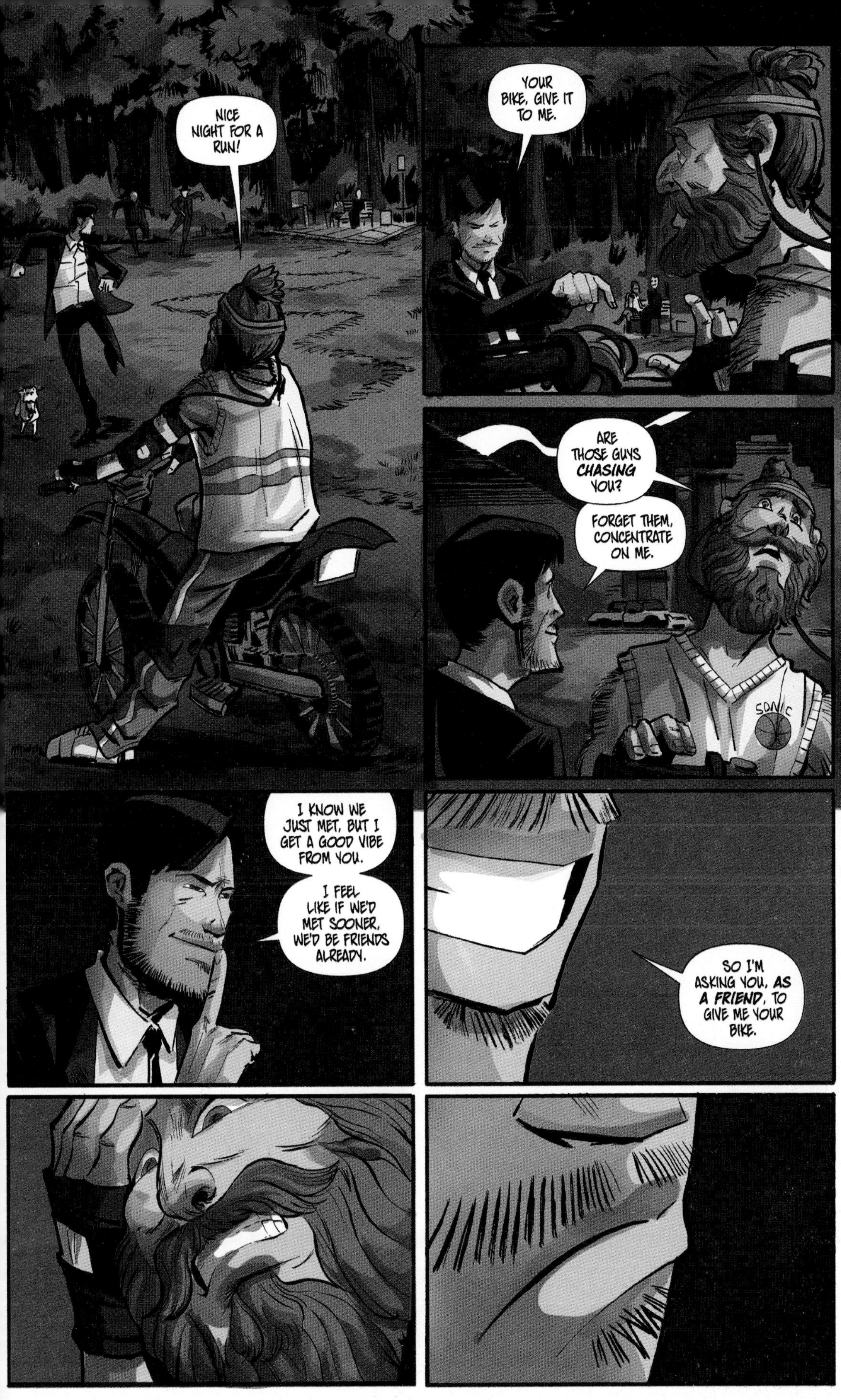

NICE NIGHT FOR A RUN!
YOUR BIKE, GIVE IT TO ME.
ARE THOSE GUYS CHASING YOU?
FORGET THEM, CONCENTRATE ON ME.
SONIC
I KNOW WE JUST MET, BUT I GET A GOOD VIBE FROM YOU.
I FEEL LIKE IF WE'D MET SOONER, WE'D BE FRIENDS ALREADY.
SO I'M ASKING YOU, AS A FRIEND, TO GIVE ME YOUR BIKE.

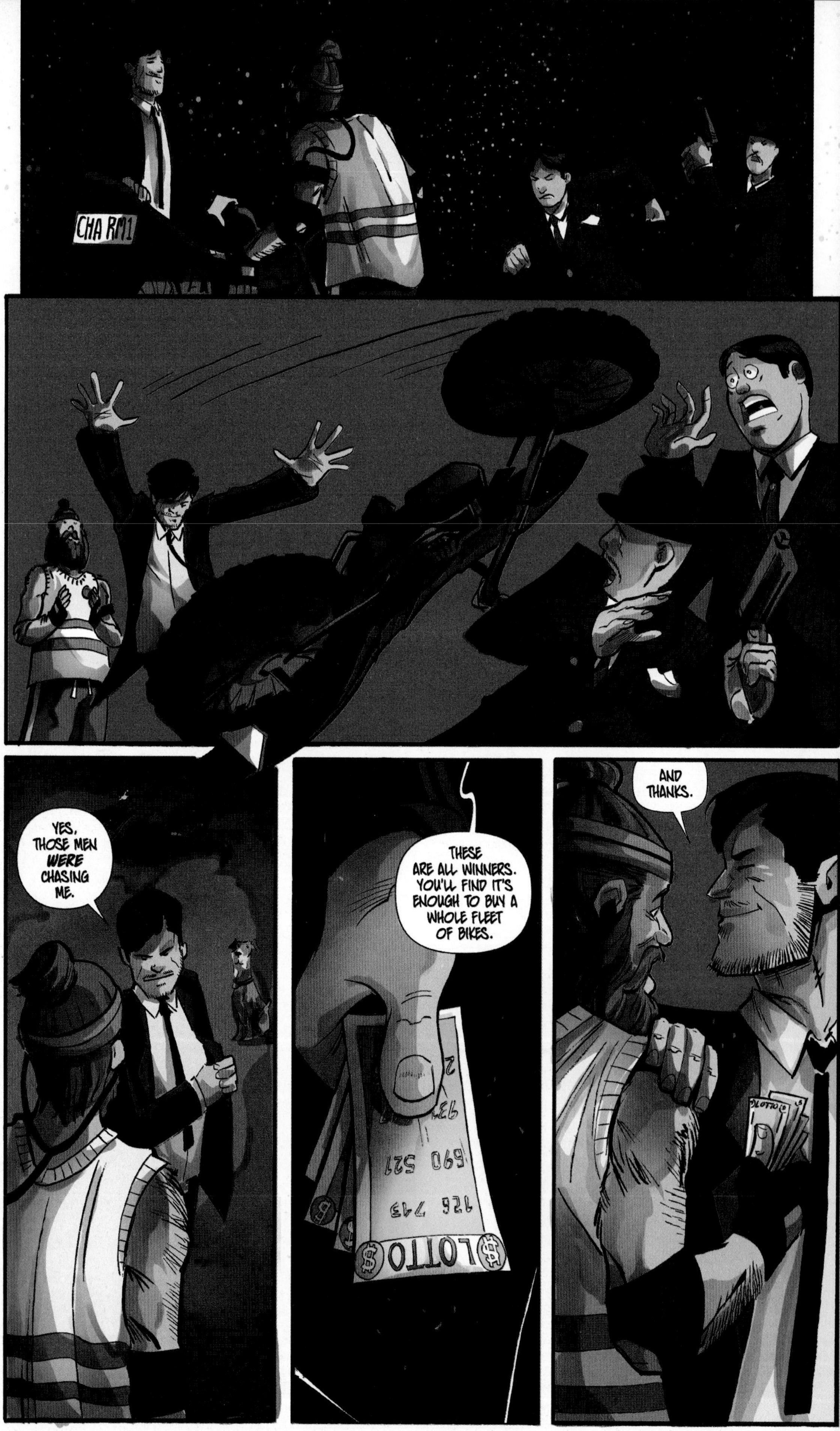
CHA RM1
YES, THOSE MEN *WERE* CHASING ME.
THESE ARE ALL WINNERS. YOU'LL FIND IT'S ENOUGH TO BUY A WHOLE FLEET OF BIKES.
AND THANKS.

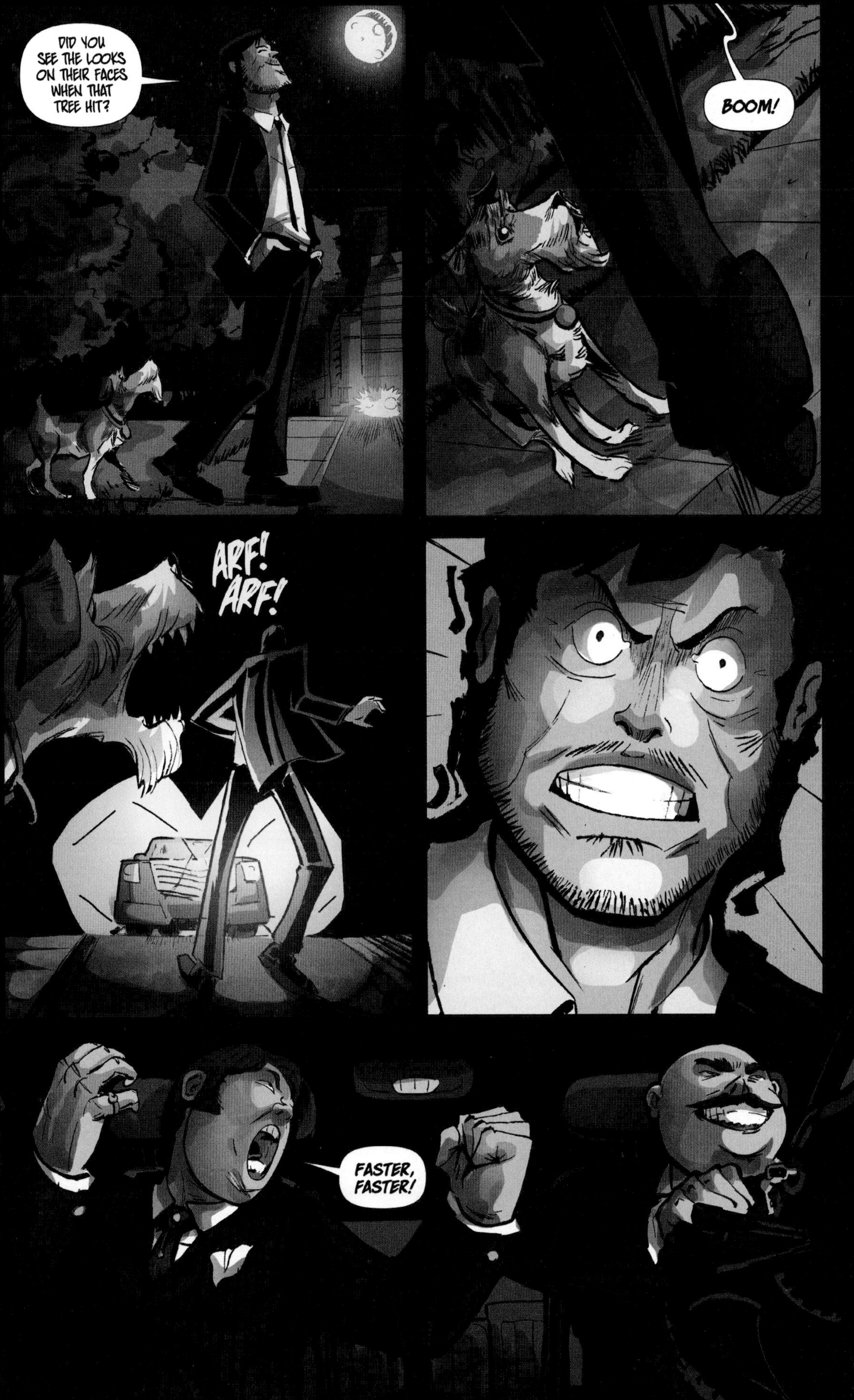
DID YOU SEE THE LOOKS ON THEIR FACES WHEN THAT TREE HIT?
BOOM!
ARF! ARF!
FASTER, FASTER!

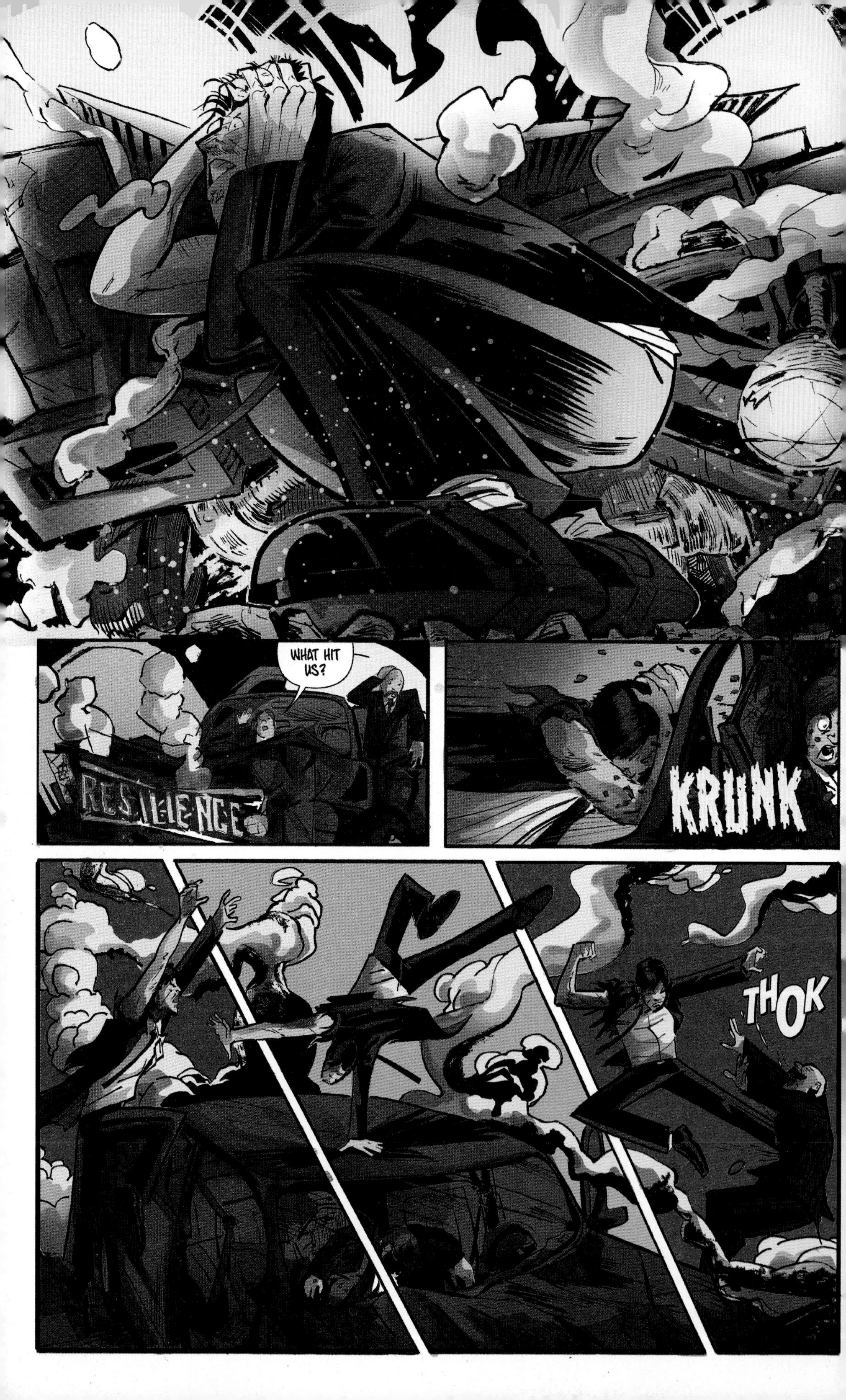
WHAT HIT US?
RESILIENCE
KRUNK
THOK

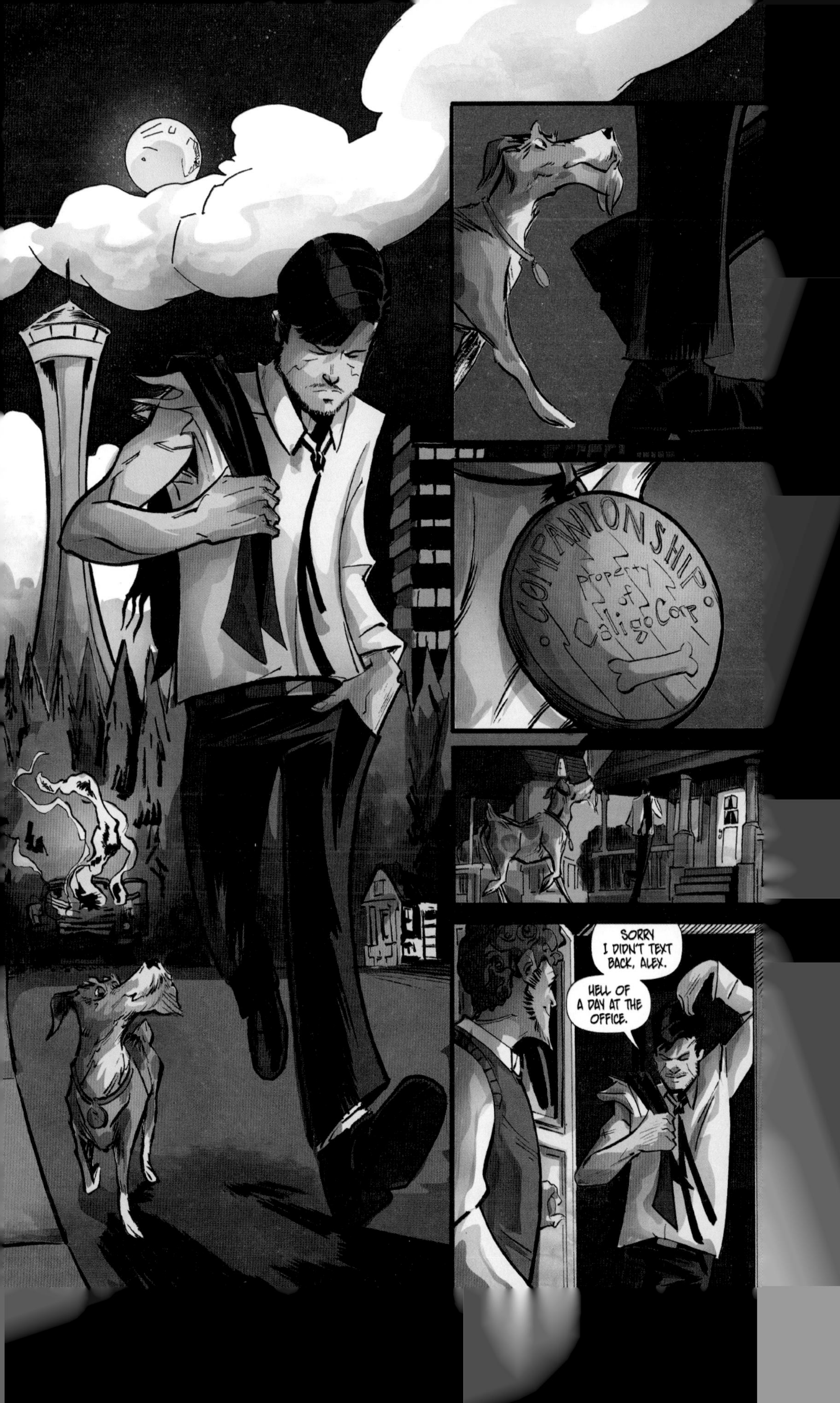
COMPANIONSHIP
Property of Caligo Corp
SORRY I DIDN'T TEXT BACK, ALEX.
HELL OF A DAY AT THE OFFICE.

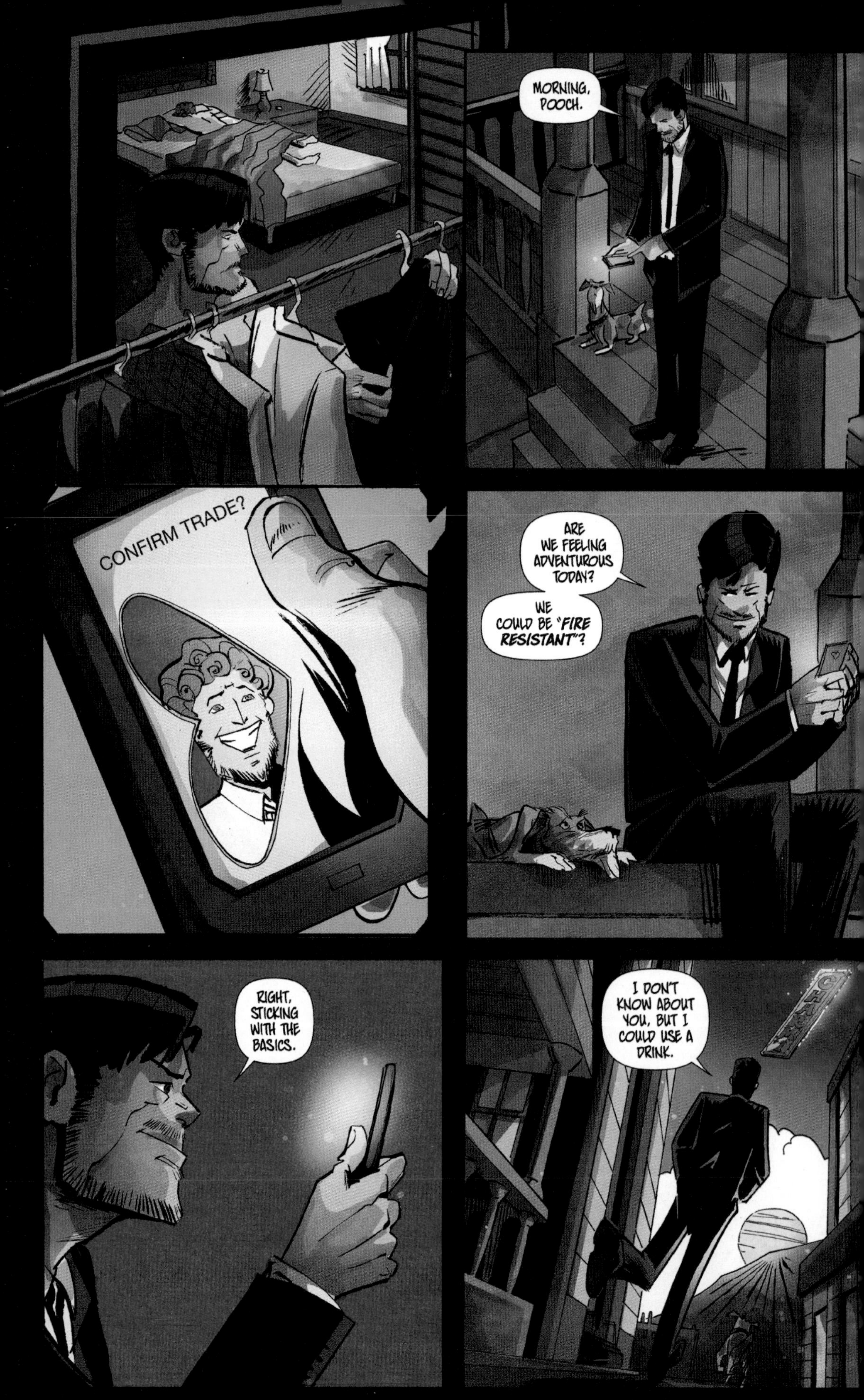
MORNING, POOCH.
CONFIRM TRADE?
ARE WE FEELING ADVENTUROUS TODAY?
WE COULD BE "FIRE RESISTANT"?
RIGHT, STICKING WITH THE BASICS.
I DON'T KNOW ABOUT YOU, BUT I COULD USE A DRINK.

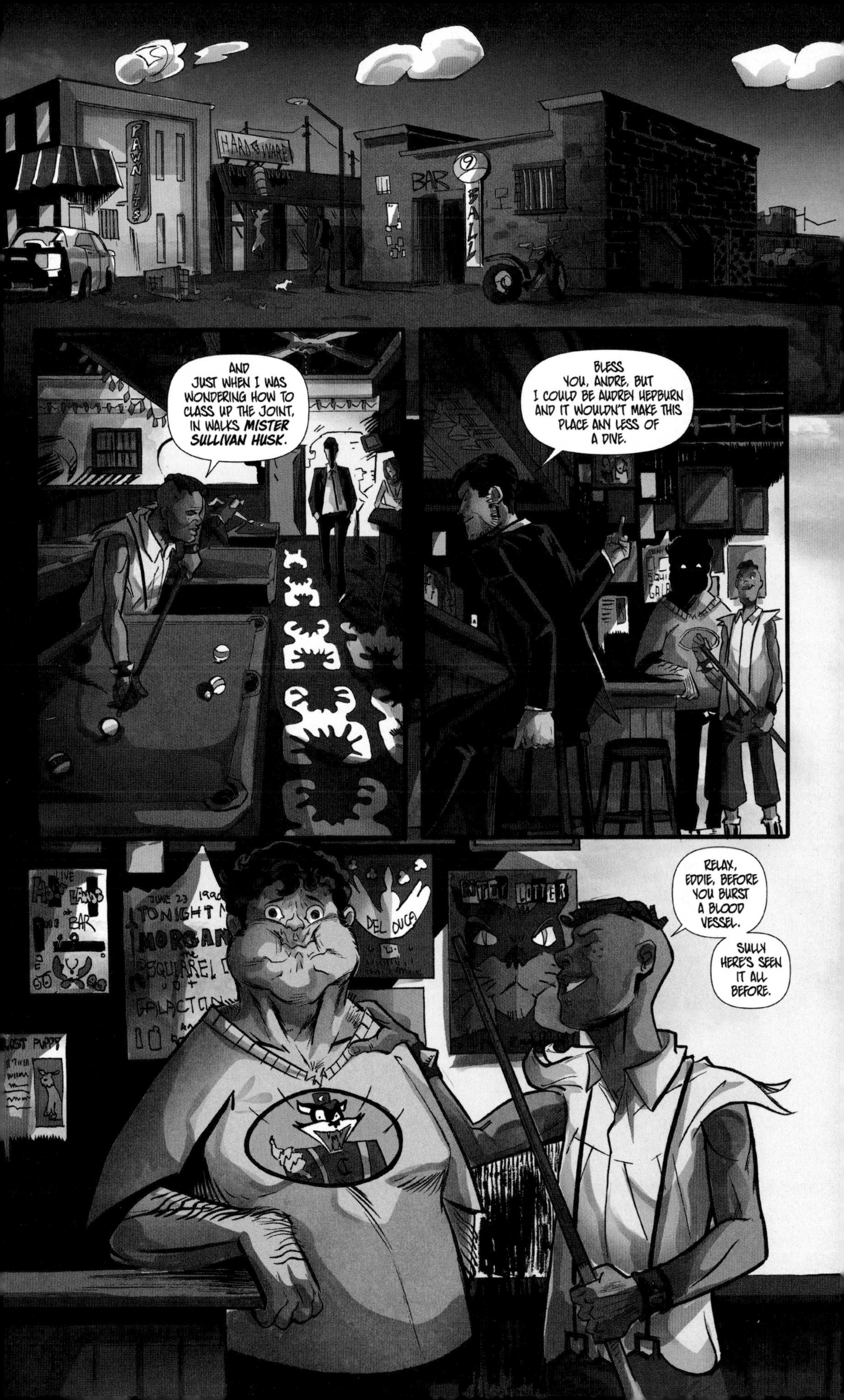
HARD WARE
PAWN IT$
BAR
9
BALL
AND JUST WHEN I WAS WONDERING HOW TO CLASS UP THE JOINT, IN WALKS MISTER SULLIVAN HUSK.
BLESS YOU, ANDRE, BUT I COULD BE AUDREY HEPBURN AND IT WOULDN'T MAKE THIS PLACE ANY LESS OF A DIVE.
TONIGHT
MORGAN
SQUIRREL
GALACTI
DEL DUCA
LOST PUPPY
RELAX, EDDIE, BEFORE YOU BURST A BLOOD VESSEL.
SULLY HERE'S SEEN IT ALL BEFORE.

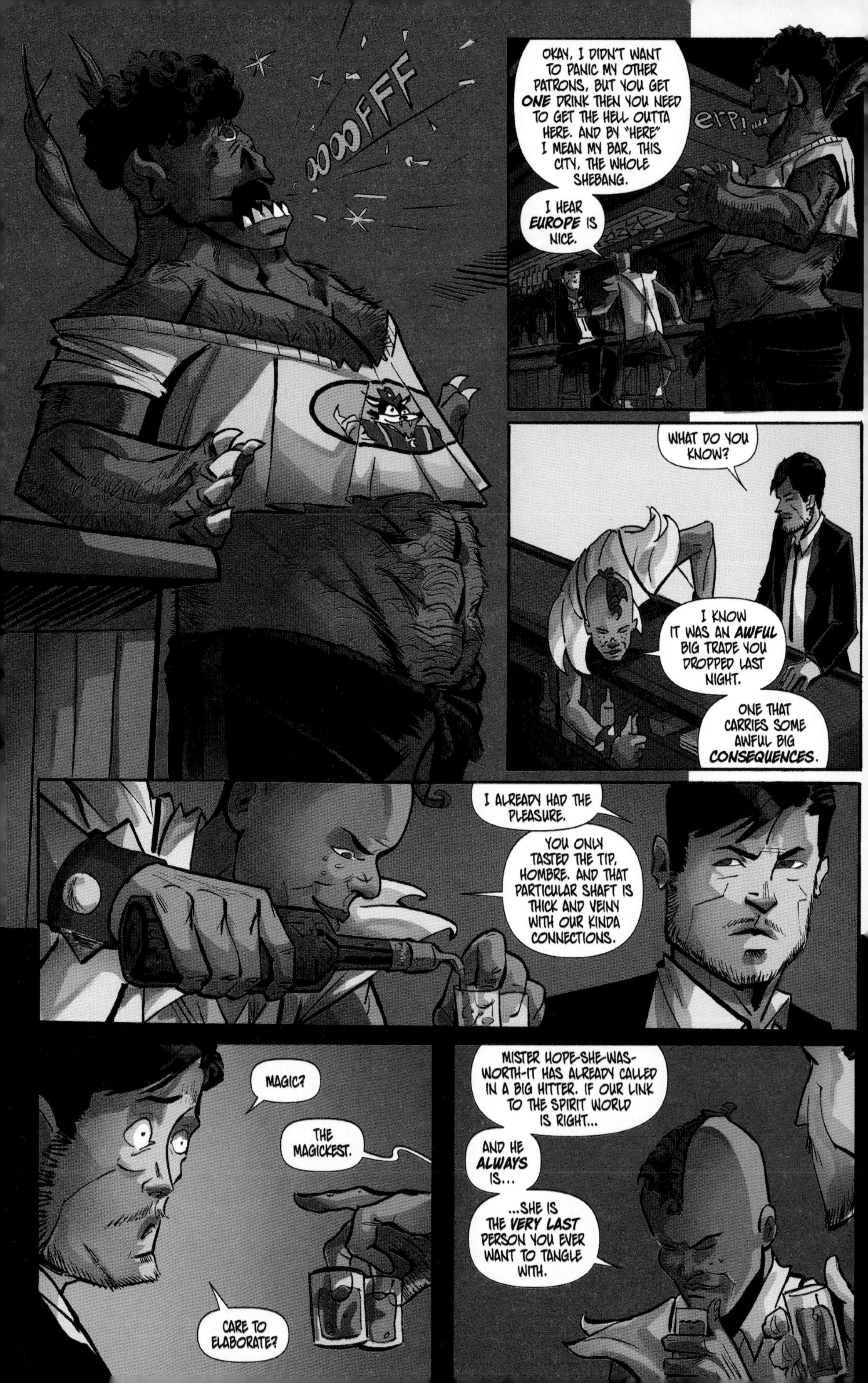
OOOOFFF
OKAY, I DIDN'T WANT TO PANIC MY OTHER PATRONS, BUT YOU GET ONE DRINK THEN YOU NEED TO GET THE HELL OUTTA HERE. AND BY "HERE" I MEAN MY BAR, THIS CITY, THE WHOLE SHEBANG.
I HEAR EUROPE IS NICE.
erp!
WHAT DO YOU KNOW?
I KNOW IT WAS AN AWFUL BIG TRADE YOU DROPPED LAST NIGHT.
ONE THAT CARRIES SOME AWFUL BIG CONSEQUENCES.
I ALREADY HAD THE PLEASURE.
YOU ONLY TASTED THE TIP, HOMBRE. AND THAT PARTICULAR SHAFT IS THICK AND VEINY WITH OUR KINDA CONNECTIONS.
MAGIC?
THE MAGICKEST.
CARE TO ELABORATE?
MISTER HOPE-SHE-WAS-WORTH-IT HAS ALREADY CALLED IN A BIG HITTER. IF OUR LINK TO THE SPIRIT WORLD IS RIGHT...
AND HE ALWAYS IS...
...SHE IS THE VERY LAST PERSON YOU EVER WANT TO TANGLE WITH.

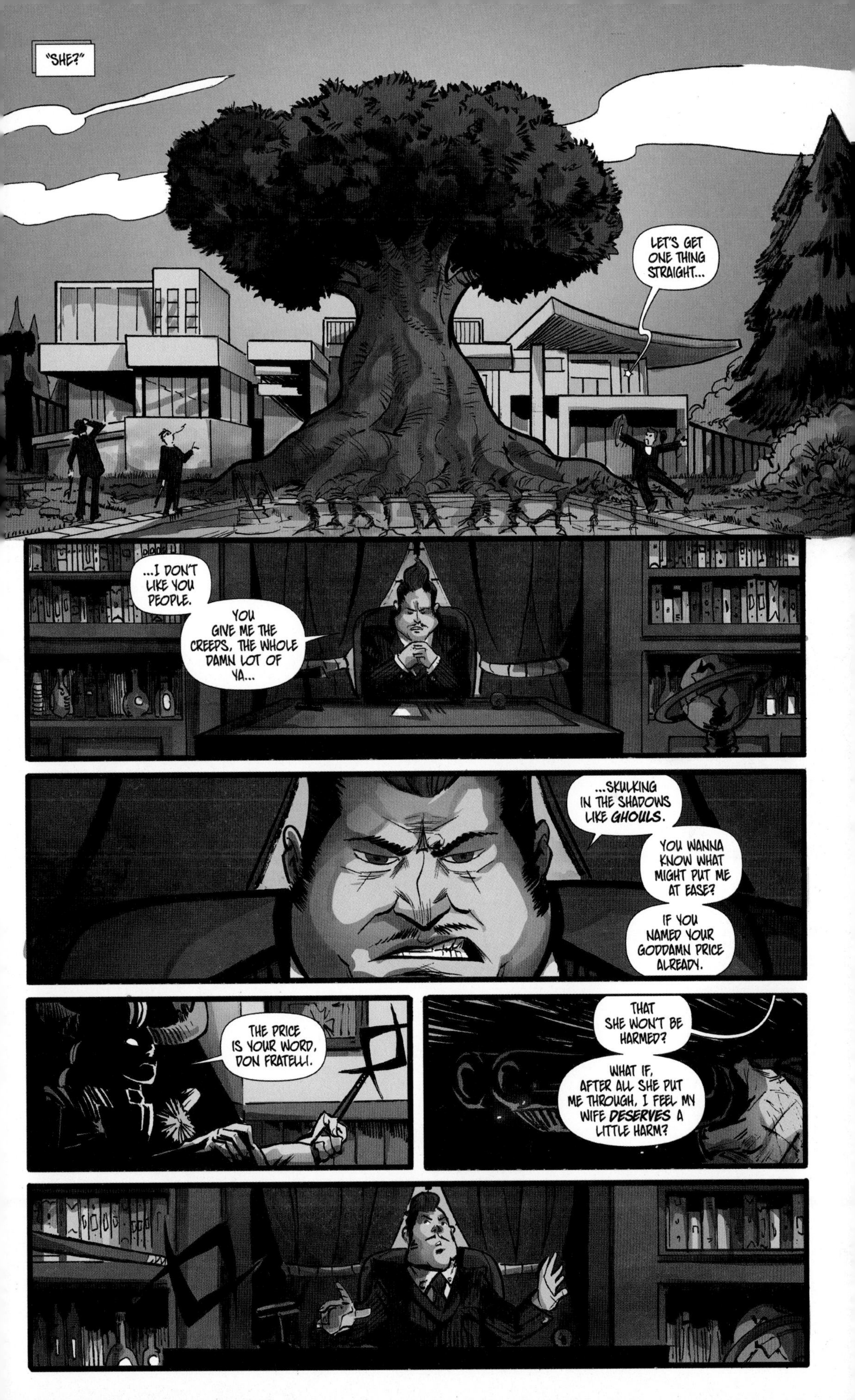
"SHE?"
LET'S GET ONE THING STRAIGHT...
...I DON'T LIKE YOU PEOPLE.
YOU GIVE ME THE CREEPS, THE WHOLE DAMN LOT OF YA...
...SKULKING IN THE SHADOWS LIKE GHOULS.
YOU WANNA KNOW WHAT MIGHT PUT ME AT EASE?
IF YOU NAMED YOUR GODDAMN PRICE ALREADY.
THE PRICE IS YOUR WORD, DON FRATELLI.
THAT SHE WON'T BE HARMED?
WHAT IF, AFTER ALL SHE PUT ME THROUGH, I FEEL MY WIFE DESERVES A LITTLE HARM?

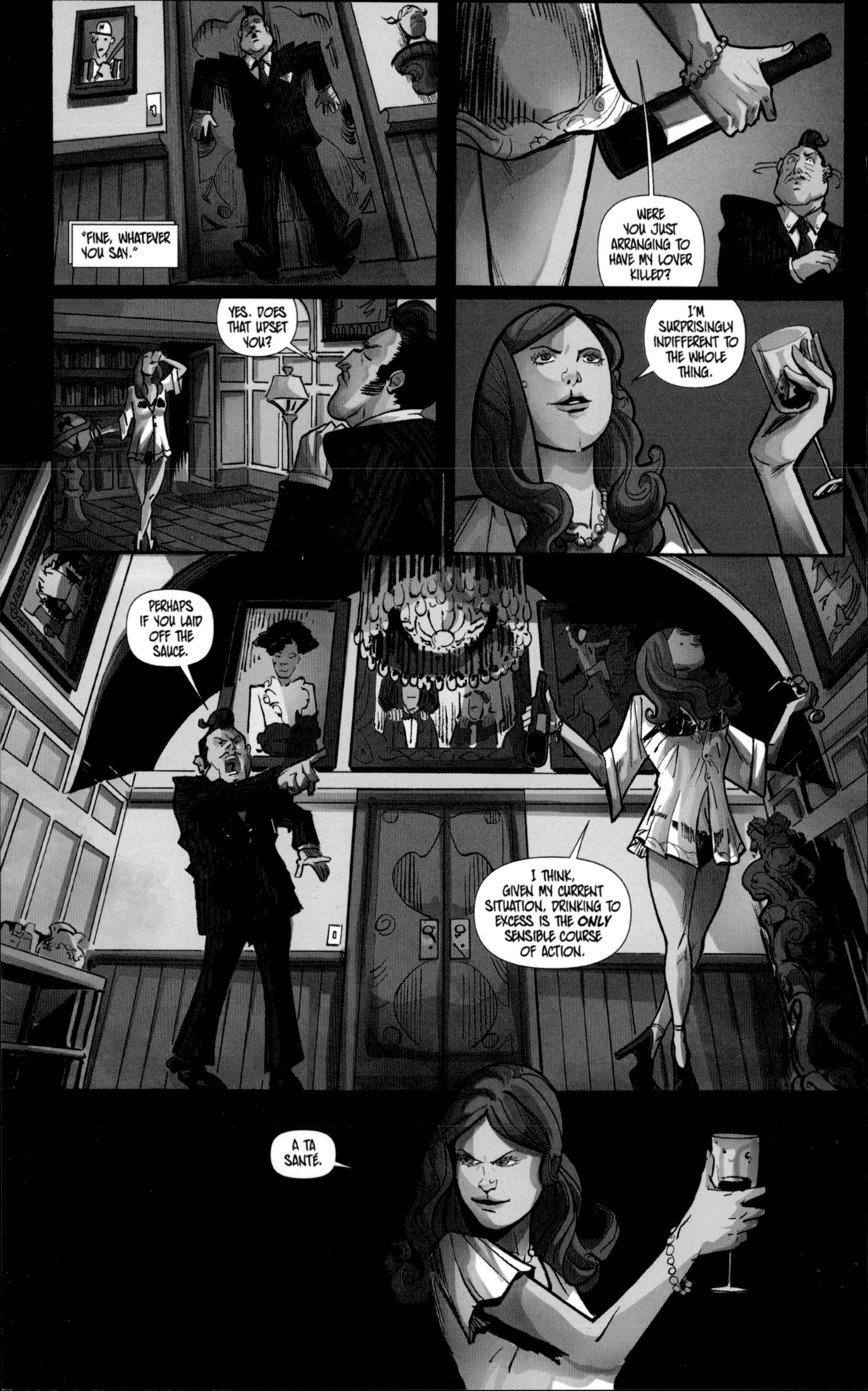
"FINE, WHATEVER YOU SAY."
WERE YOU JUST ARRANGING TO HAVE MY LOVER KILLED?
YES. DOES THAT UPSET YOU?
I'M SURPRISINGLY INDIFFERENT TO THE WHOLE THING.
PERHAPS IF YOU LAID OFF THE SAUCE.
I THINK, GIVEN MY CURRENT SITUATION, DRINKING TO EXCESS IS THE **ONLY** SENSIBLE COURSE OF ACTION.
A TA SANTÉ.

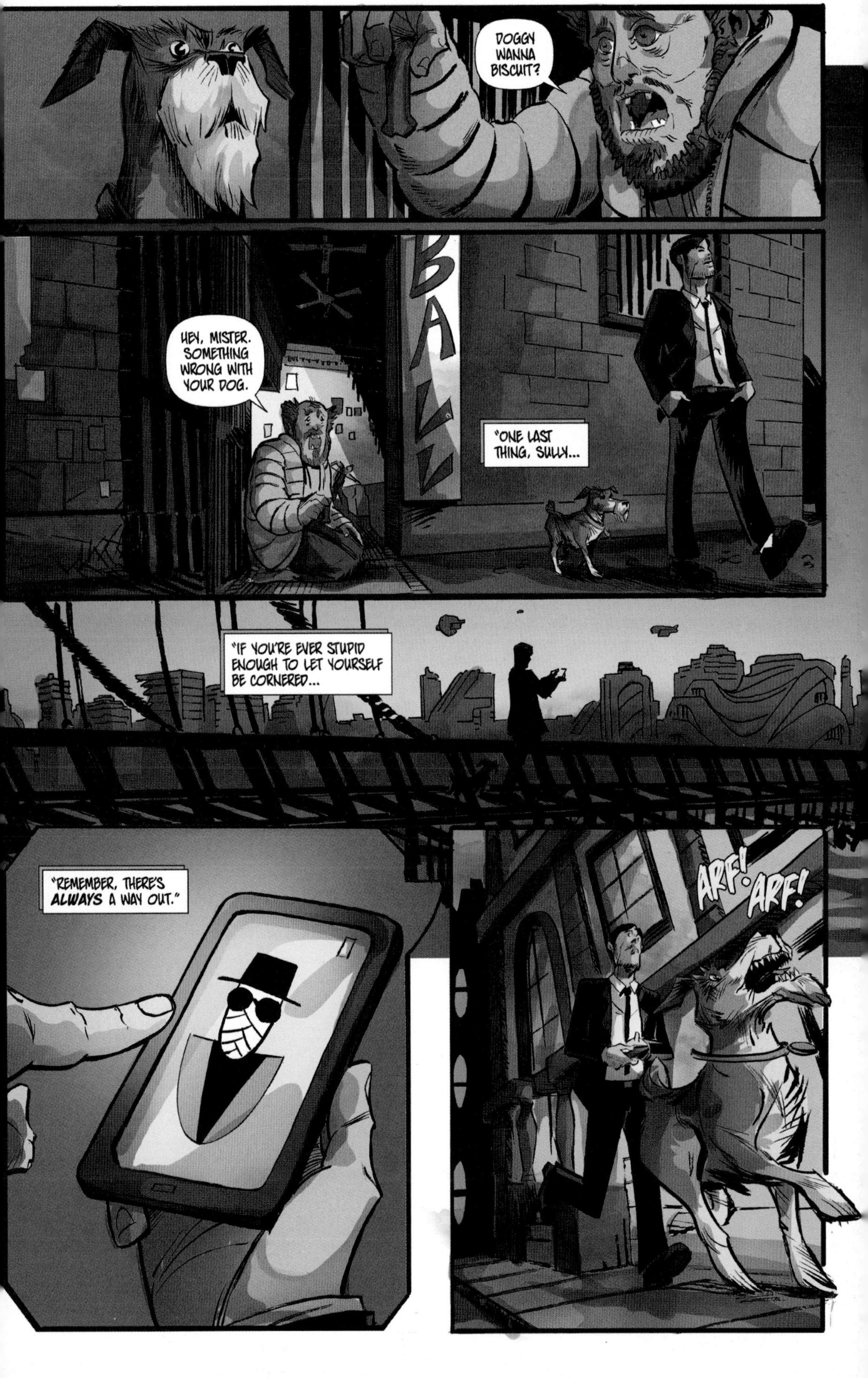
DOGGY WANNA BISCUIT?
HEY, MISTER. SOMETHING WRONG WITH YOUR DOG.
"ONE LAST THING, SULLY...
"IF YOU'RE EVER STUPID ENOUGH TO LET YOURSELF BE CORNERED...
"REMEMBER, THERE'S ALWAYS A WAY OUT."
ARF! ARF!

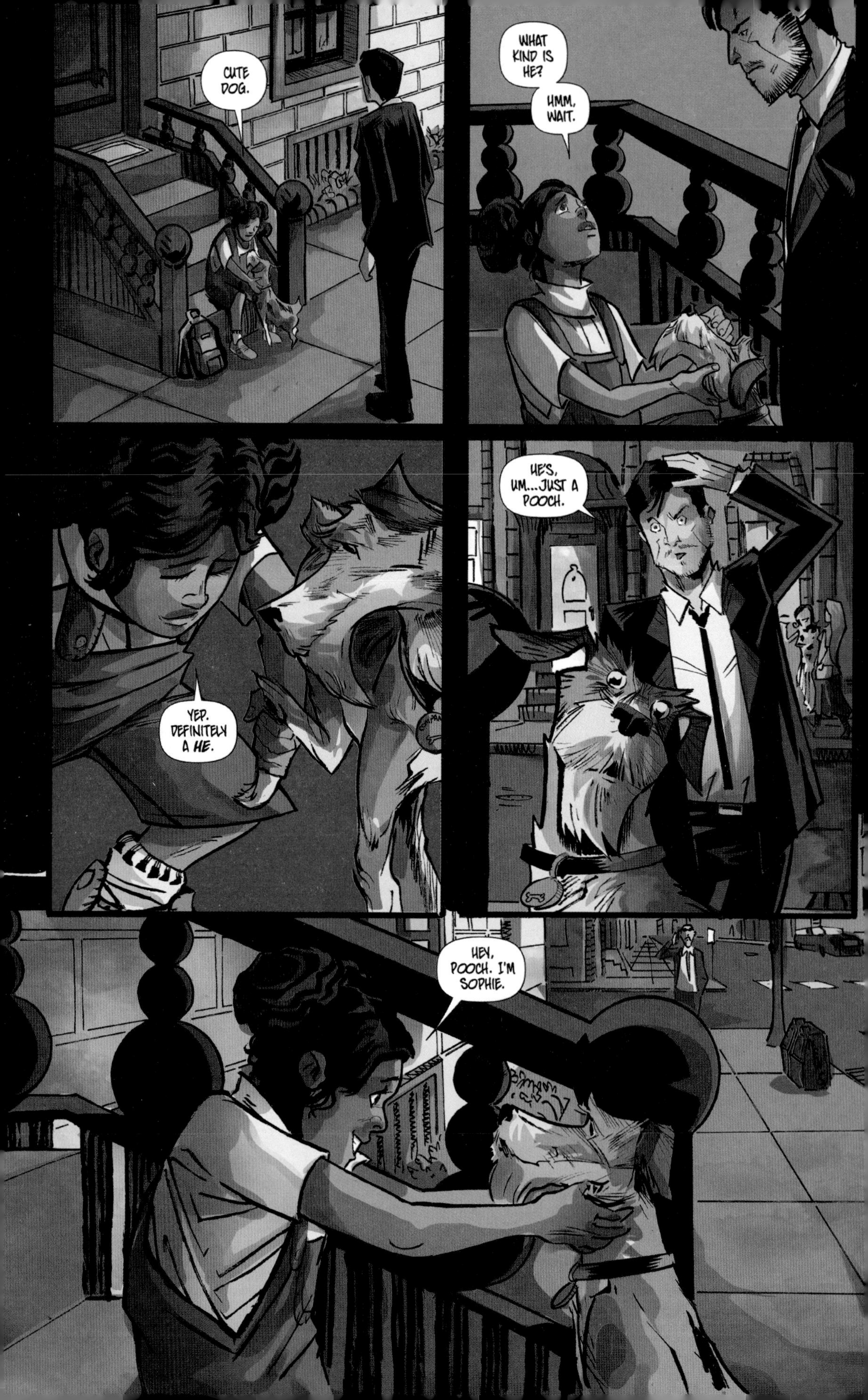
CUTE DOG.
WHAT KIND IS HE?
HMM, WAIT.
YEP. DEFINITELY A HE.
HE'S, UM...JUST A POOCH.
HEY, POOCH. I'M SOPHIE.

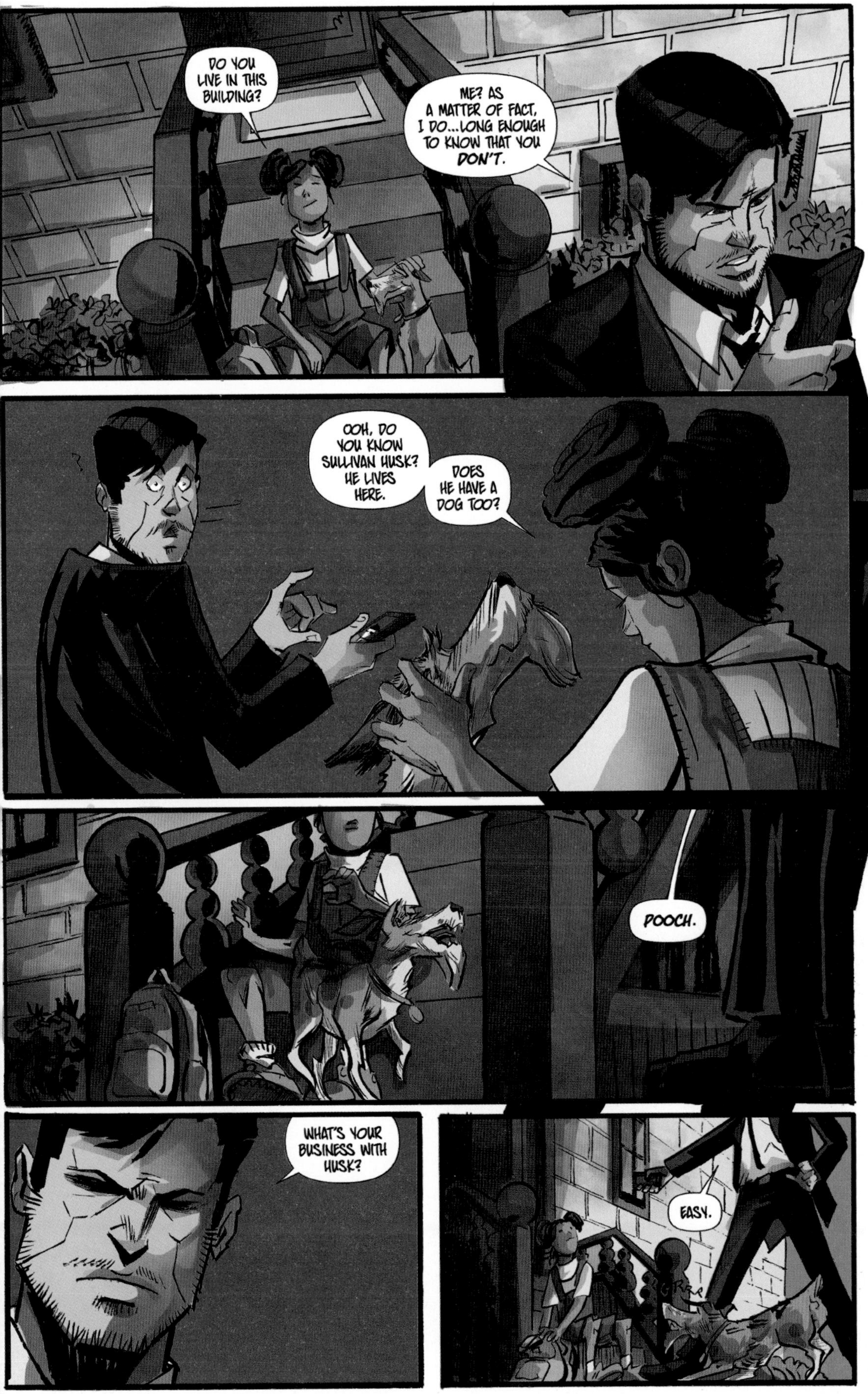
DO YOU LIVE IN THIS BUILDING?
ME? AS A MATTER OF FACT, I DO...LONG ENOUGH TO KNOW THAT YOU DON'T.
OOH, DO YOU KNOW SULLIVAN HUSK? HE LIVES HERE.
DOES HE HAVE A DOG TOO?
POOCH.
WHAT'S YOUR BUSINESS WITH HUSK?
EASY.

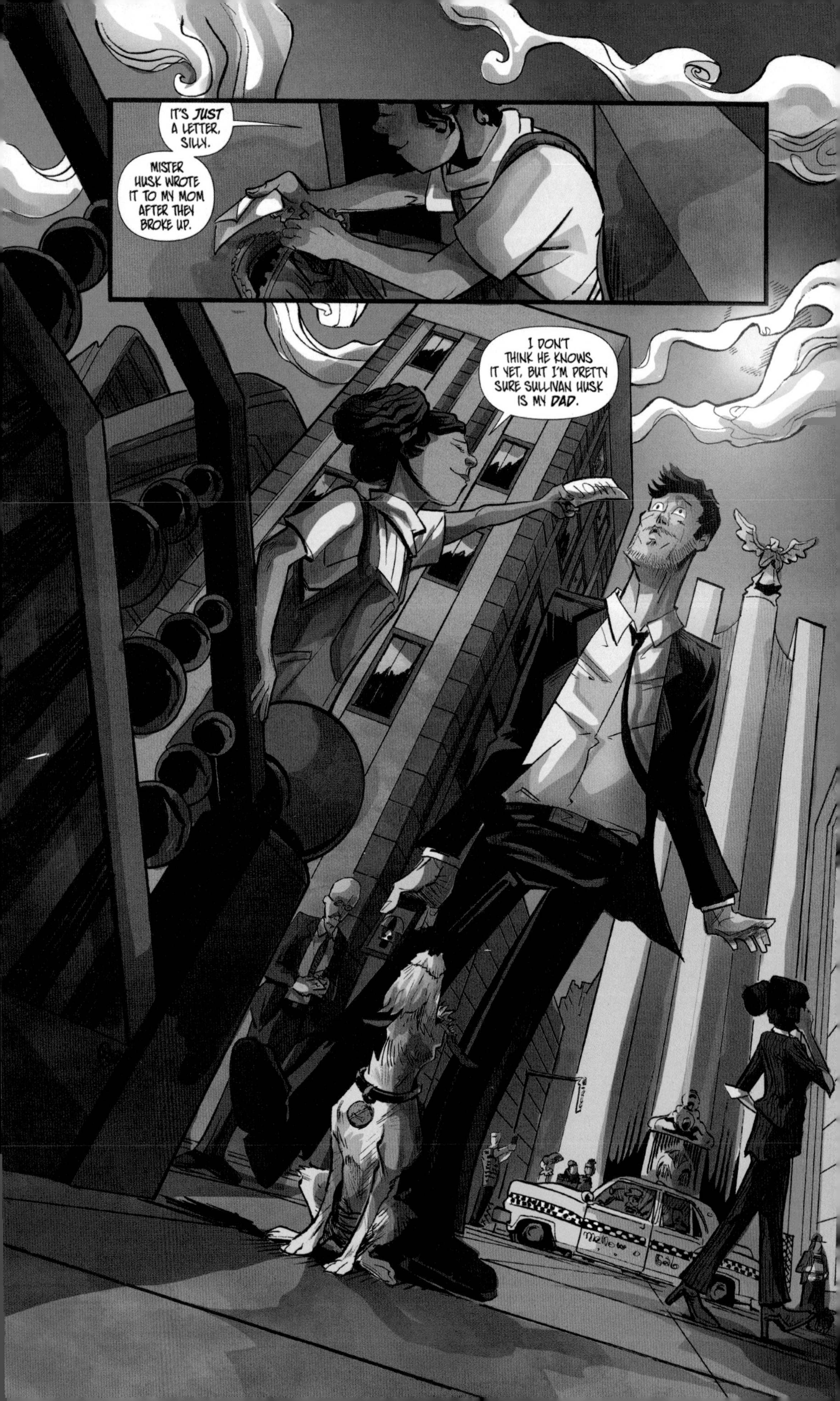
IT'S JUST A LETTER, SILLY.
MISTER HUSK WROTE IT TO MY MOM AFTER THEY BROKE UP.
I DON'T THINK HE KNOWS IT YET, BUT I'M PRETTY SURE SULLIVAN HUSK IS MY DAD.

CHAPTER 2

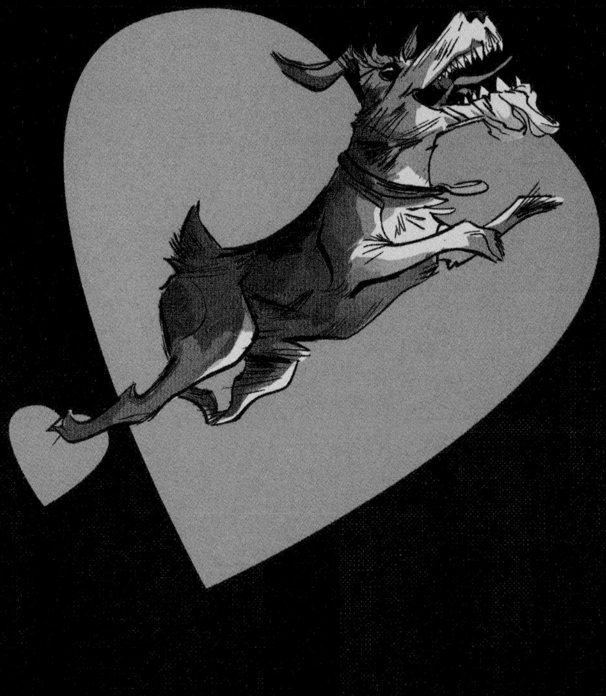

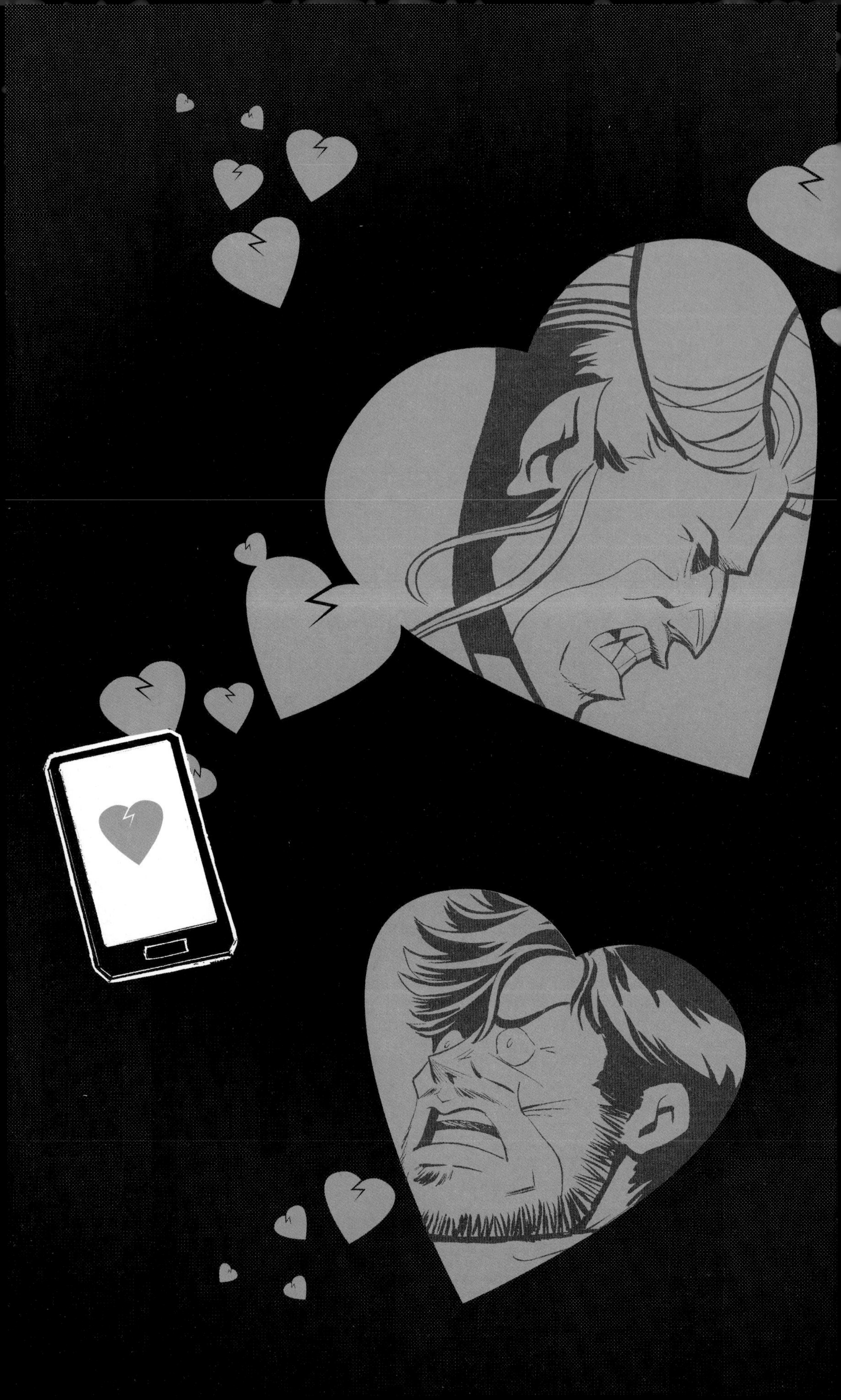

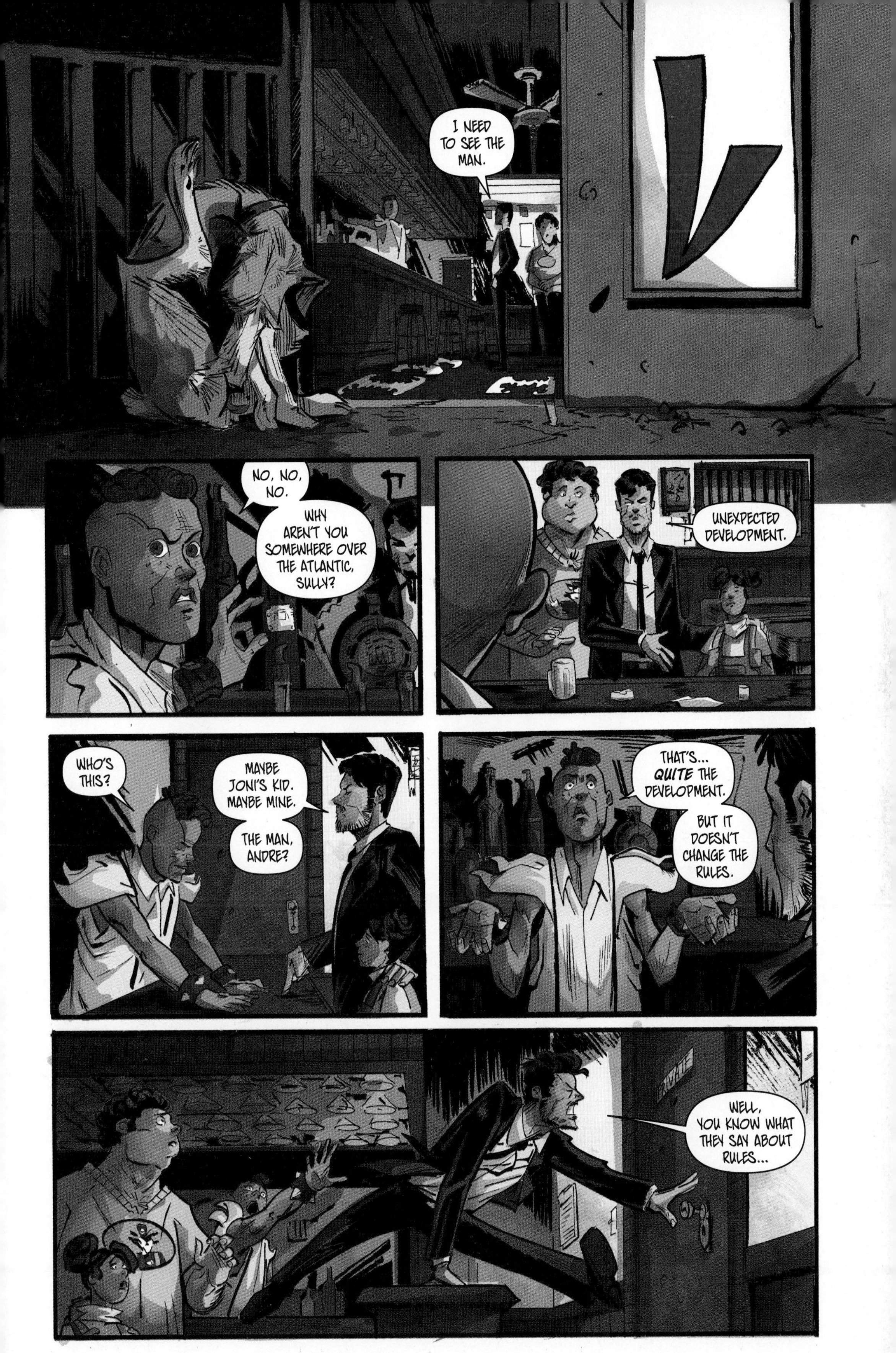

I NEED TO SEE THE MAN.
NO, NO, NO.
WHY AREN'T YOU SOMEWHERE OVER THE ATLANTIC, SULLY?
UNEXPECTED DEVELOPMENT.
WHO'S THIS?
MAYBE JONI'S KID. MAYBE MINE.
THE MAN, ANDRE?
THAT'S... QUITE THE DEVELOPMENT.
BUT IT DOESN'T CHANGE THE RULES.
PRIVATE
WELL, YOU KNOW WHAT THEY SAY ABOUT RULES...

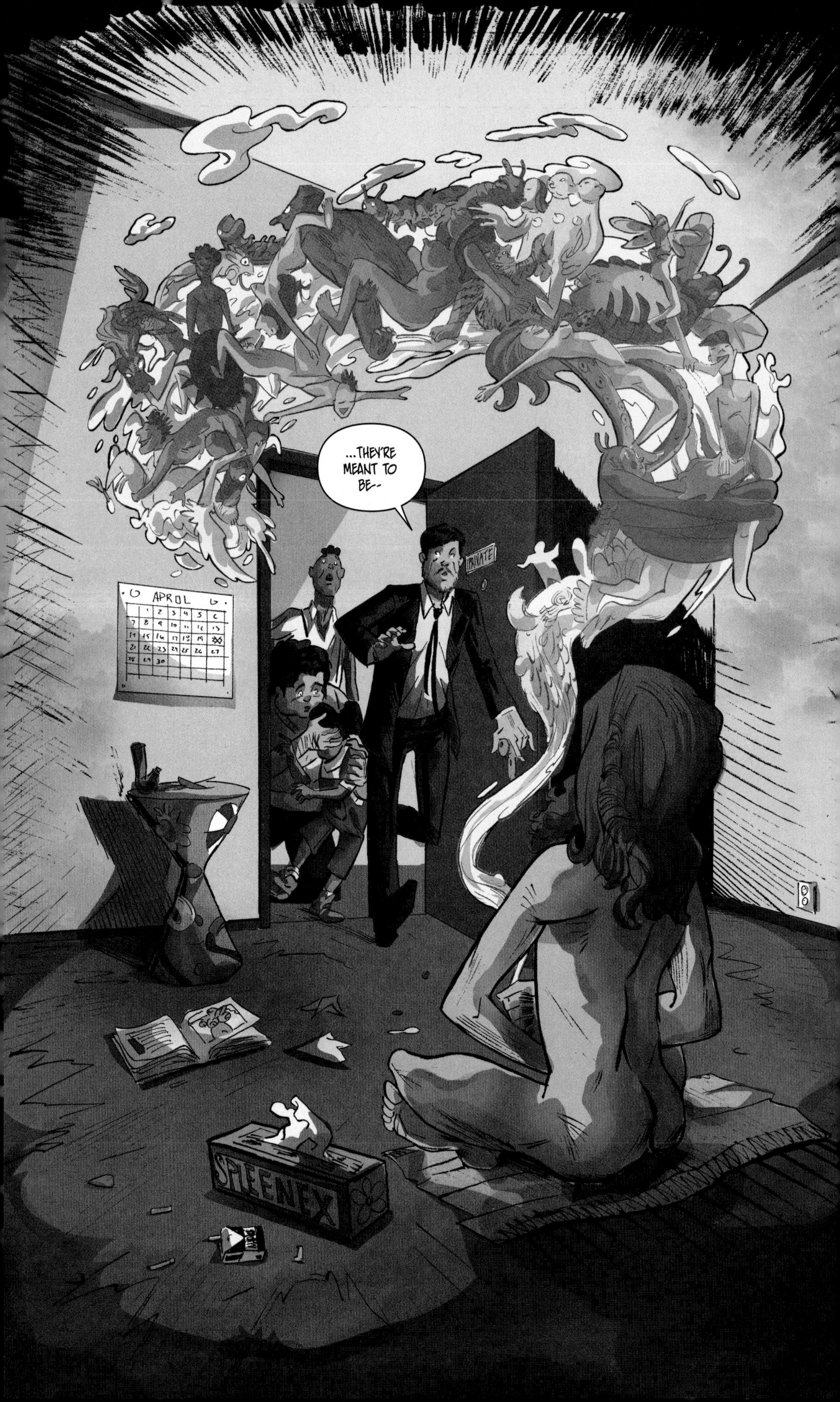
...THEY'RE MEANT TO BE--
APROL
PRIVATE
SPLEENEX

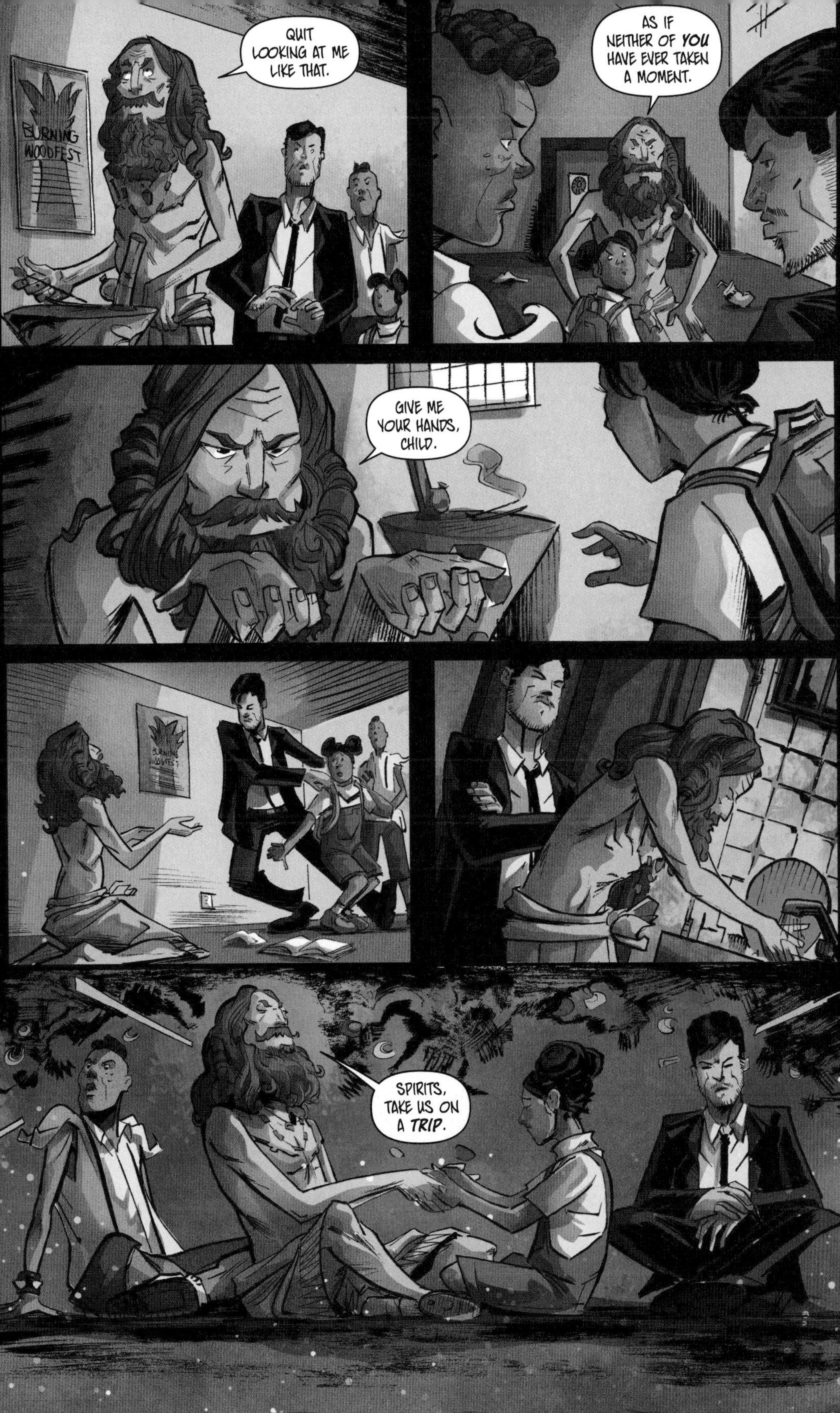
BURNING WOODFEST
QUIT LOOKING AT ME LIKE THAT.
AS IF NEITHER OF *YOU* HAVE EVER TAKEN A MOMENT.
GIVE ME YOUR HANDS, CHILD.
BURNING WOODFEST
SPIRITS, TAKE US ON A *TRIP*.

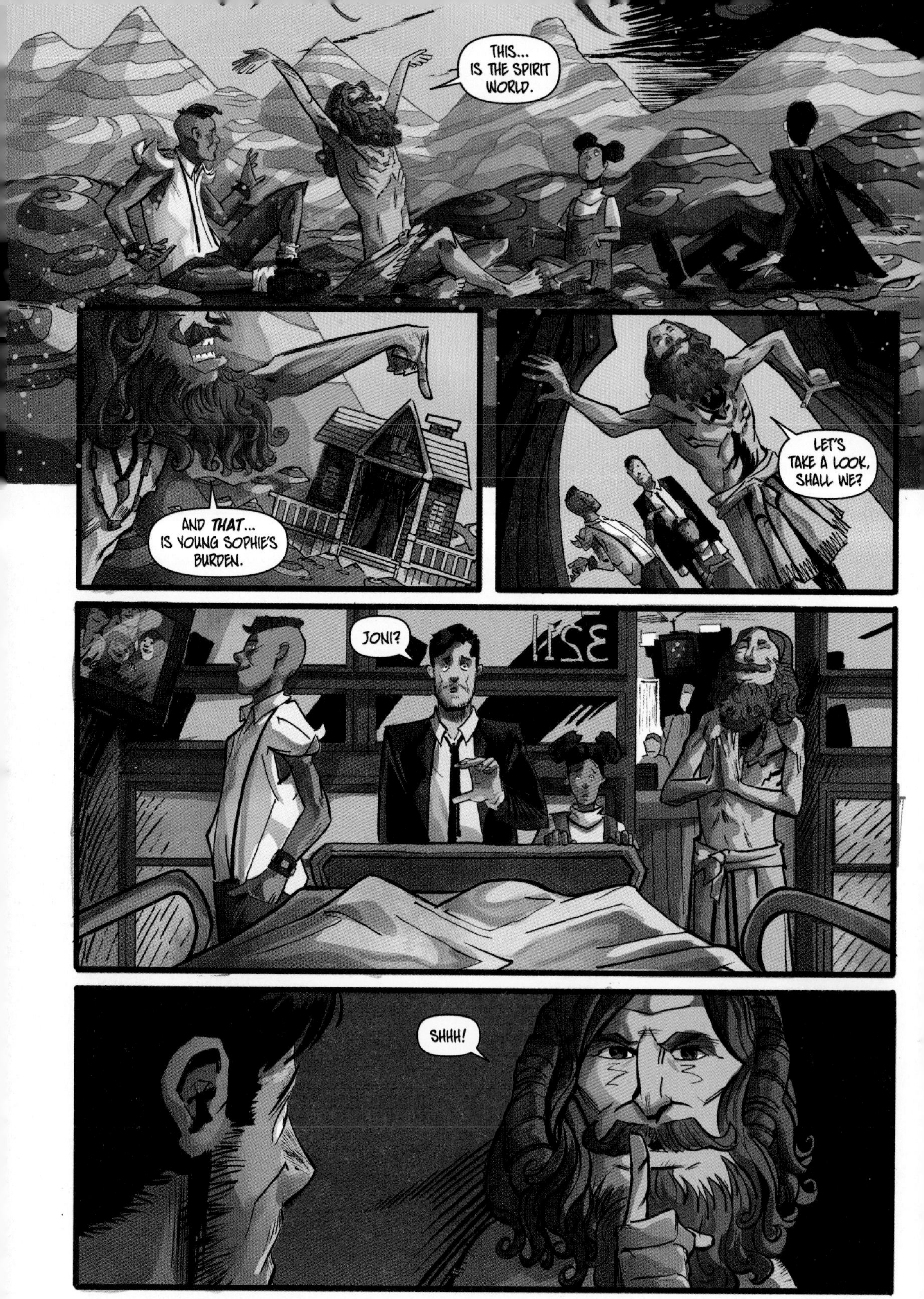
THIS... IS THE SPIRIT WORLD.
AND THAT... IS YOUNG SOPHIE'S BURDEN.
LET'S TAKE A LOOK, SHALL WE?
JONI?
SHHH!

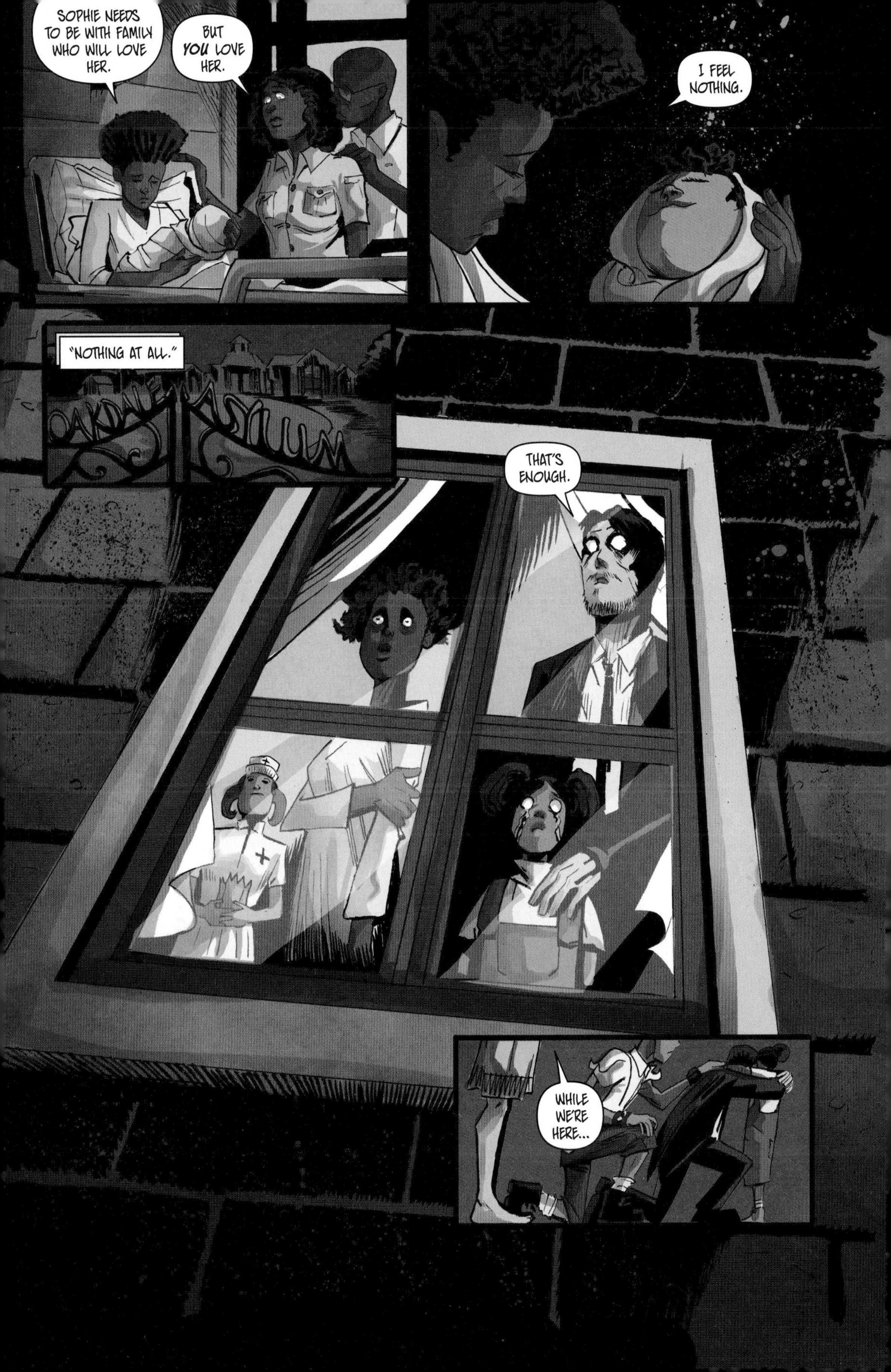
SOPHIE NEEDS TO BE WITH FAMILY WHO WILL LOVE HER.
BUT YOU LOVE HER.
I FEEL NOTHING.
"NOTHING AT ALL."
OAKDALE ASYLUM
THAT'S ENOUGH.
WHILE WE'RE HERE...

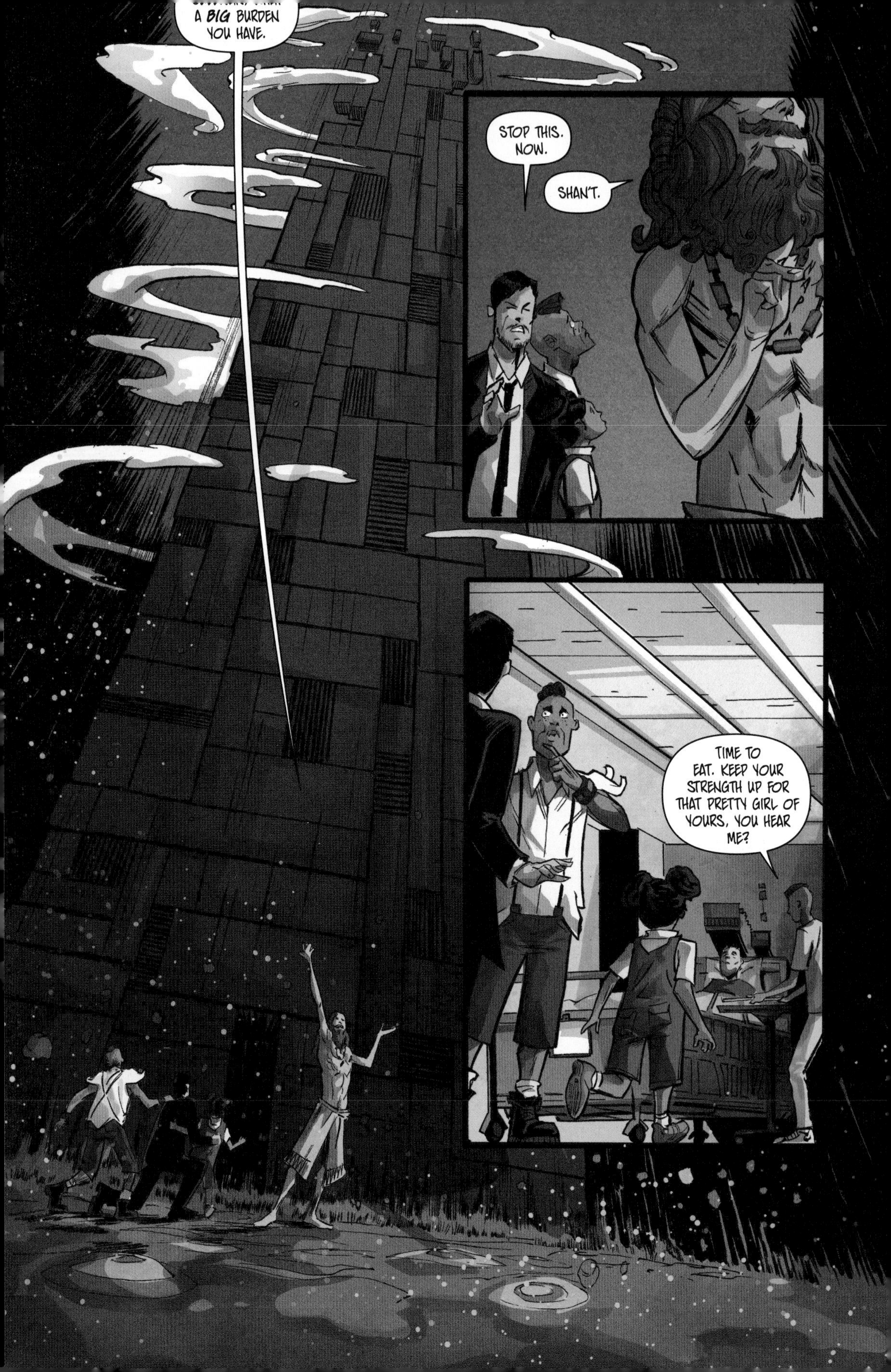
A BIG BURDEN YOU HAVE.
STOP THIS. NOW.
SHAN'T.
TIME TO EAT. KEEP YOUR STRENGTH UP FOR THAT PRETTY GIRL OF YOURS, YOU HEAR ME?

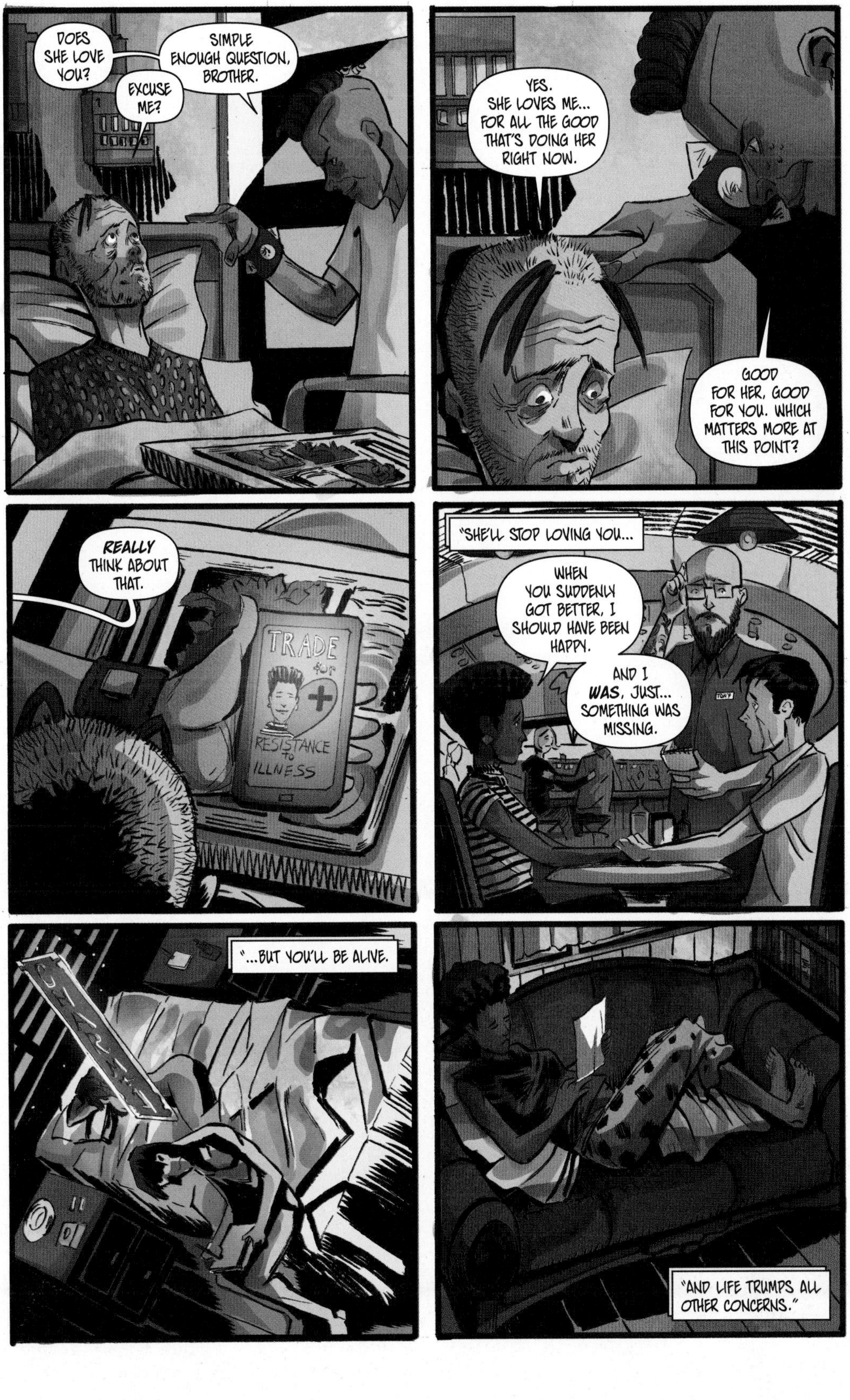
DOES SHE LOVE YOU?
SIMPLE ENOUGH QUESTION, BROTHER.
EXCUSE ME?
YES. SHE LOVES ME... FOR ALL THE GOOD THAT'S DOING HER RIGHT NOW.
GOOD FOR HER, GOOD FOR YOU. WHICH MATTERS MORE AT THIS POINT?
REALLY THINK ABOUT THAT.
TRADE for RESISTANCE to ILLNESS
"SHE'LL STOP LOVING YOU...
WHEN YOU SUDDENLY GOT BETTER, I SHOULD HAVE BEEN HAPPY.
AND I WAS, JUST... SOMETHING WAS MISSING.
TONY
"...BUT YOU'LL BE ALIVE.
"AND LIFE TRUMPS ALL OTHER CONCERNS."

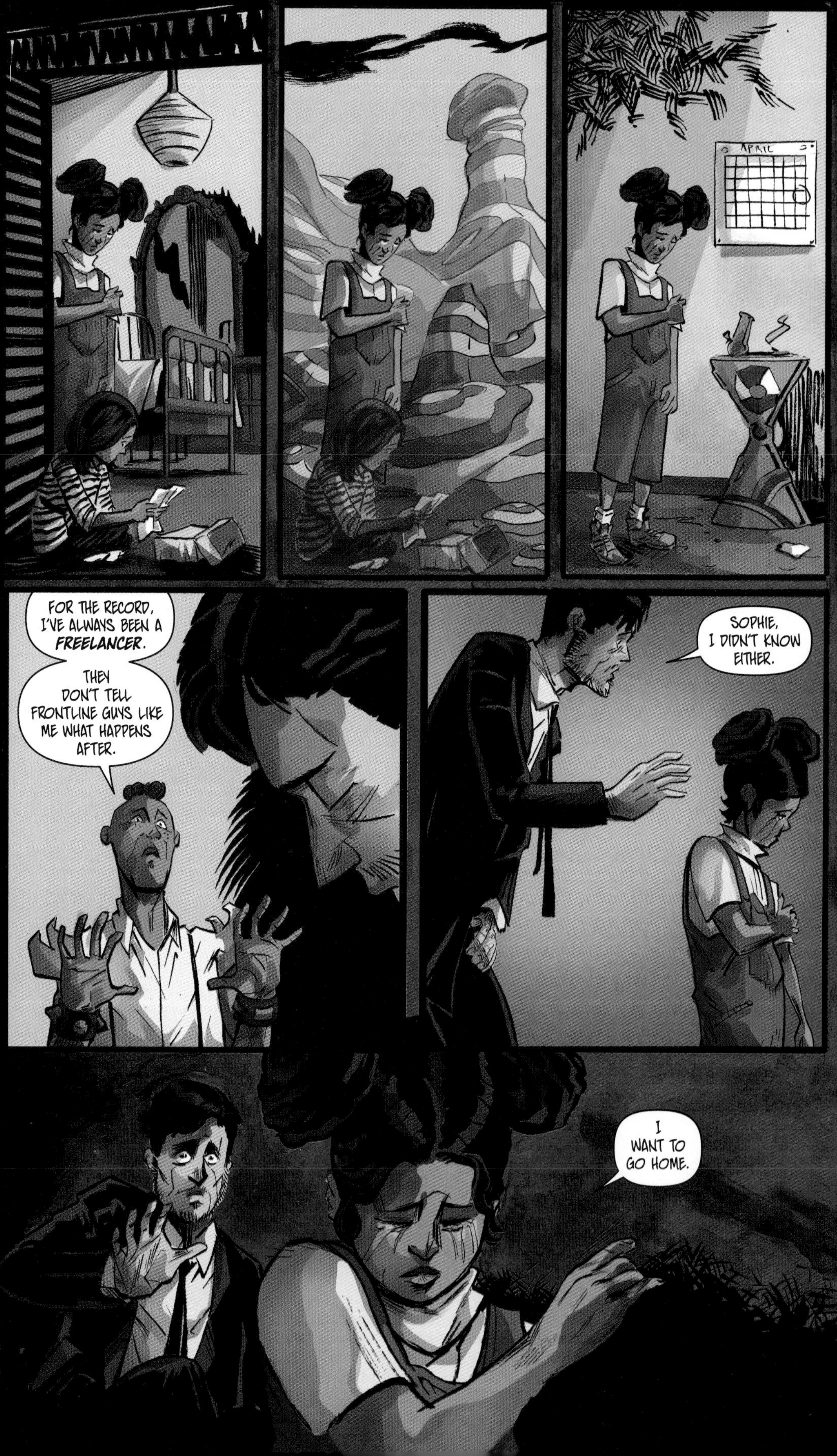
APRIL
FOR THE RECORD, I'VE ALWAYS BEEN A **FREELANCER**.
THEY DON'T TELL FRONTLINE GUYS LIKE ME WHAT HAPPENS AFTER.
SOPHIE, I DIDN'T KNOW EITHER.
I WANT TO GO HOME.

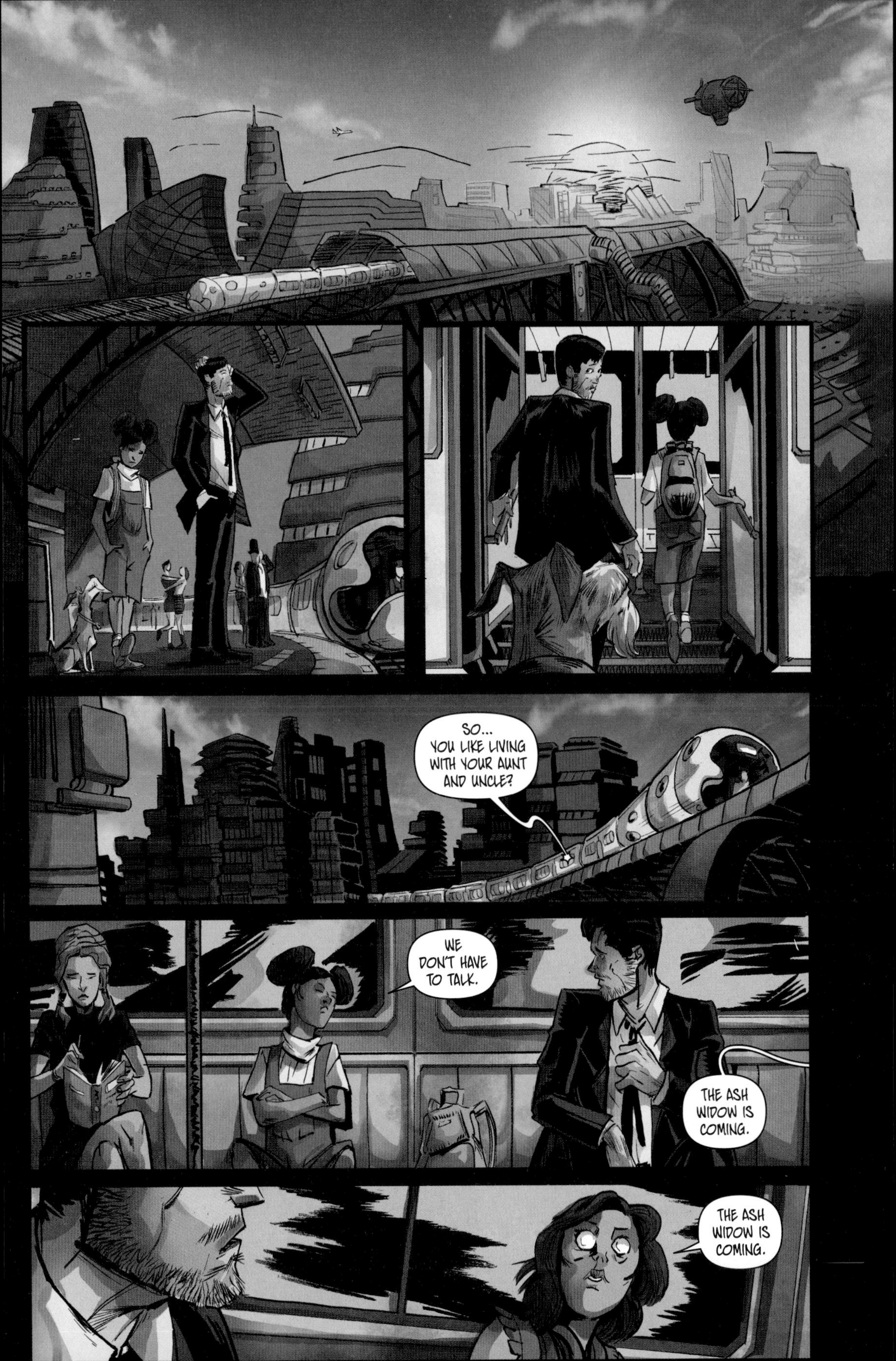
SO... YOU LIKE LIVING WITH YOUR AUNT AND UNCLE?
WE DON'T HAVE TO TALK.
THE ASH WIDOW IS COMING.
THE ASH WIDOW IS COMING.

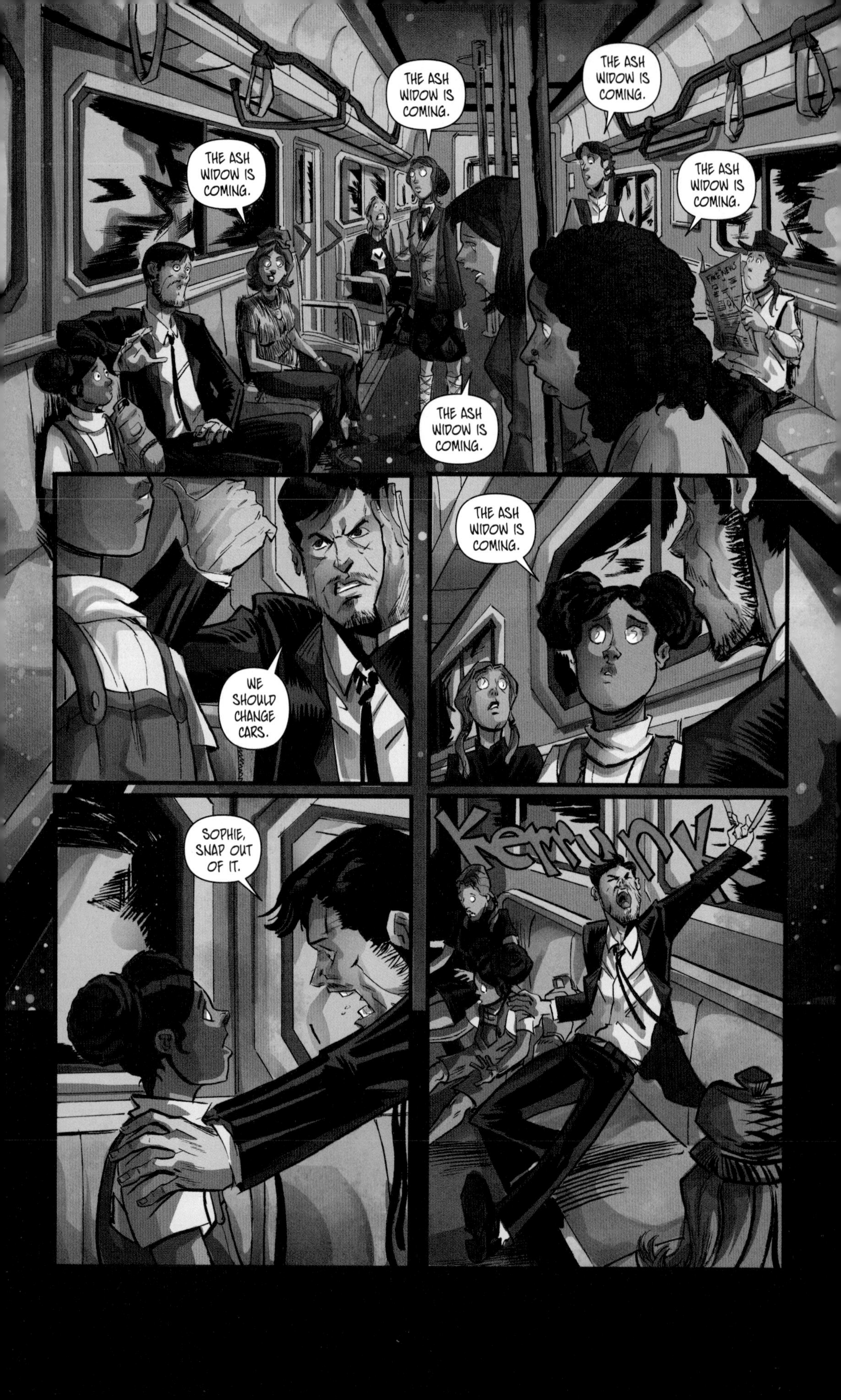
THE ASH WIDOW IS COMING.
THE ASH WIDOW IS COMING.
THE ASH WIDOW IS COMING.
THE ASH WIDOW IS COMING.
THE ASH WIDOW IS COMING.
WE SHOULD CHANGE CARS.
THE ASH WIDOW IS COMING.
SOPHIE, SNAP OUT OF IT.
KERRUNK

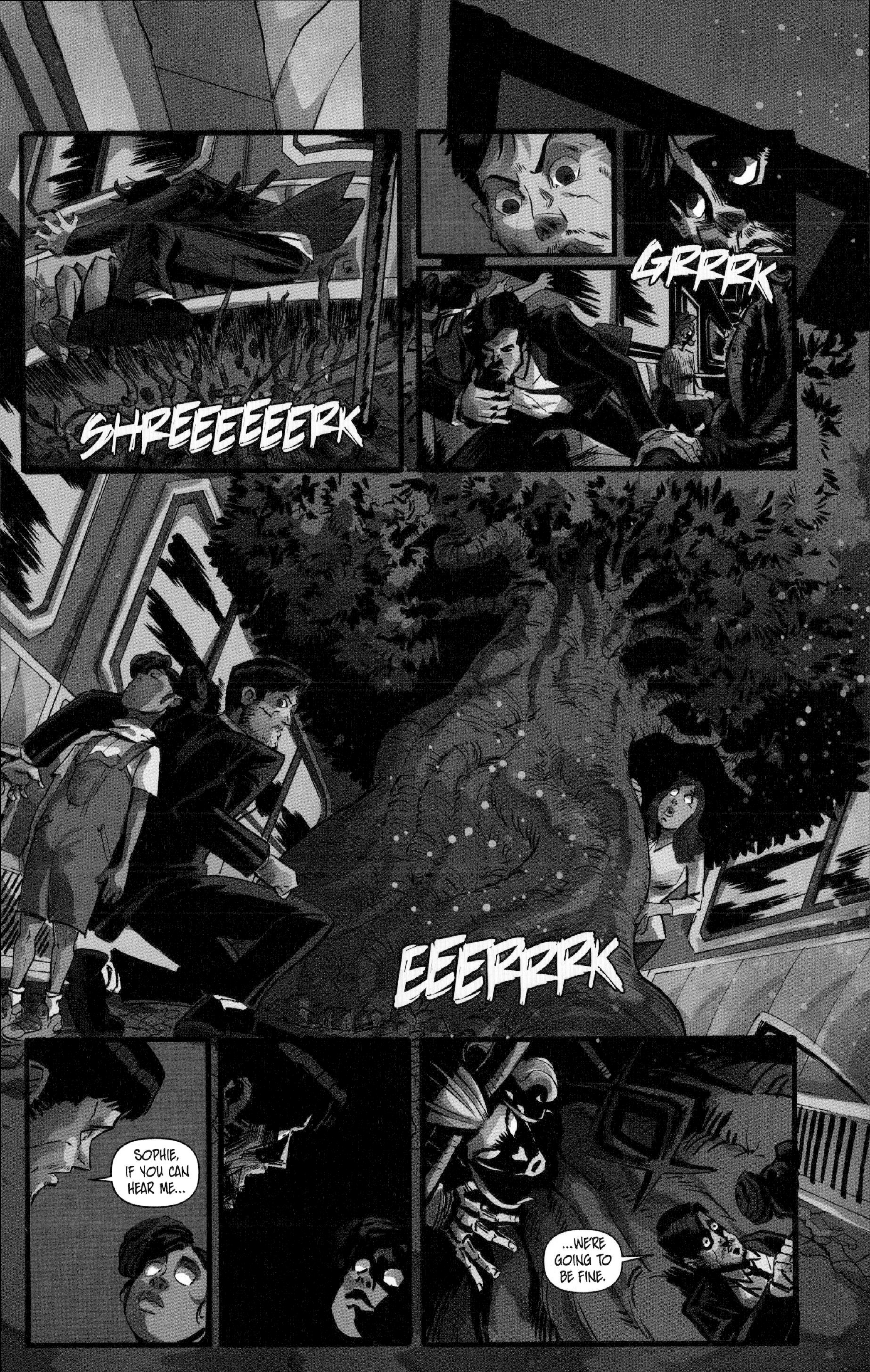
SHREEEEEEERK
GRRRK
EEERRRK
SOPHIE, IF YOU CAN HEAR ME...
...WE'RE GOING TO BE FINE.

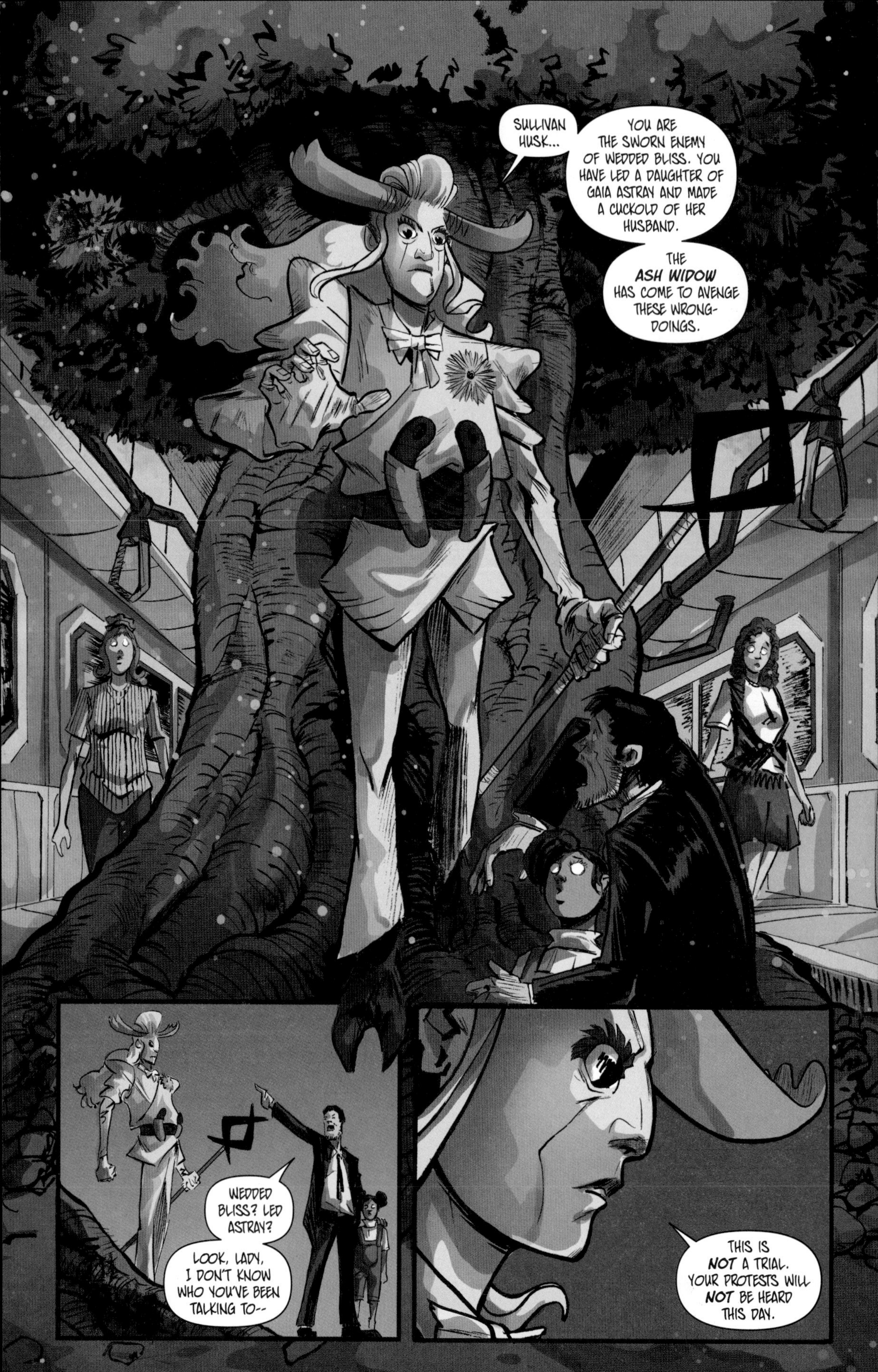

SULLIVAN HUSK...
YOU ARE THE SWORN ENEMY OF WEDDED BLISS. YOU HAVE LED A DAUGHTER OF GAIA ASTRAY AND MADE A CUCKOLD OF HER HUSBAND.
THE **ASH WIDOW** HAS COME TO AVENGE THESE WRONG-DOINGS.
WEDDED BLISS? LED ASTRAY?
LOOK, LADY, I DON'T KNOW WHO YOU'VE BEEN TALKING TO--
THIS IS **NOT** A TRIAL. YOUR PROTESTS WILL **NOT** BE HEARD THIS DAY.

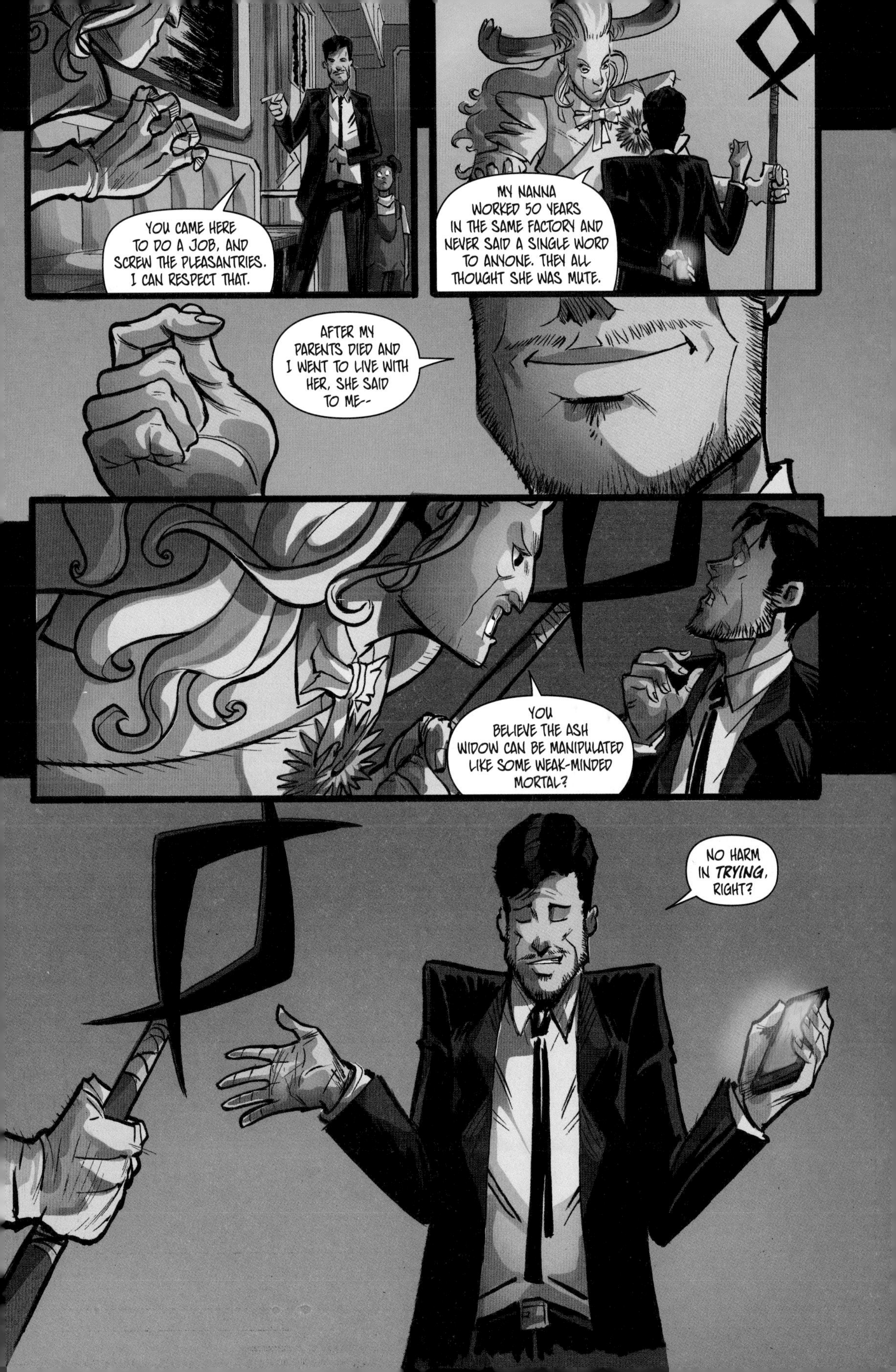
YOU CAME HERE TO DO A JOB, AND SCREW THE PLEASANTRIES. I CAN RESPECT THAT.
MY NANNA WORKED 50 YEARS IN THE SAME FACTORY AND NEVER SAID A SINGLE WORD TO ANYONE. THEY ALL THOUGHT SHE WAS MUTE.
AFTER MY PARENTS DIED AND I WENT TO LIVE WITH HER, SHE SAID TO ME--
YOU BELIEVE THE ASH WIDOW CAN BE MANIPULATED LIKE SOME WEAK-MINDED MORTAL?
NO HARM IN *TRYING*, RIGHT?

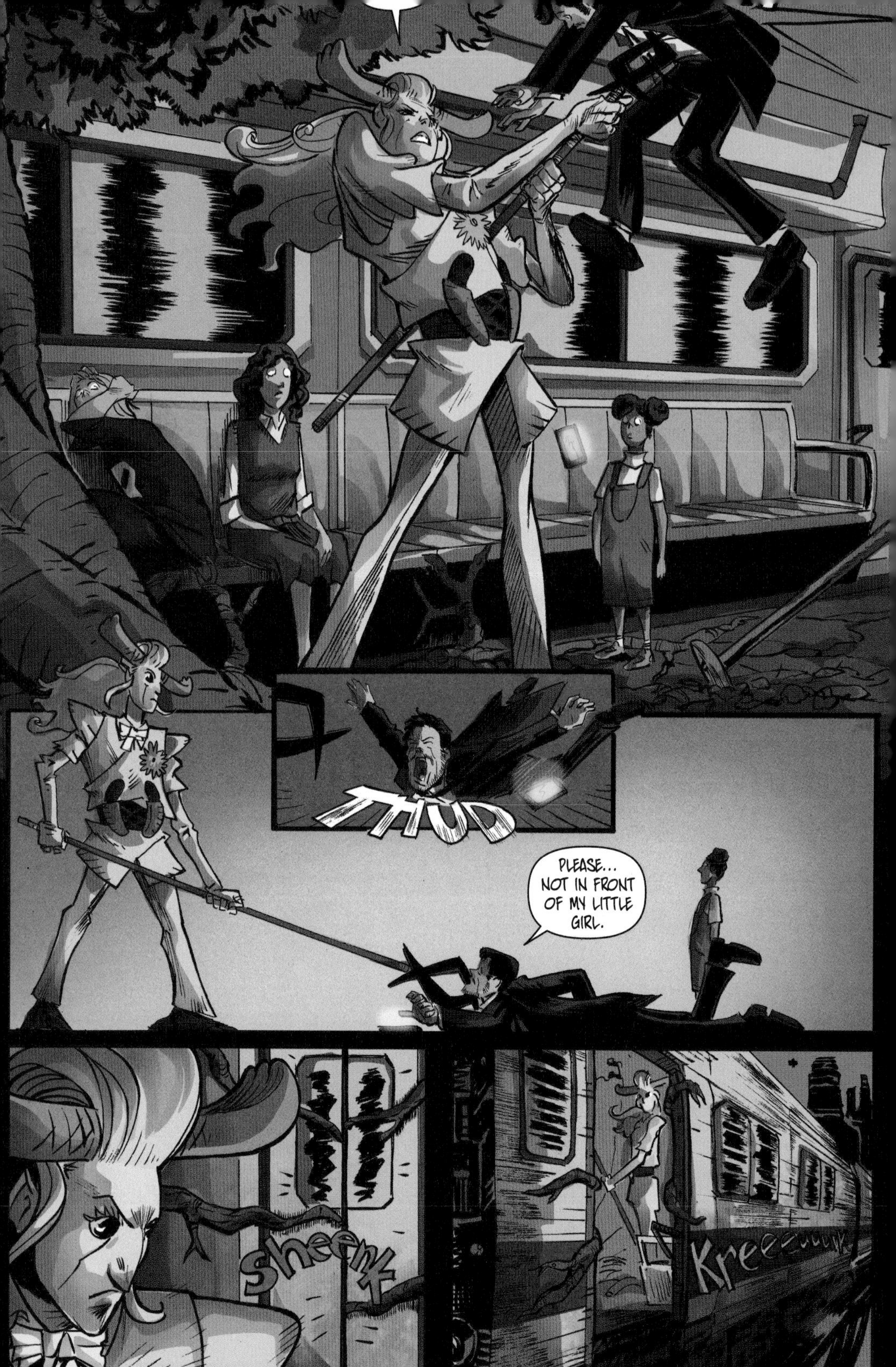
THUD
PLEASE... NOT IN FRONT OF MY LITTLE GIRL.
sheenk
Kreeeuuuk

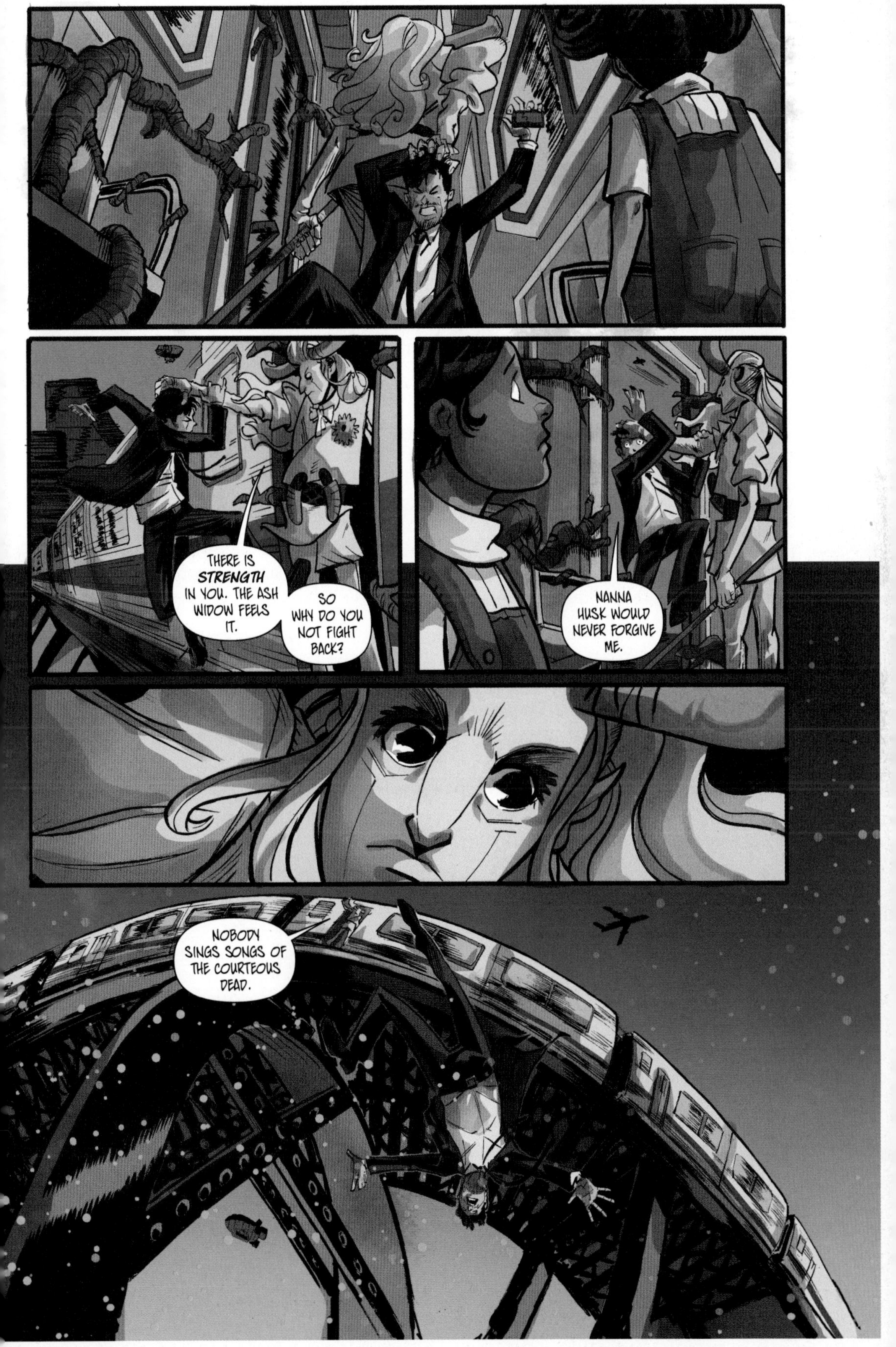

THERE IS STRENGTH IN YOU. THE ASH WIDOW FEELS IT.
SO WHY DO YOU NOT FIGHT BACK?
NANNA HUSK WOULD NEVER FORGIVE ME.
NOBODY SINGS SONGS OF THE COURTEOUS DEAD.

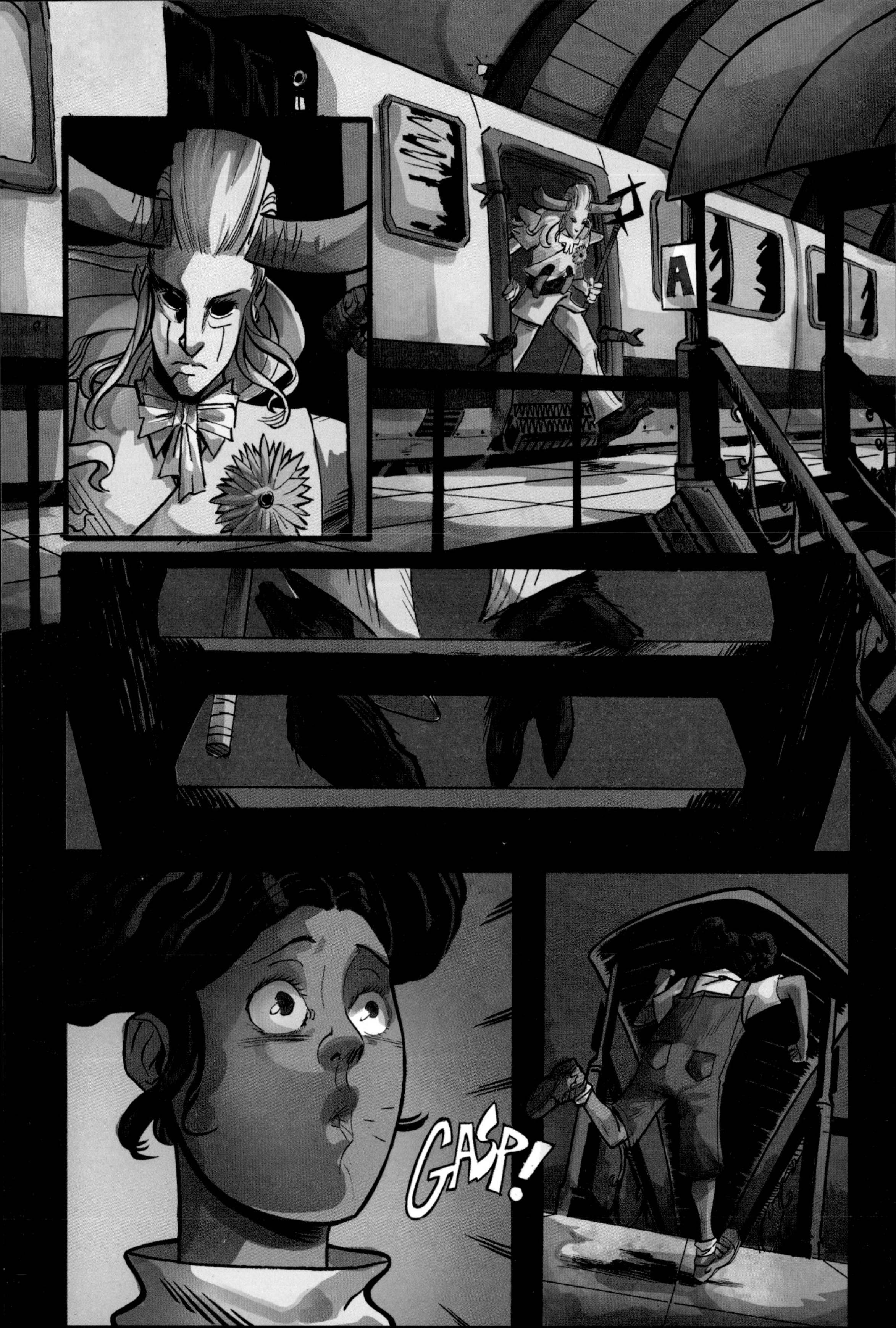
A
GASP!

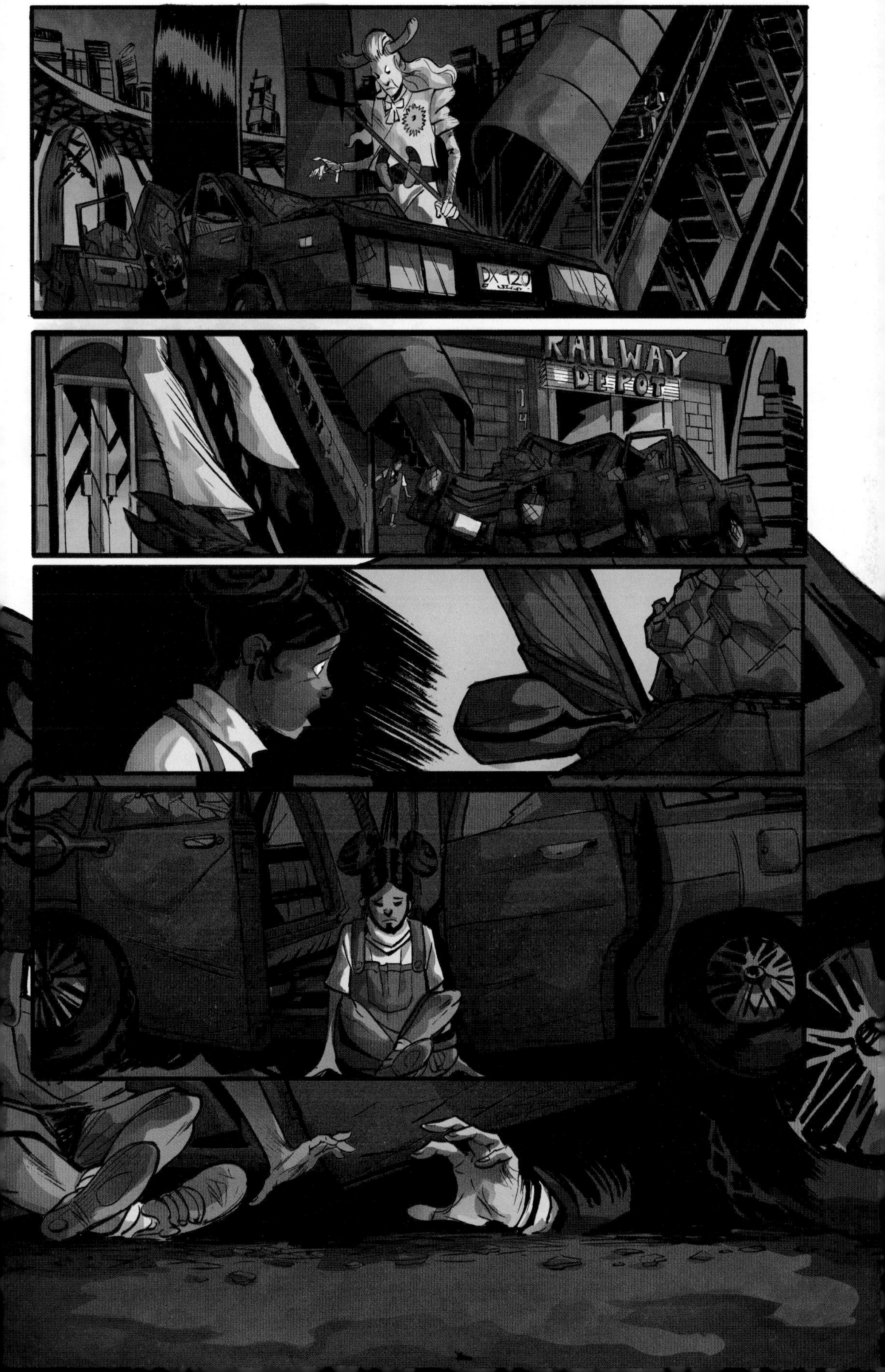
DX 420
RAILWAY
DEPOT
14

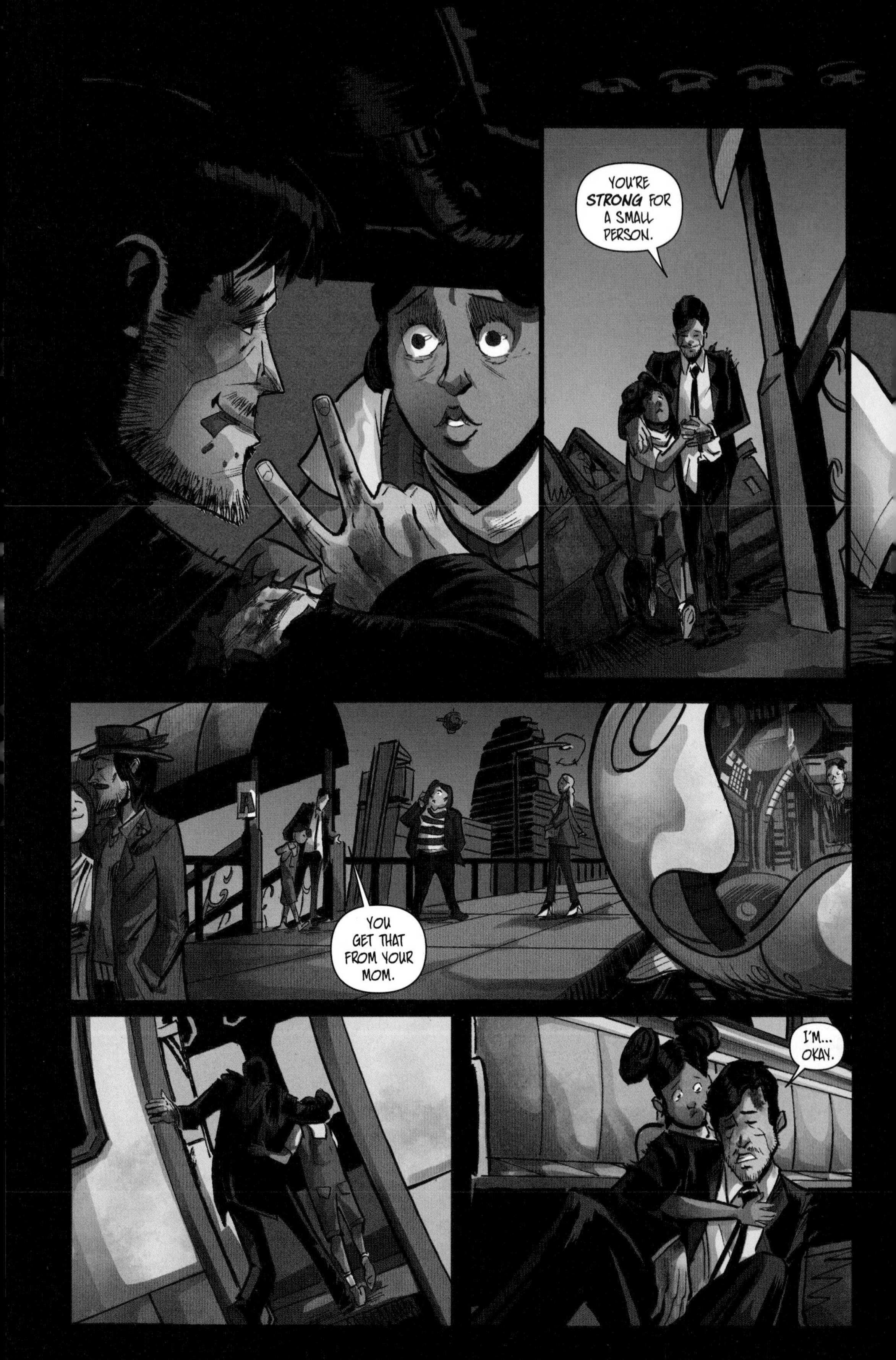
YOU'RE STRONG FOR A SMALL PERSON.
YOU GET THAT FROM YOUR MOM.
I'M... OKAY.

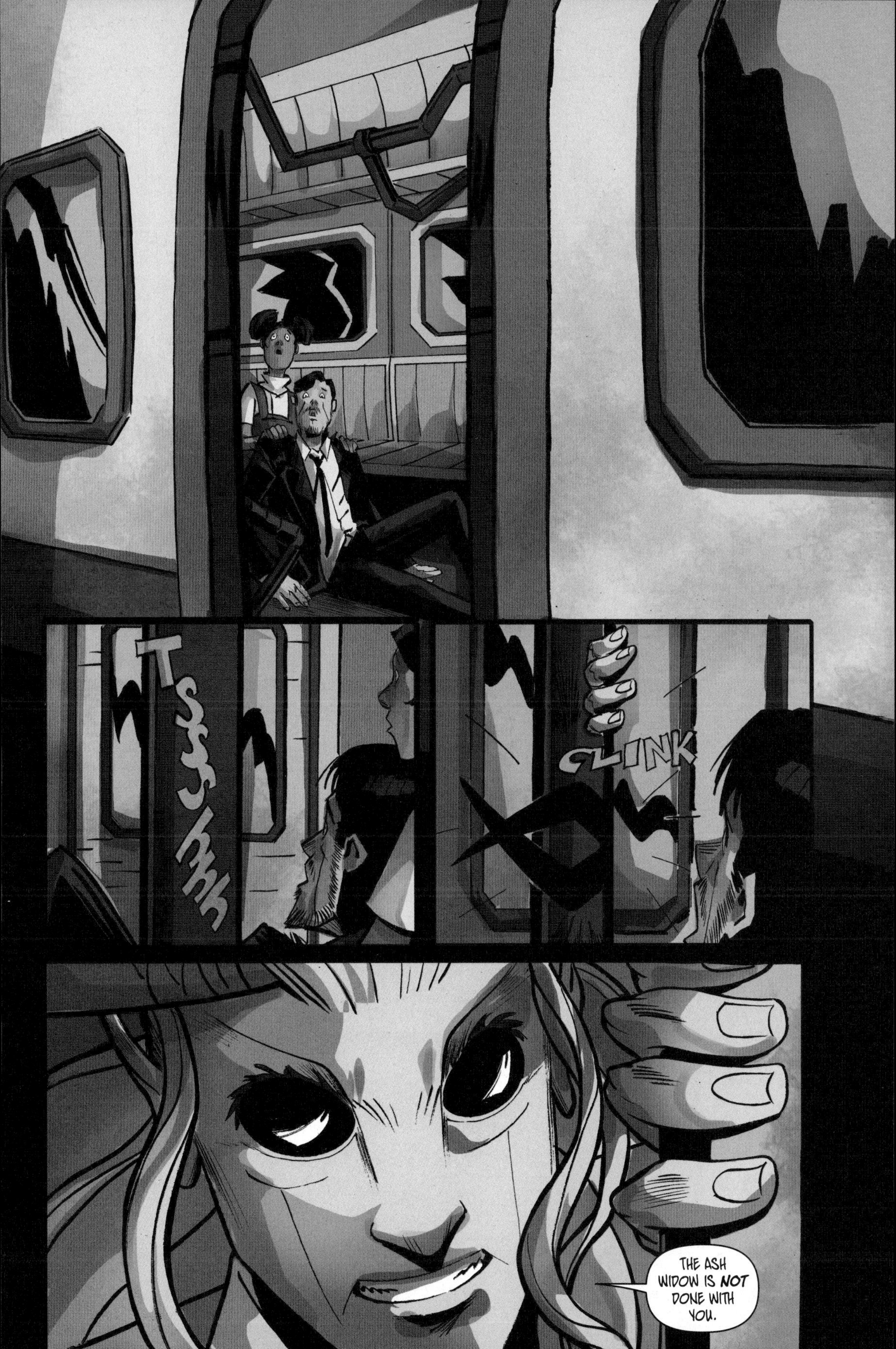
TSSSHHH
CLINK
THE ASH WIDOW IS NOT DONE WITH YOU.

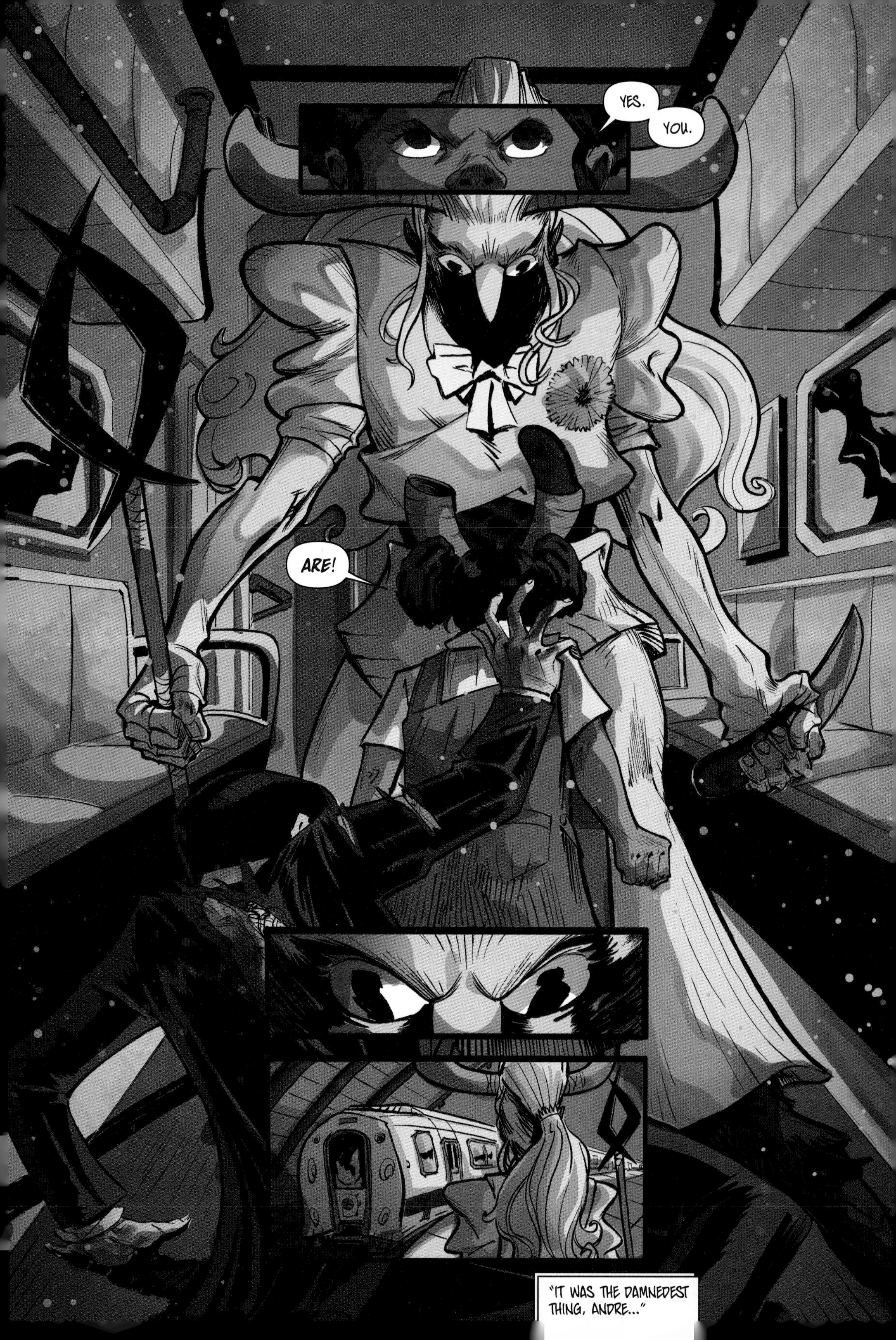
YES.
YOU.
ARE!
"IT WAS THE DAMNEDEST THING, ANDRE..."

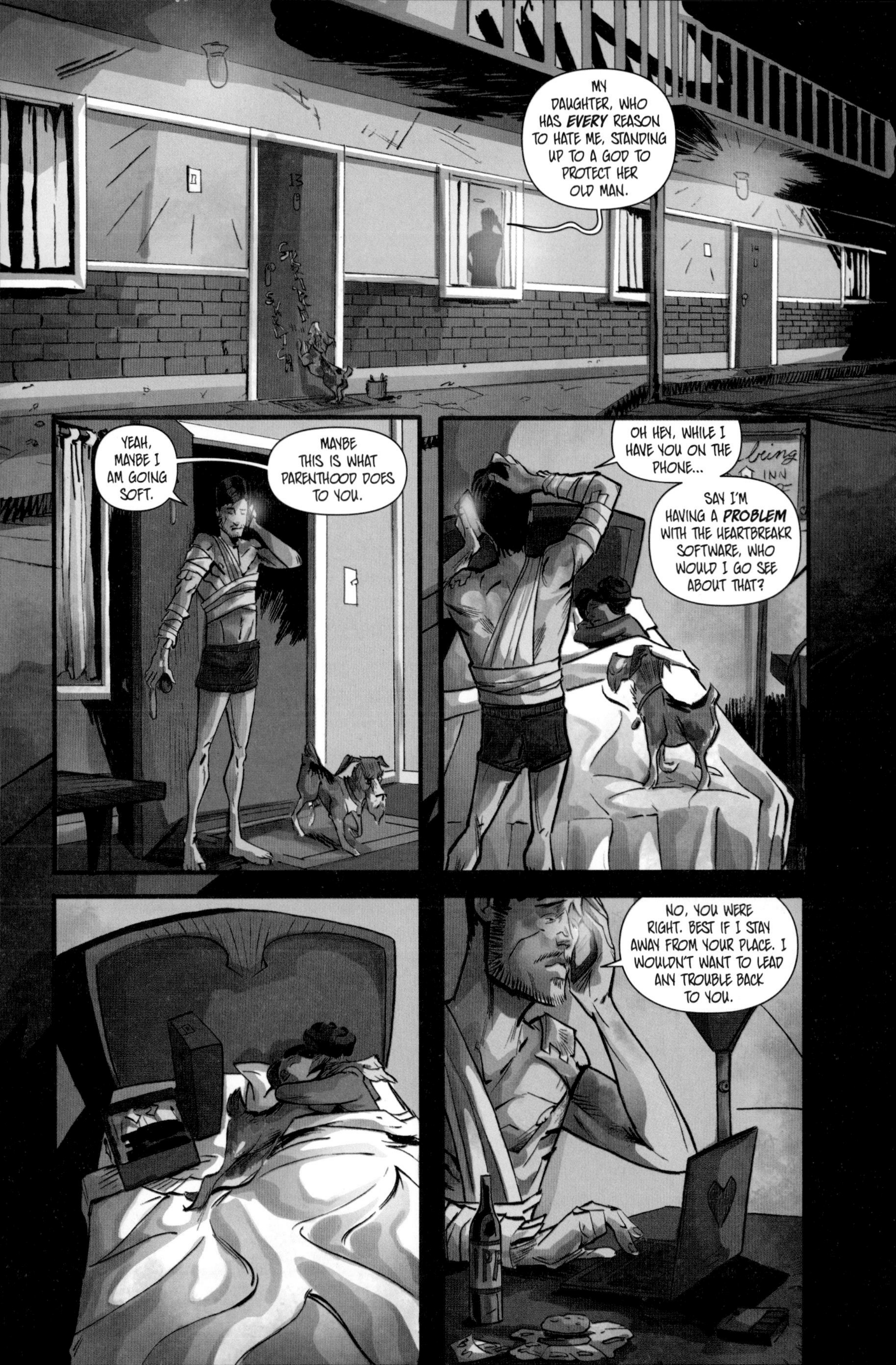
MY DAUGHTER, WHO HAS EVERY REASON TO HATE ME, STANDING UP TO A GOD TO PROTECT HER OLD MAN.
YEAH, MAYBE I AM GOING SOFT.
MAYBE THIS IS WHAT PARENTHOOD DOES TO YOU.
OH HEY, WHILE I HAVE YOU ON THE PHONE...
SAY I'M HAVING A PROBLEM WITH THE HEARTBREAKR SOFTWARE, WHO WOULD I GO SEE ABOUT THAT?
NO, YOU WERE RIGHT. BEST IF I STAY AWAY FROM YOUR PLACE. I WOULDN'T WANT TO LEAD ANY TROUBLE BACK TO YOU.

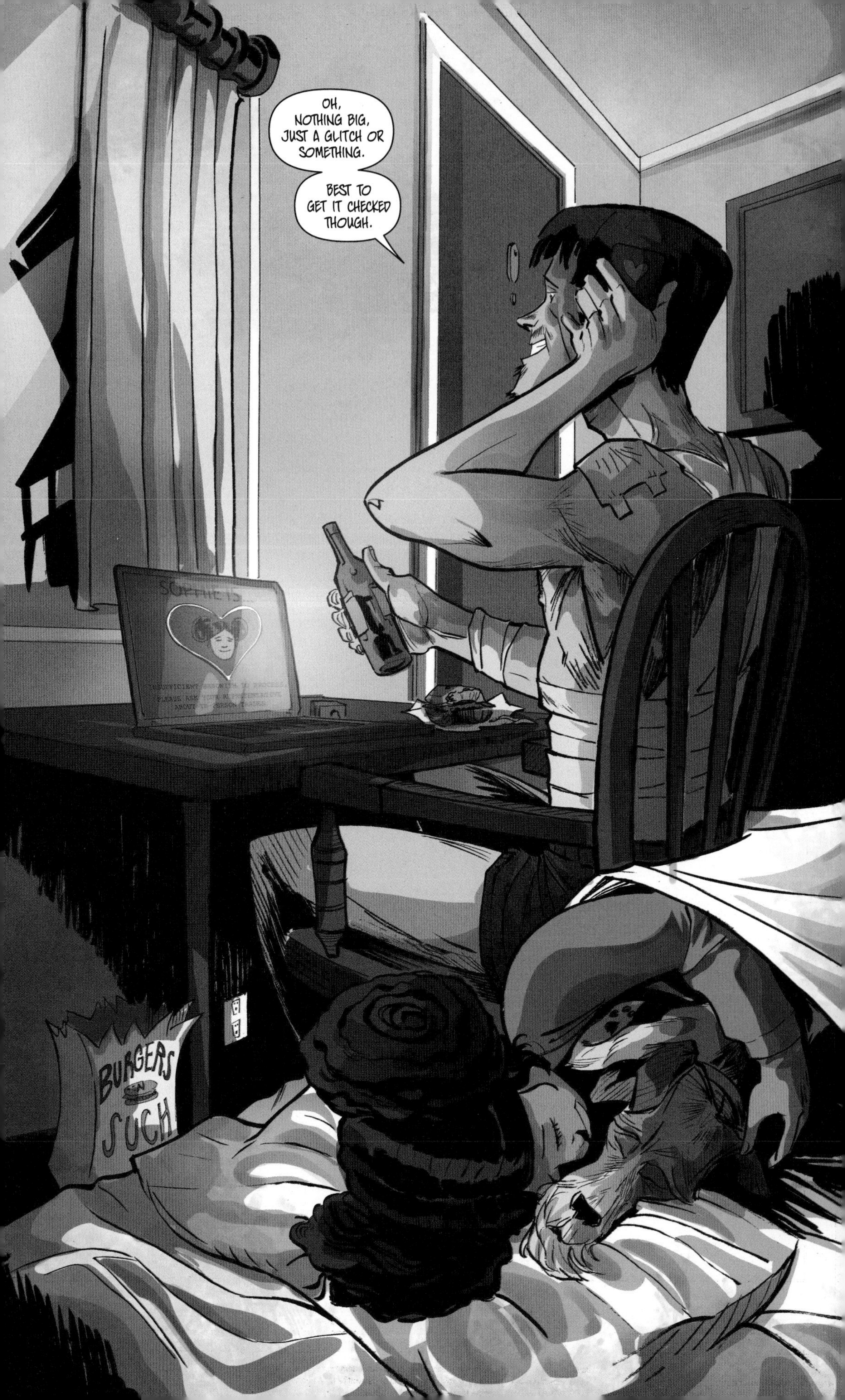
OH, NOTHING BIG, JUST A GLITCH OR SOMETHING.
BEST TO GET IT CHECKED THOUGH.
BURGERS 'N SUCH

CHAPTER 3

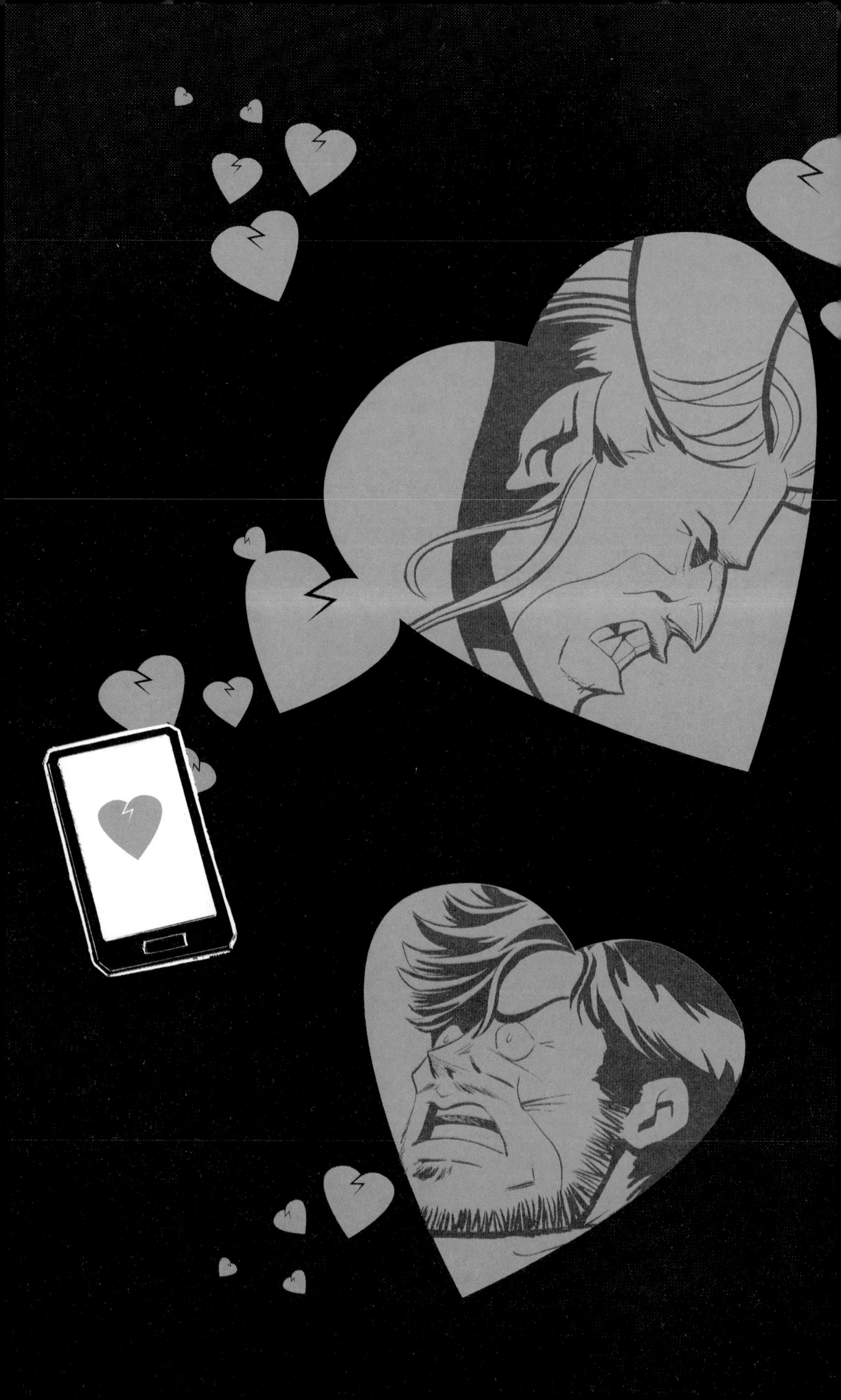

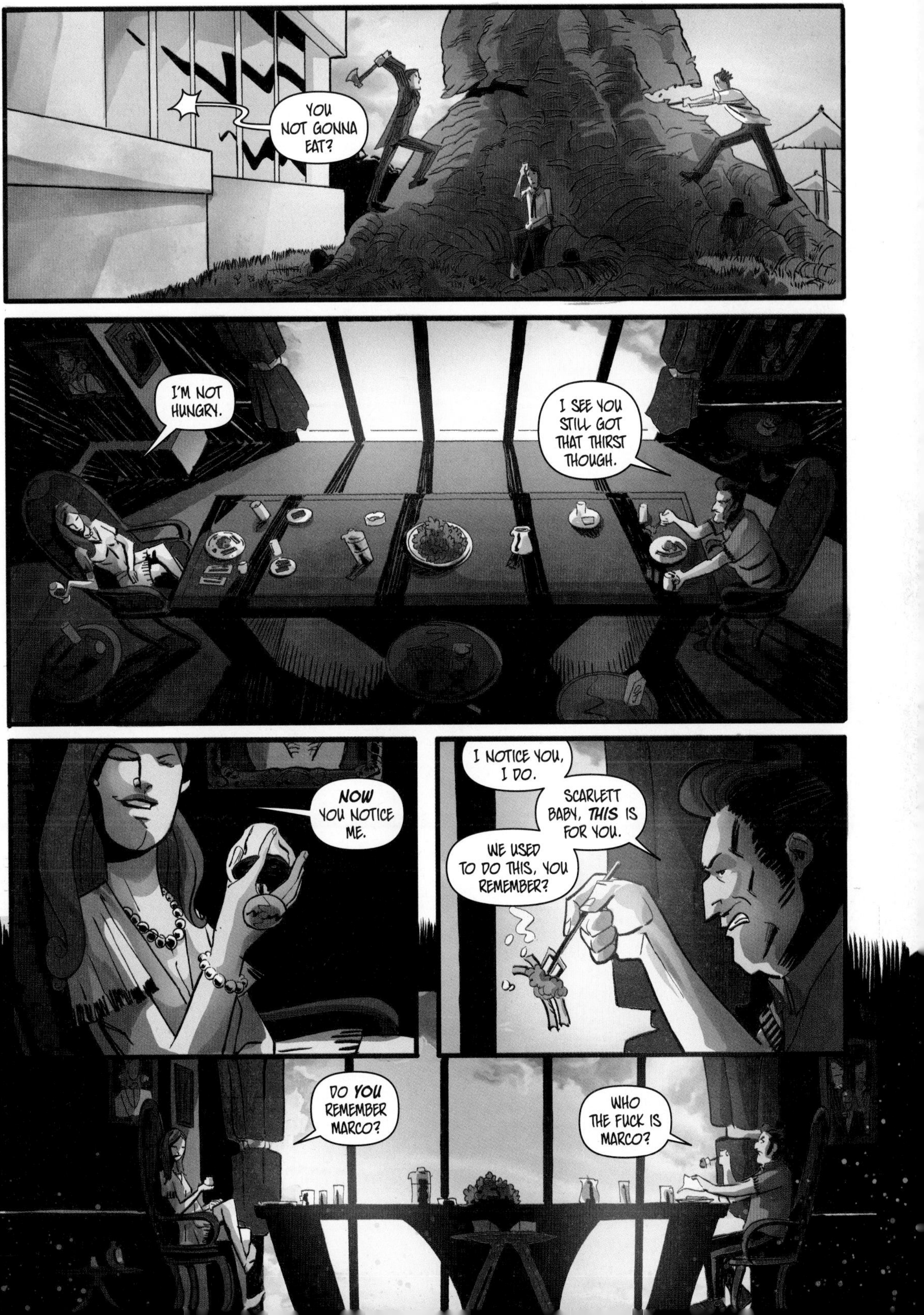
YOU NOT GONNA EAT?
I'M NOT HUNGRY.
I SEE YOU STILL GOT THAT THIRST THOUGH.
NOW YOU NOTICE ME.
I NOTICE YOU, I DO.
SCARLETT BABY, THIS IS FOR YOU.
WE USED TO DO THIS, YOU REMEMBER?
DO YOU REMEMBER MARCO?
WHO THE FUCK IS MARCO?

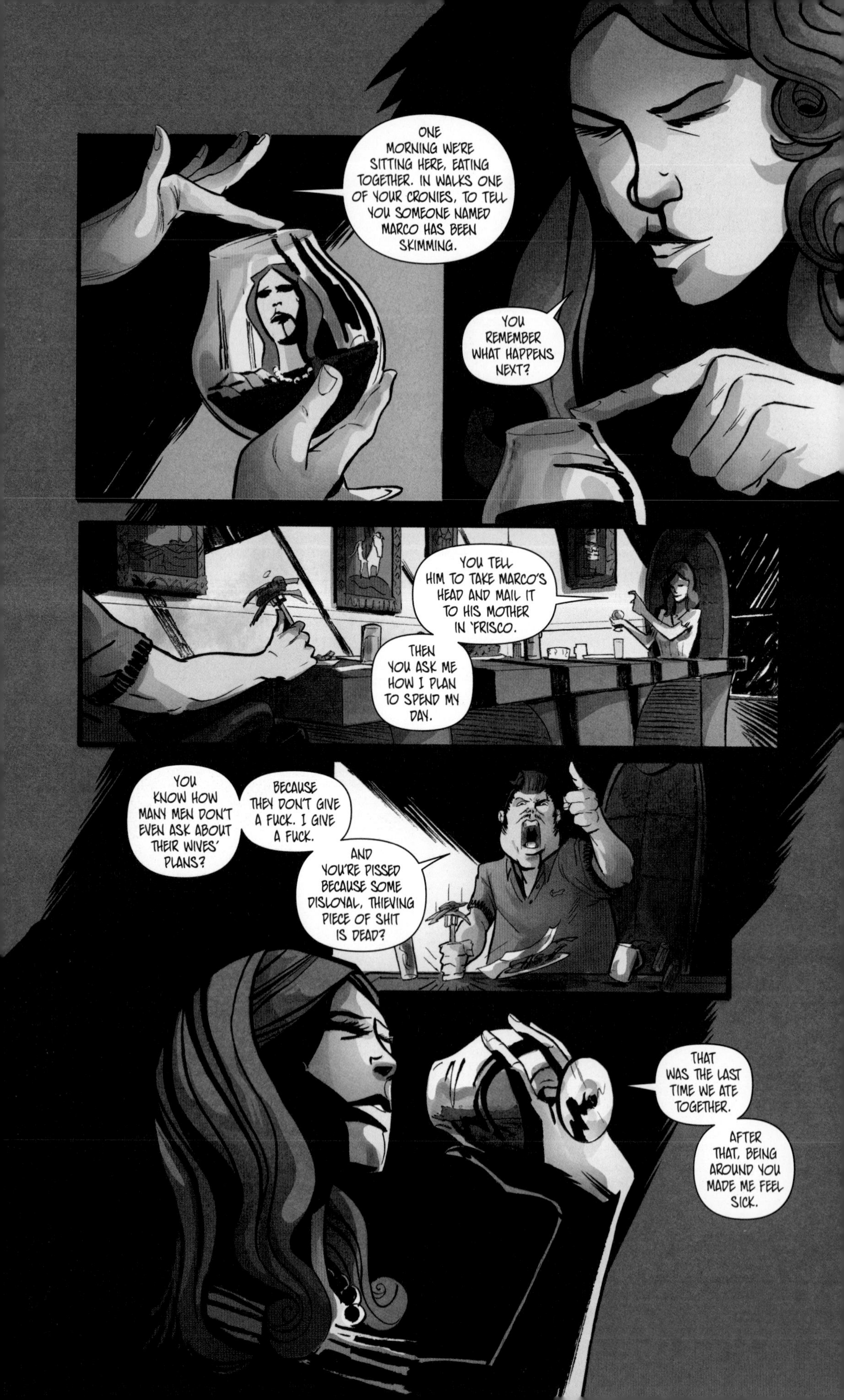
ONE MORNING WE'RE SITTING HERE, EATING TOGETHER. IN WALKS ONE OF YOUR CRONIES, TO TELL YOU SOMEONE NAMED MARCO HAS BEEN SKIMMING.
YOU REMEMBER WHAT HAPPENS NEXT?
YOU TELL HIM TO TAKE MARCO'S HEAD AND MAIL IT TO HIS MOTHER IN 'FRISCO.
THEN YOU ASK ME HOW I PLAN TO SPEND MY DAY.
YOU KNOW HOW MANY MEN DON'T EVEN ASK ABOUT THEIR WIVES' PLANS?
BECAUSE THEY DON'T GIVE A FUCK. I GIVE A FUCK.
AND YOU'RE PISSED BECAUSE SOME DISLOYAL, THIEVING PIECE OF SHIT IS DEAD?
THAT WAS THE LAST TIME WE ATE TOGETHER.
AFTER THAT, BEING AROUND YOU MADE ME FEEL SICK.

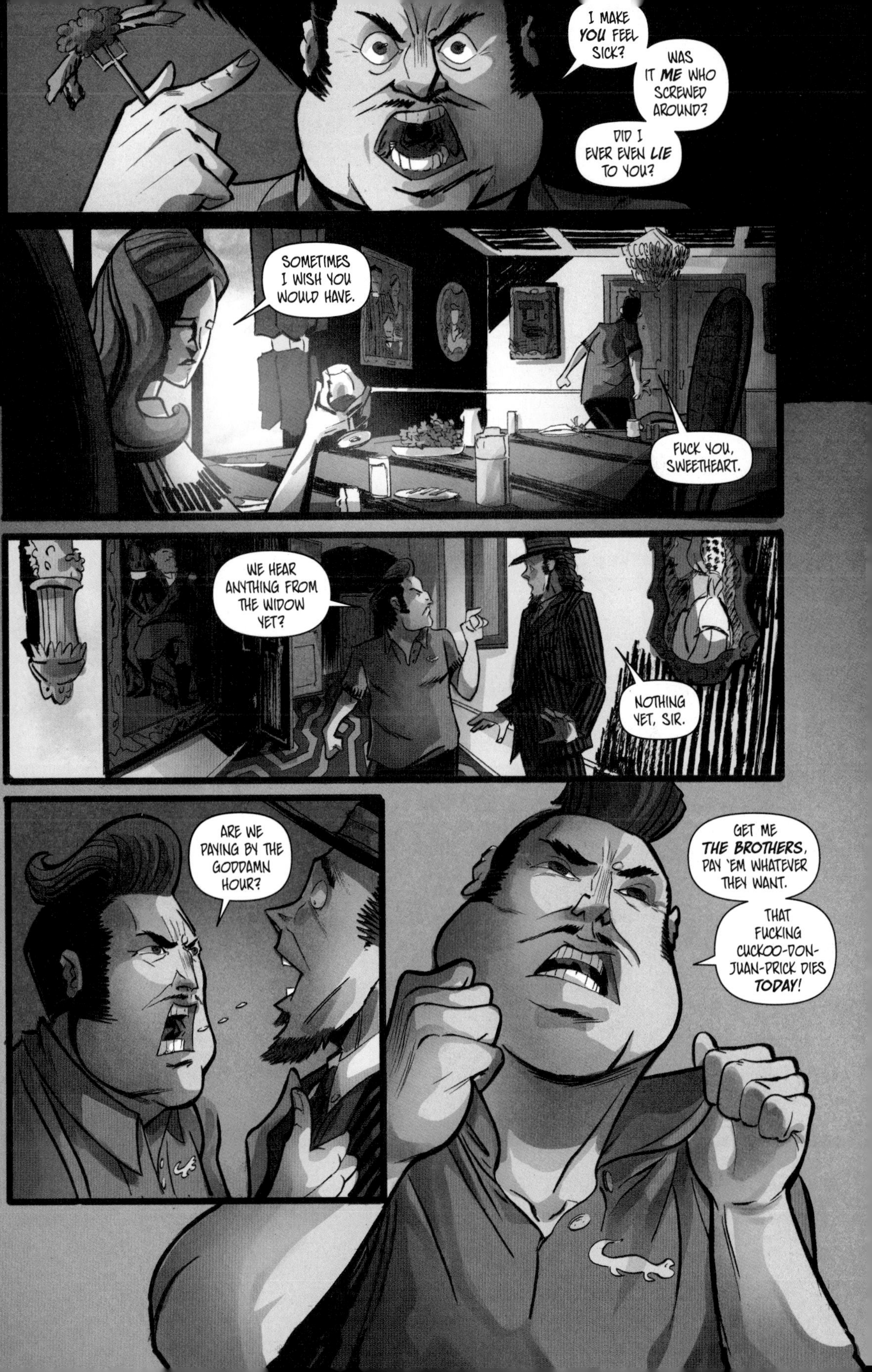
I MAKE *YOU* FEEL SICK?
WAS IT *ME* WHO SCREWED AROUND?
DID I EVER EVEN *LIE* TO YOU?
SOMETIMES I WISH YOU WOULD HAVE.
FUCK YOU, SWEETHEART.
WE HEAR ANYTHING FROM THE WIDOW YET?
NOTHING YET, SIR.
ARE WE PAYING BY THE GODDAMN HOUR?
GET ME *THE BROTHERS*, PAY 'EM WHATEVER THEY WANT.
THAT FUCKING CUCKOO-DON-JUAN-PRICK DIES *TODAY*!

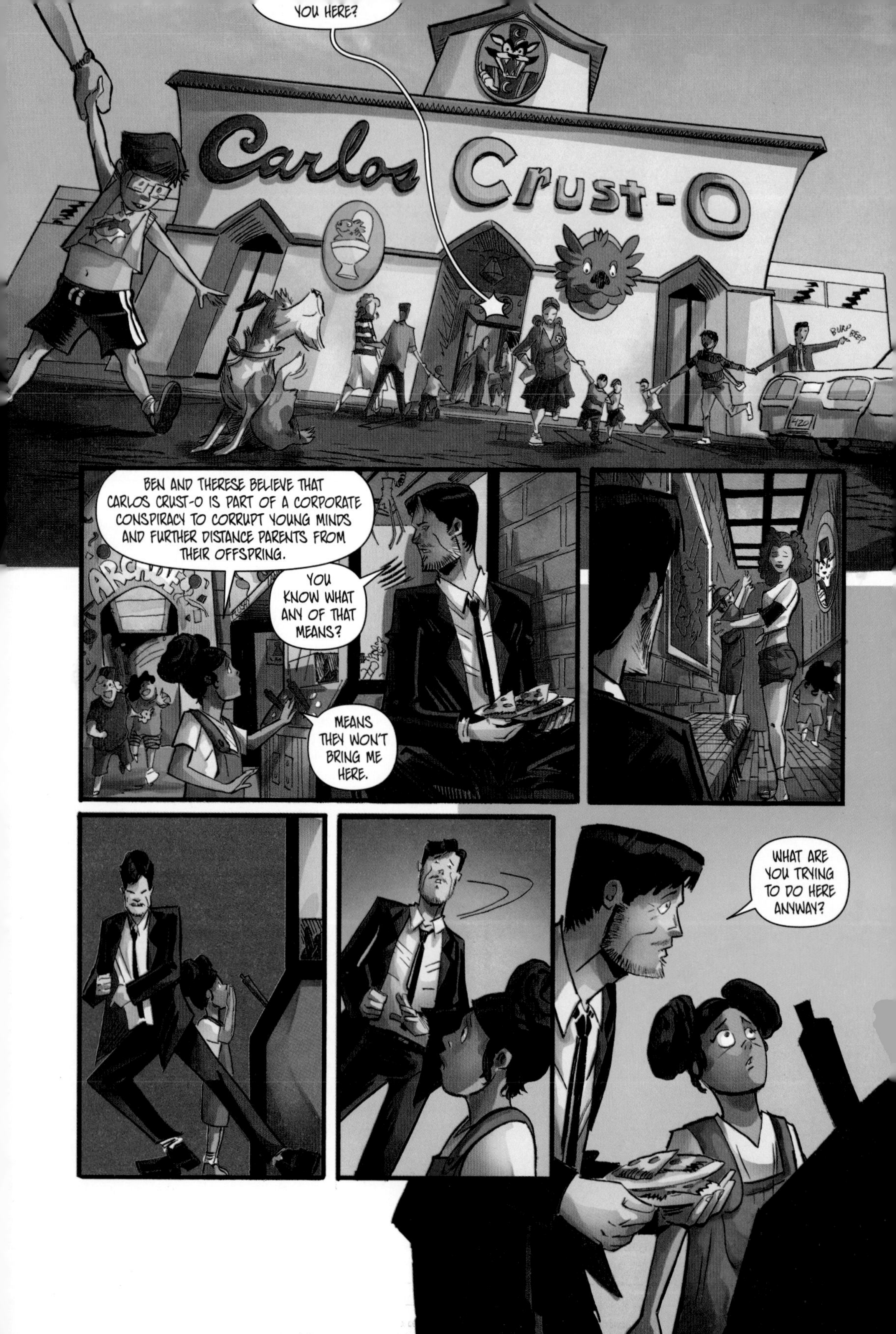
YOU HERE?
Carlos Crust-O
BURP BEEP
420
BEN AND THERESE BELIEVE THAT CARLOS CRUST-O IS PART OF A CORPORATE CONSPIRACY TO CORRUPT YOUNG MINDS AND FURTHER DISTANCE PARENTS FROM THEIR OFFSPRING.
YOU KNOW WHAT ANY OF THAT MEANS?
MEANS THEY WON'T BRING ME HERE.
WHAT ARE YOU TRYING TO DO HERE ANYWAY?

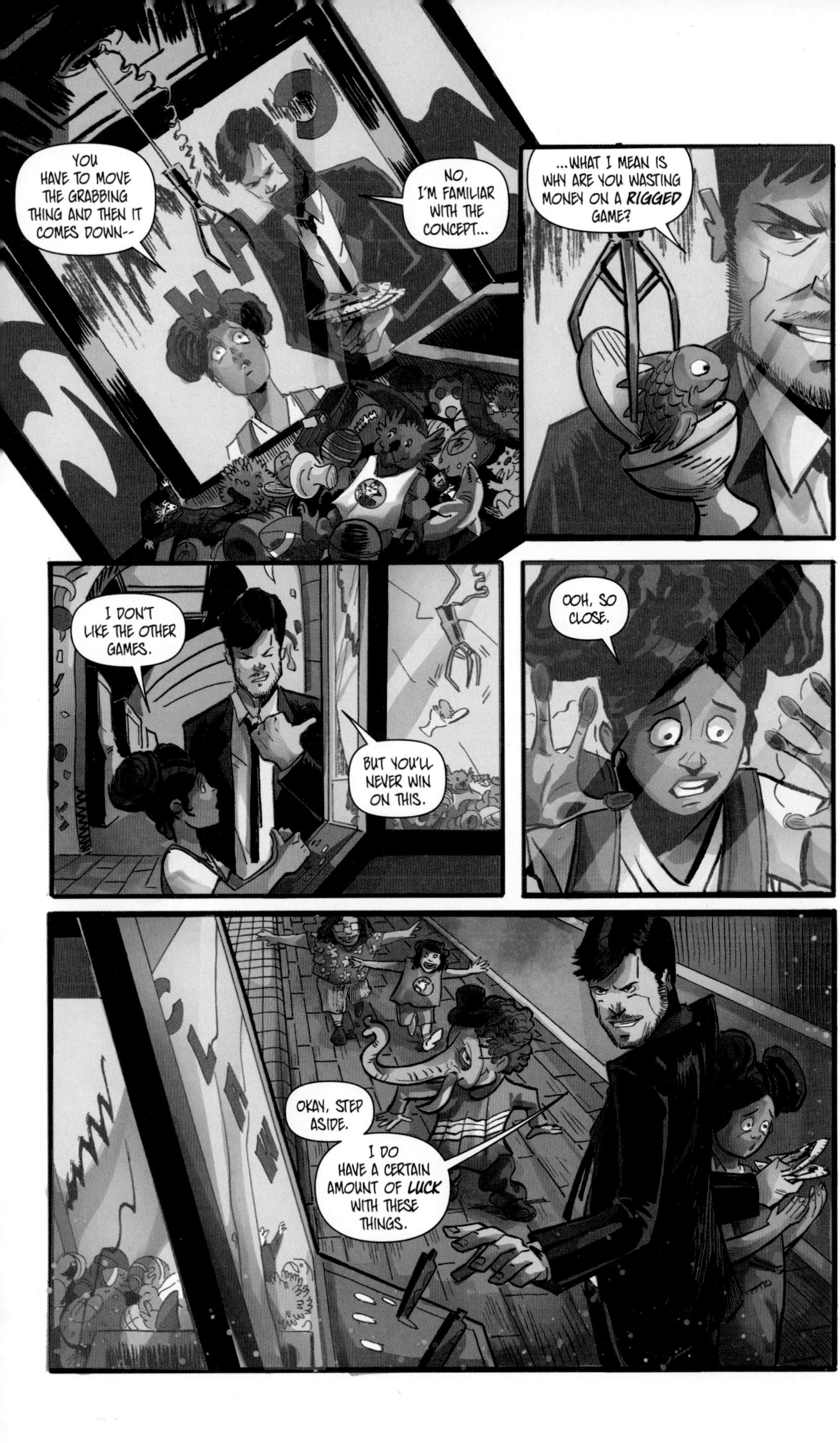
YOU HAVE TO MOVE THE GRABBING THING AND THEN IT COMES DOWN--
NO, I'M FAMILIAR WITH THE CONCEPT...
...WHAT I MEAN IS WHY ARE YOU WASTING MONEY ON A RIGGED GAME?
I DON'T LIKE THE OTHER GAMES.
BUT YOU'LL NEVER WIN ON THIS.
OOH, SO CLOSE.
OKAY, STEP ASIDE.
I DO HAVE A CERTAIN AMOUNT OF LUCK WITH THESE THINGS.

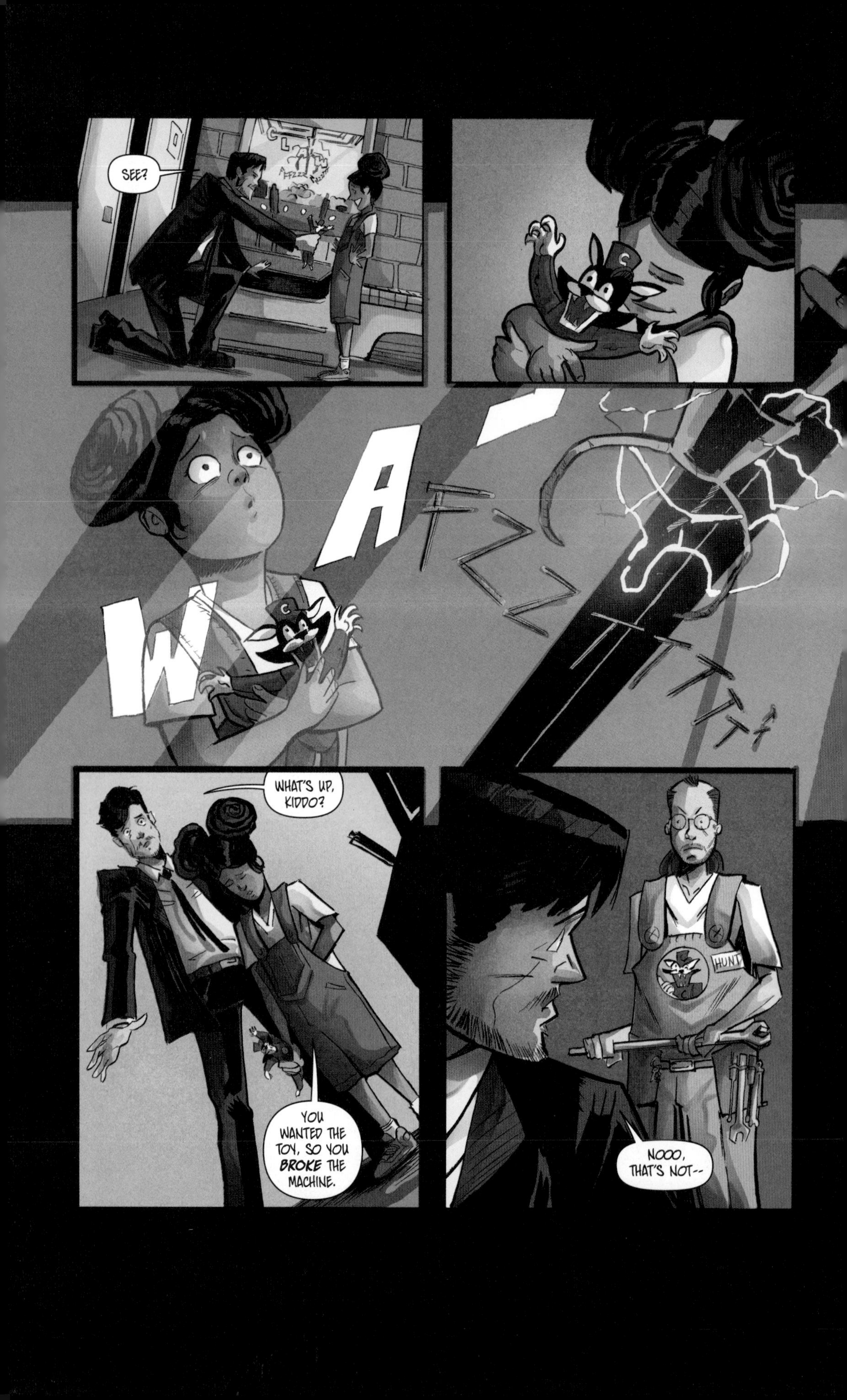
SEE?
AFZZZ
WA
AFZZZTTTT
WHAT'S UP, KIDDO?
YOU WANTED THE TOY, SO YOU BROKE THE MACHINE.
HUNT
NOOO, THAT'S NOT--

LIKE HOW YOU WANTED A NEW LIFE, SO YOU **BROKE** MY MOM.
HUNT
SOMETIMES GROWN-UPS HAVE **NO CHOICE** BUT TO MAKE WHAT SEEM LIKE REALLY BAD DECISIONS.
AND SOMETIMES OTHER PEOPLE GET HURT AS A RESULT.
NOT THAT I KNEW--
ARCADE
SOPHIE... WAIT!
FLUSHY
GOOD JOB, JERK.

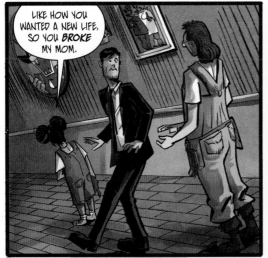

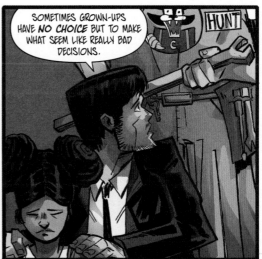

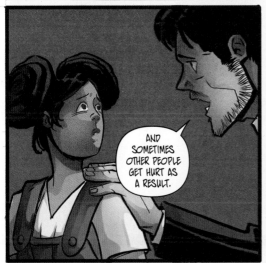

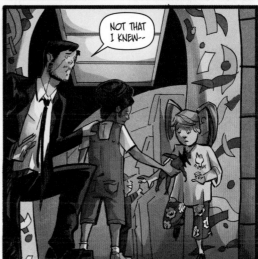

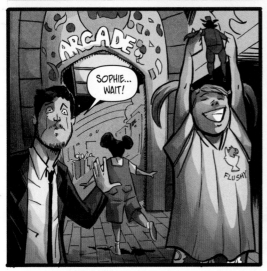

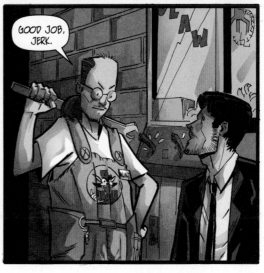

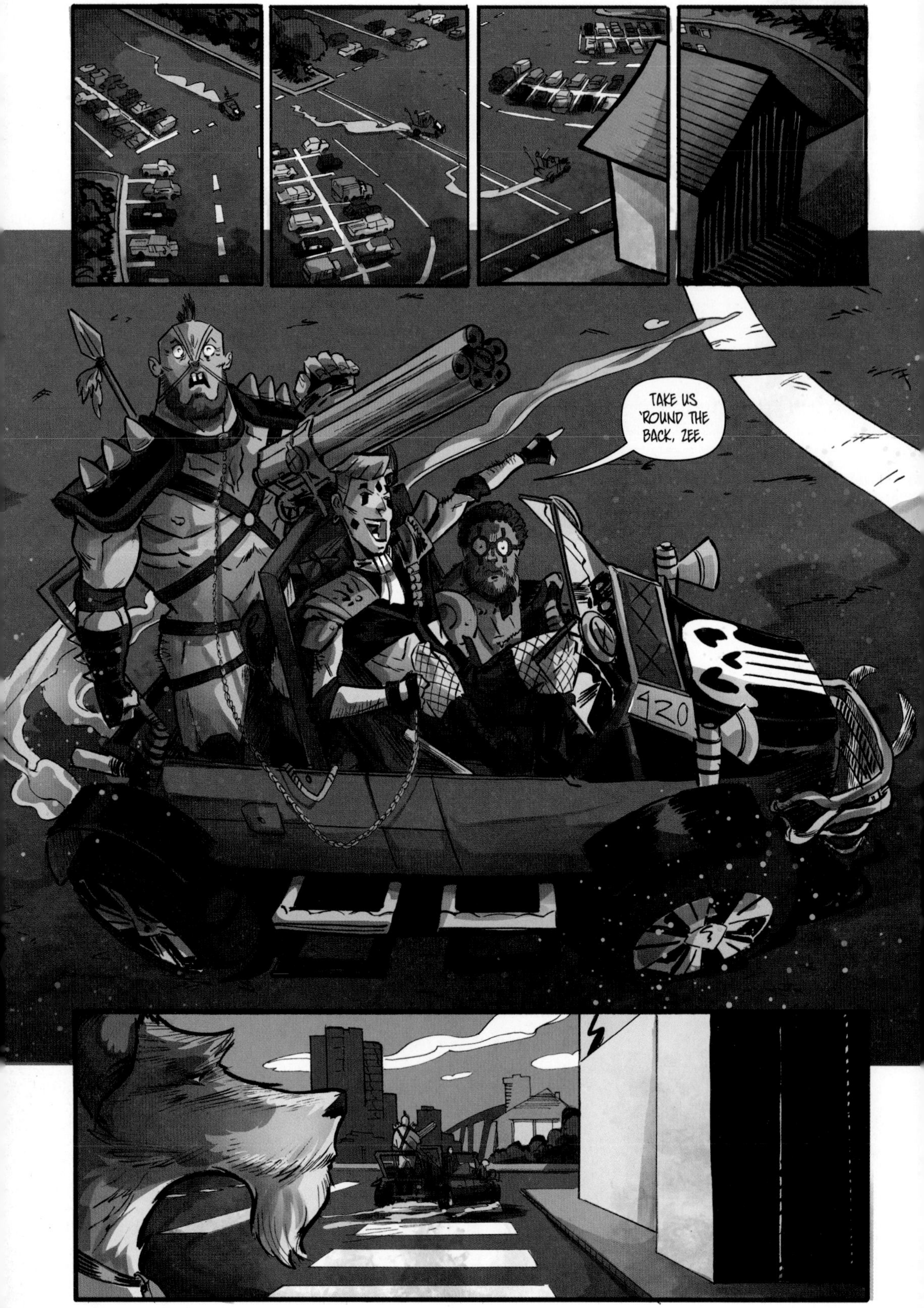
TAKE US 'ROUND THE BACK, ZEE.
420

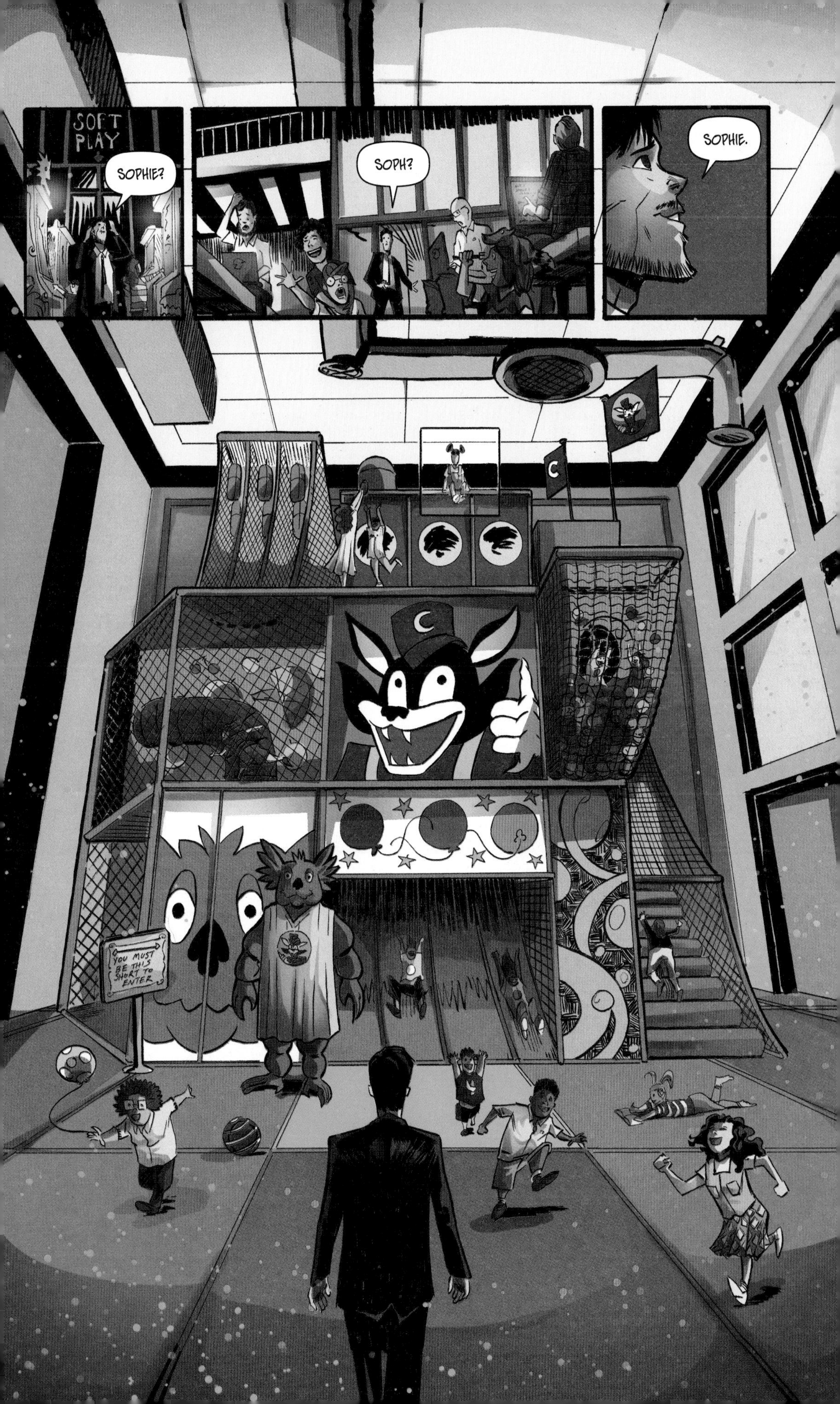

SOFT PLAY
SOPHIE?
SOPH?
SOPHIE.
C
C
YOU MUST BE THIS SHORT TO ENTER

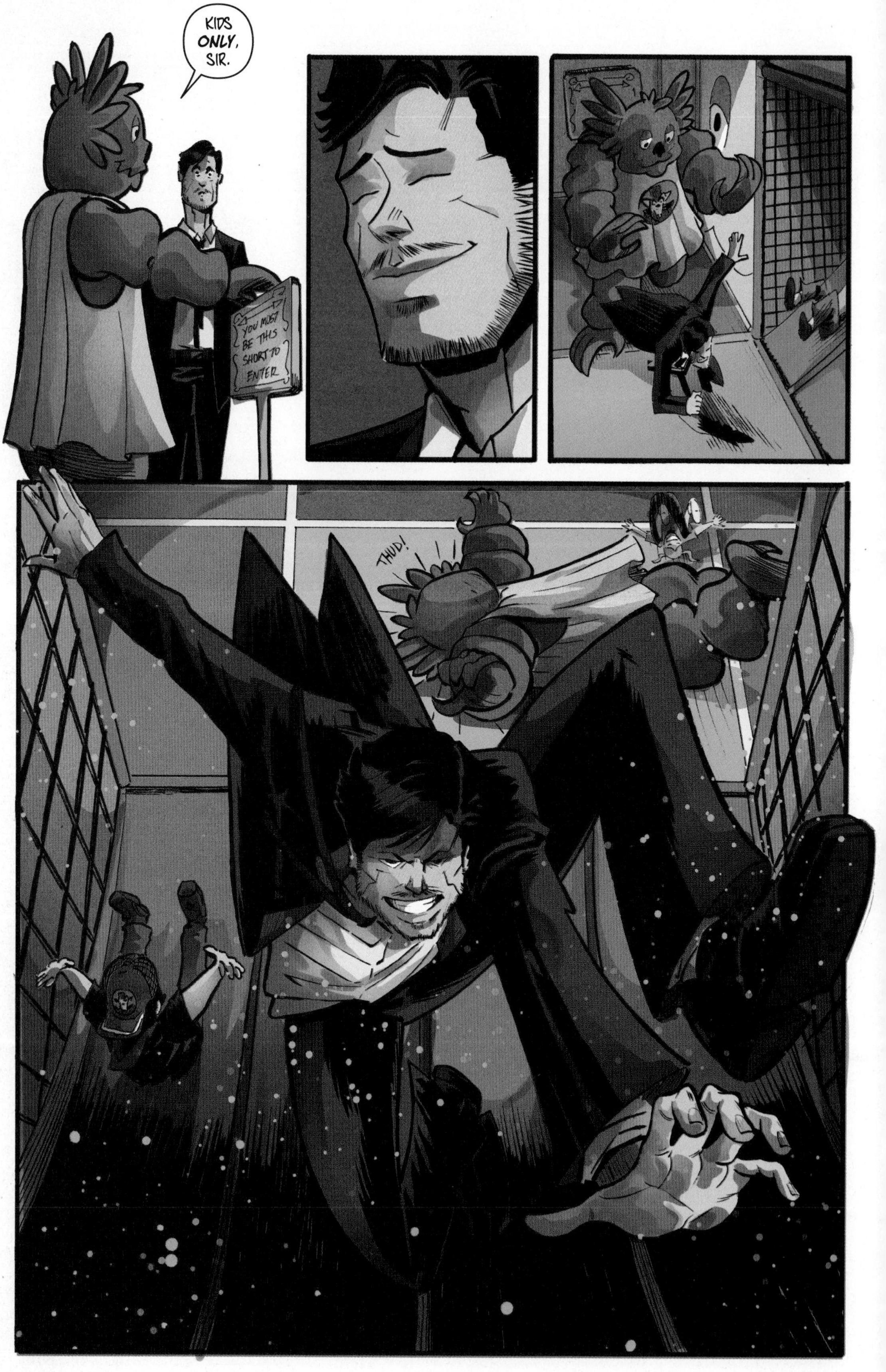
KIDS ONLY, SIR.
YOU MUST BE THIS SHORT TO ENTER
THUD!

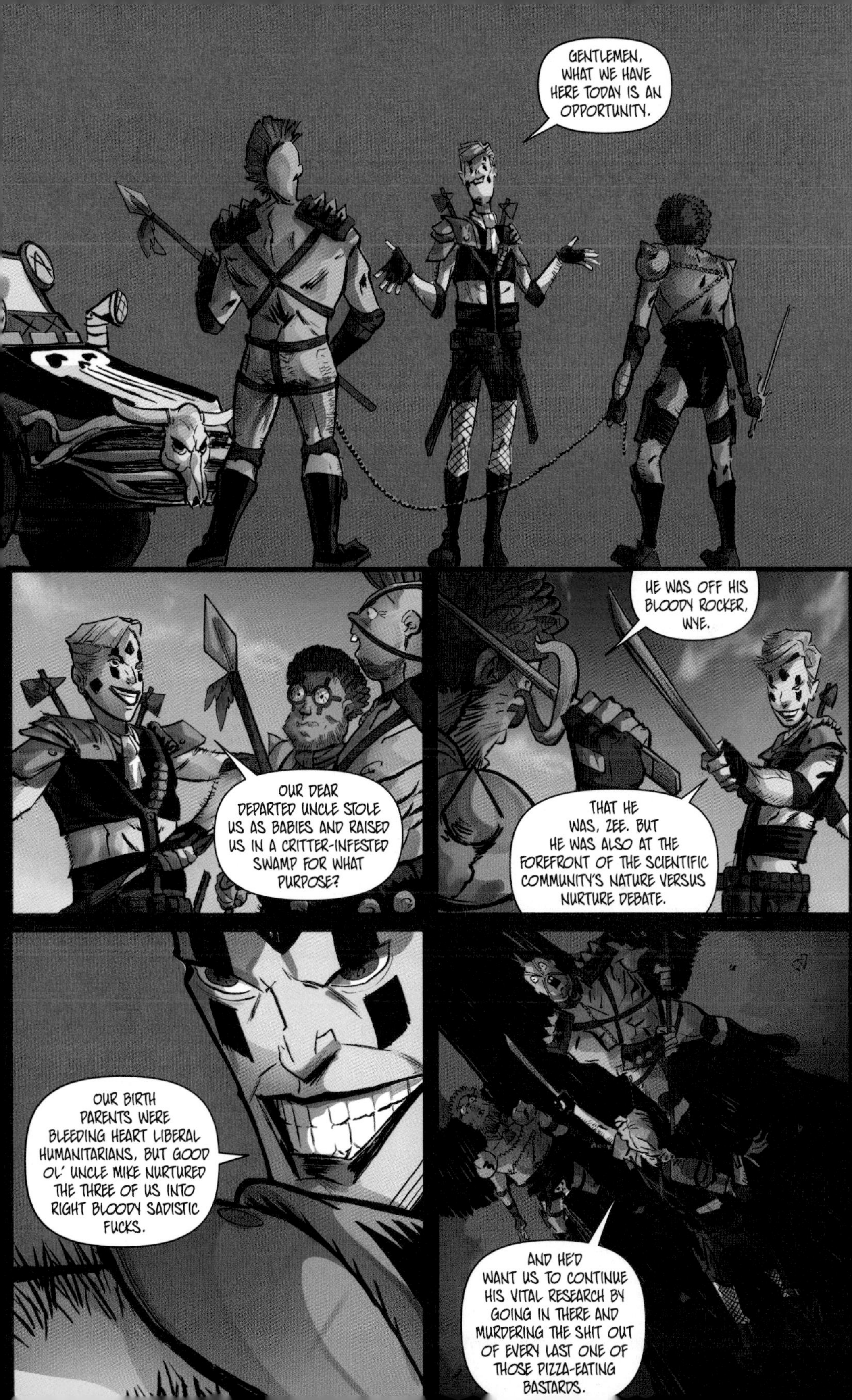
GENTLEMEN, WHAT WE HAVE HERE TODAY IS AN OPPORTUNITY.
OUR DEAR DEPARTED UNCLE STOLE US AS BABIES AND RAISED US IN A CRITTER-INFESTED SWAMP FOR WHAT PURPOSE?
HE WAS OFF HIS BLOODY ROCKER, WYE.
THAT HE WAS, ZEE. BUT HE WAS ALSO AT THE FOREFRONT OF THE SCIENTIFIC COMMUNITY'S NATURE VERSUS NURTURE DEBATE.
OUR BIRTH PARENTS WERE BLEEDING HEART LIBERAL HUMANITARIANS, BUT GOOD OL' UNCLE MIKE NURTURED THE THREE OF US INTO RIGHT BLOODY SADISTIC FUCKS.
AND HE'D WANT US TO CONTINUE HIS VITAL RESEARCH BY GOING IN THERE AND MURDERING THE SHIT OUT OF EVERY LAST ONE OF THOSE PIZZA-EATING BASTARDS.

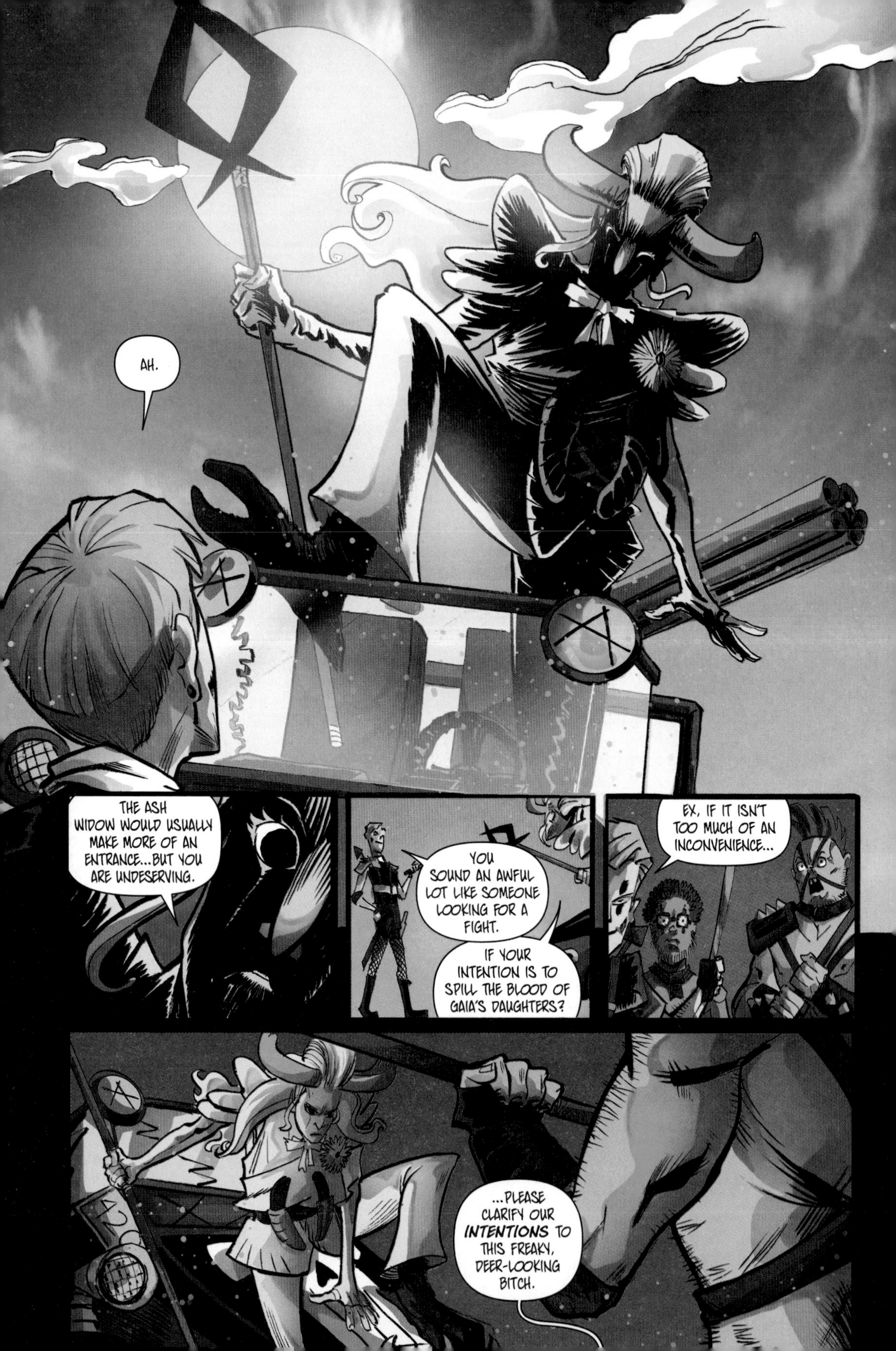
AH.
THE ASH WIDOW WOULD USUALLY MAKE MORE OF AN ENTRANCE...BUT YOU ARE UNDESERVING.
YOU SOUND AN AWFUL LOT LIKE SOMEONE LOOKING FOR A FIGHT.
IF YOUR INTENTION IS TO SPILL THE BLOOD OF GAIA'S DAUGHTERS?
EX, IF IT ISN'T TOO MUCH OF AN INCONVENIENCE...
...PLEASE CLARIFY OUR **INTENTIONS** TO THIS FREAKY, DEER-LOOKING BITCH.

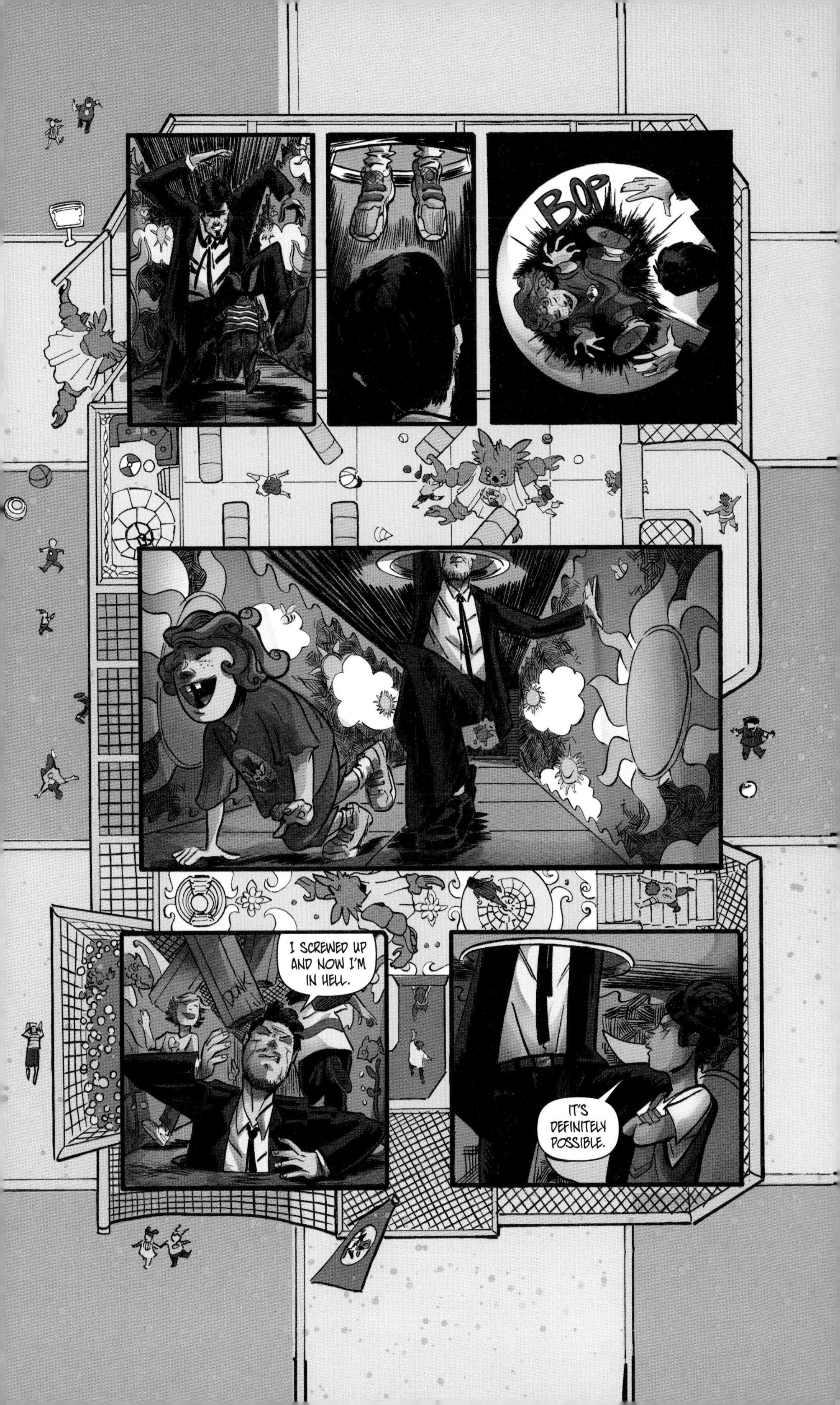
BOP
DONK
I SCREWED UP AND NOW I'M IN HELL.
IT'S DEFINITELY POSSIBLE.

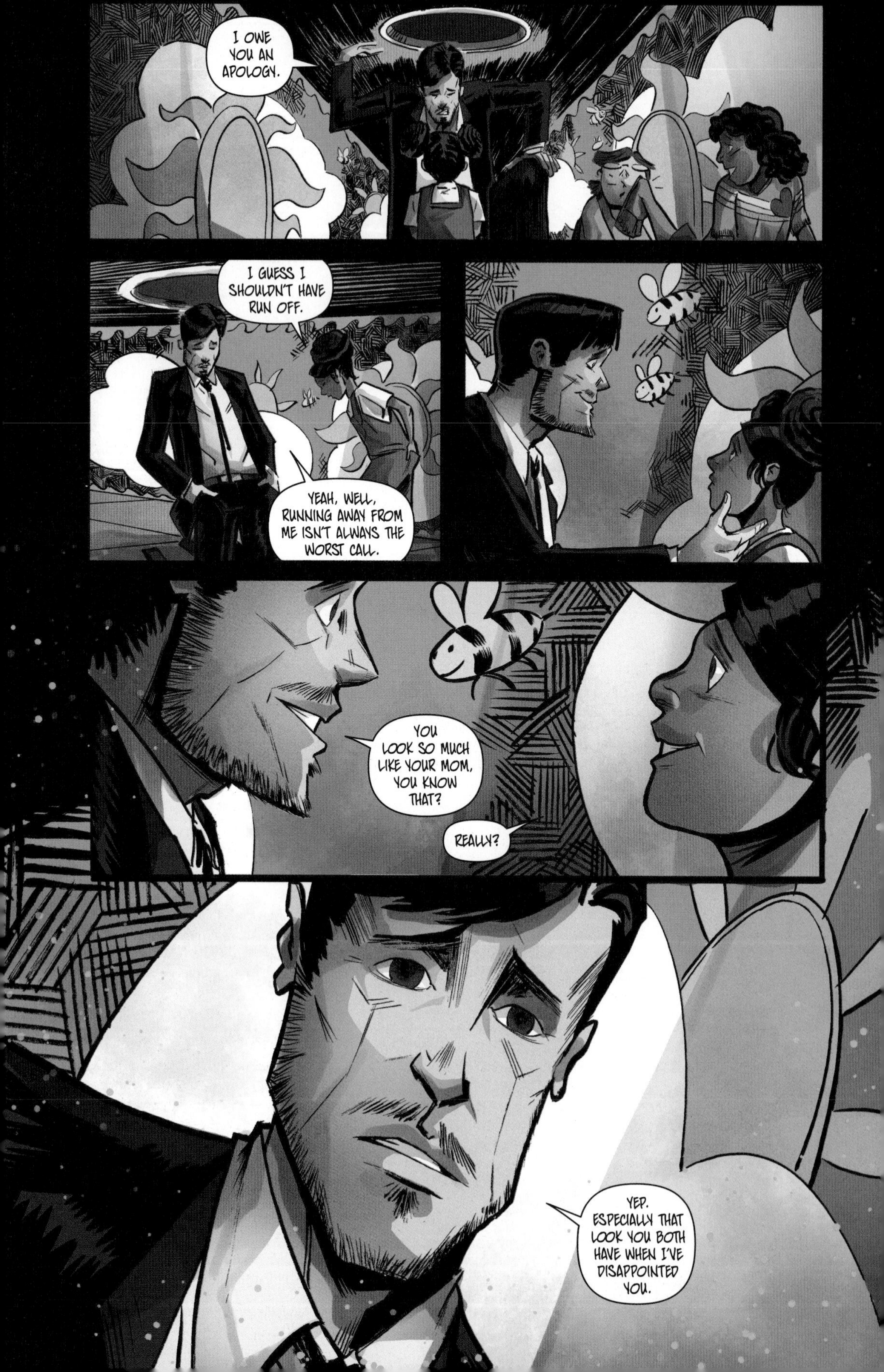
I OWE YOU AN APOLOGY.
I GUESS I SHOULDN'T HAVE RUN OFF.
YEAH, WELL, RUNNING AWAY FROM ME ISN'T ALWAYS THE WORST CALL.
YOU LOOK SO MUCH LIKE YOUR MOM, YOU KNOW THAT?
REALLY?
YEP. ESPECIALLY THAT LOOK YOU BOTH HAVE WHEN I'VE DISAPPOINTED YOU.

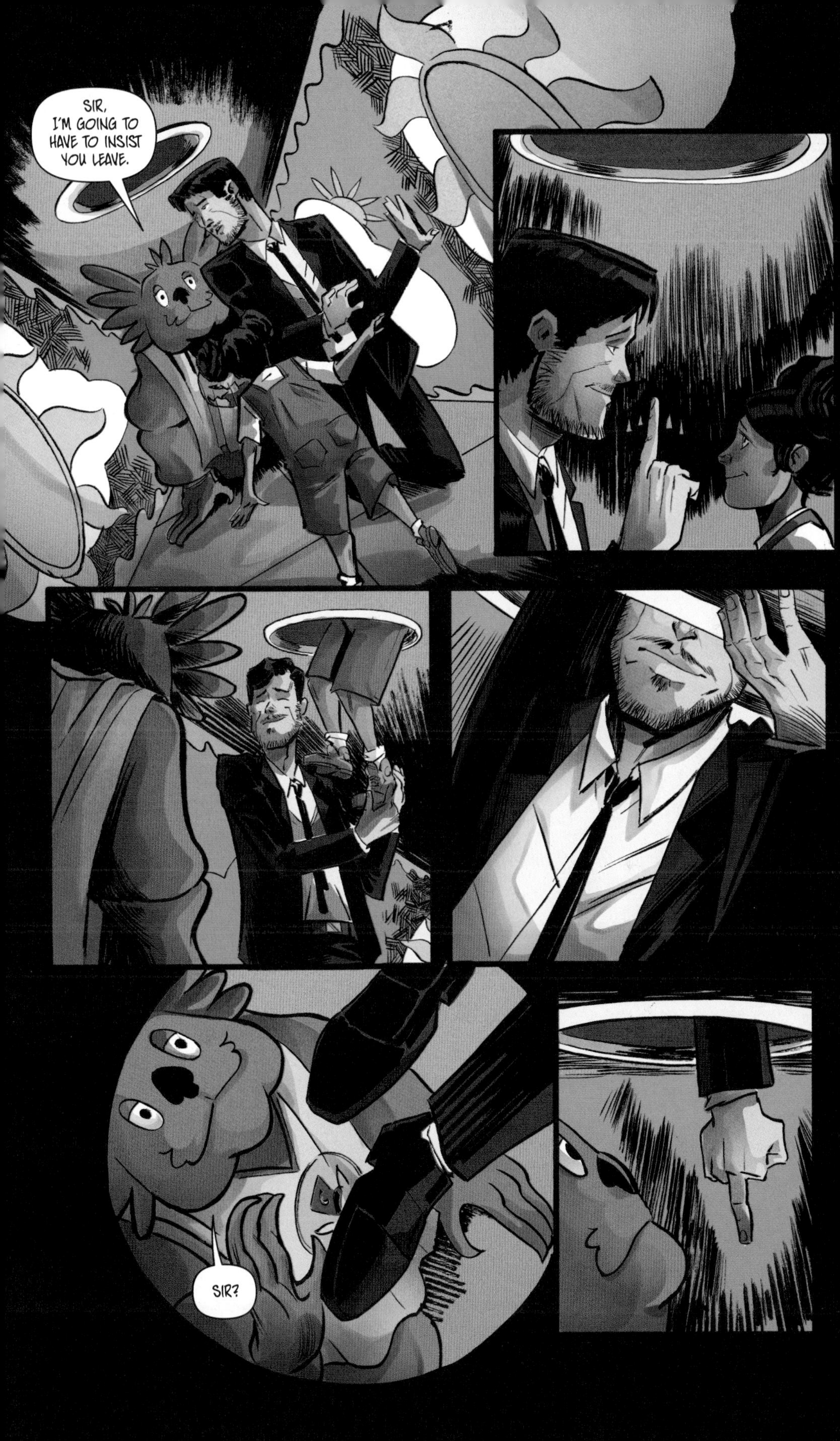
SIR, I'M GOING TO HAVE TO INSIST YOU LEAVE.
SIR?

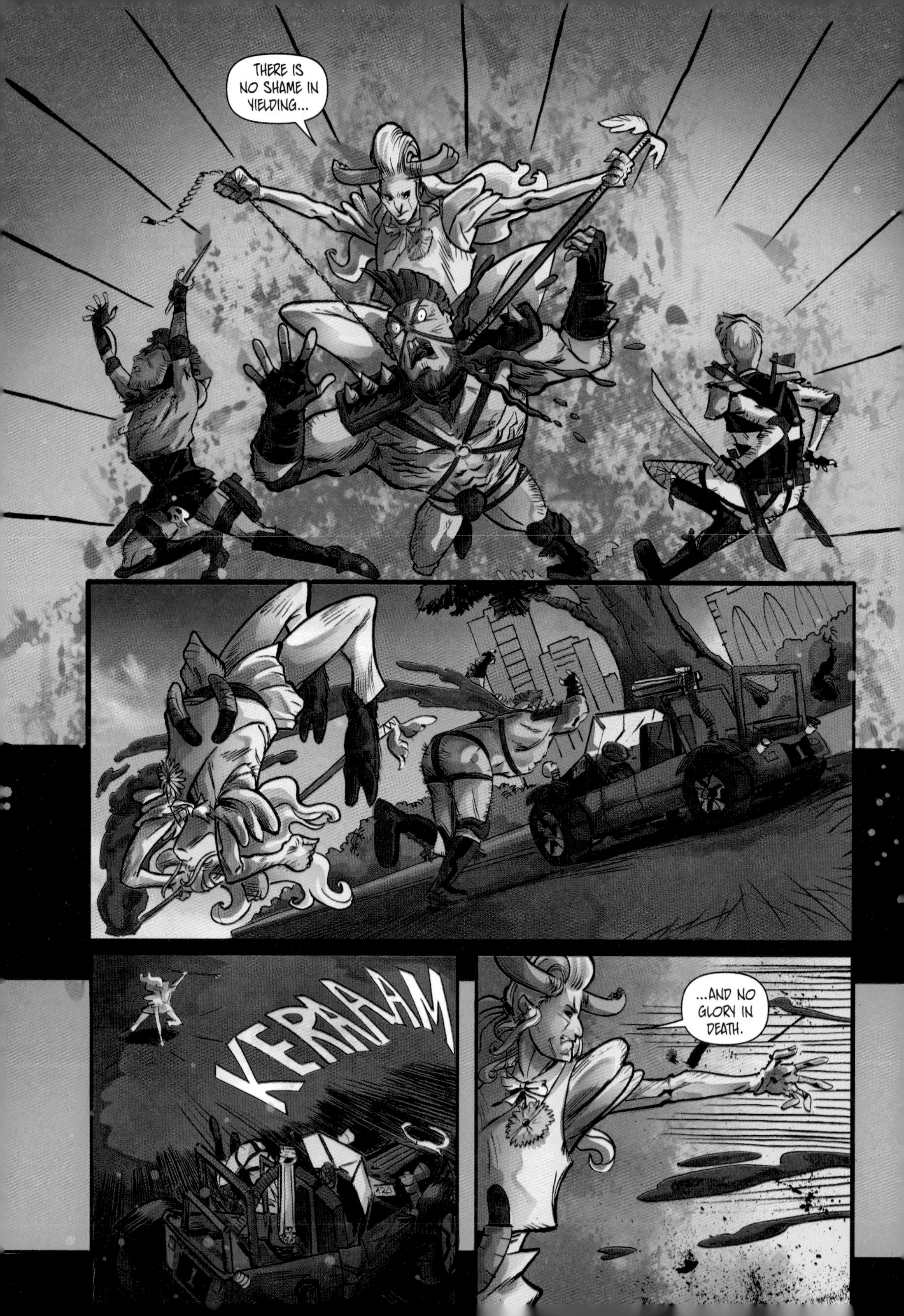
THERE IS NO SHAME IN YIELDING...
KERRAAM
...AND NO GLORY IN DEATH.

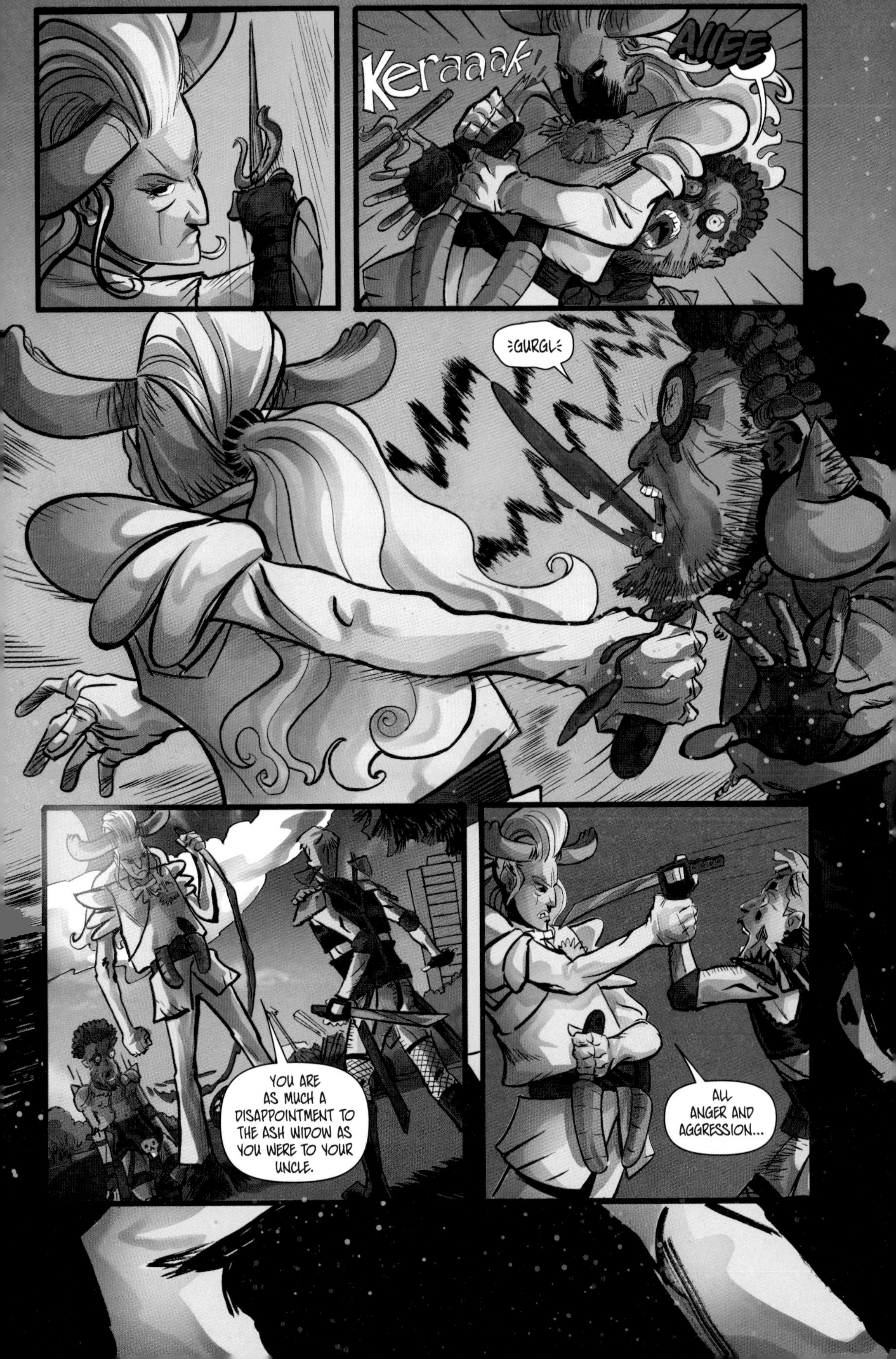
Keraaak
AIIEE
GURGL
YOU ARE AS MUCH A DISAPPOINTMENT TO THE ASH WIDOW AS YOU WERE TO YOUR UNCLE.
ALL ANGER AND AGGRESSION...

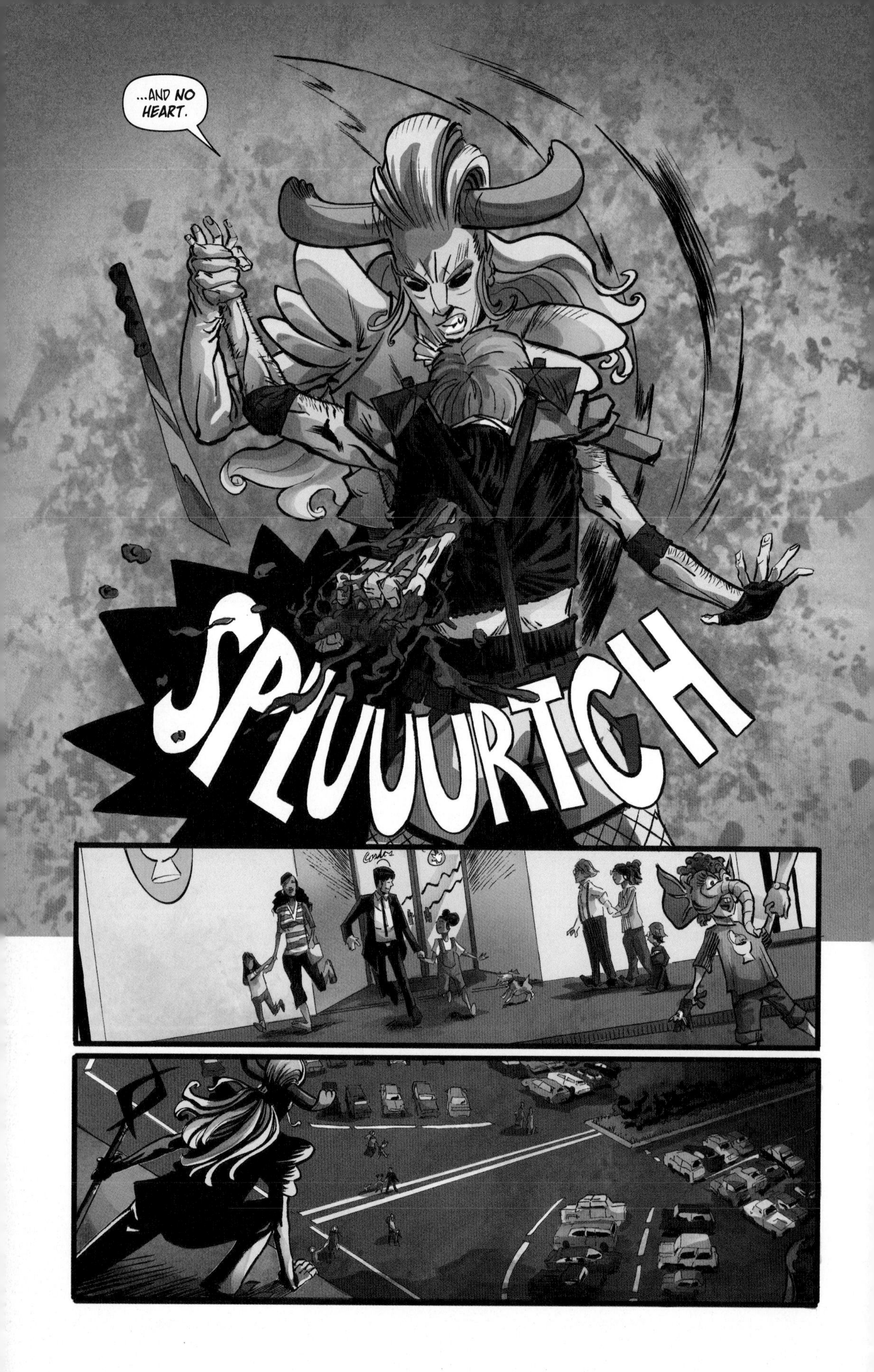
...AND NO HEART.
SPLUUURTCH

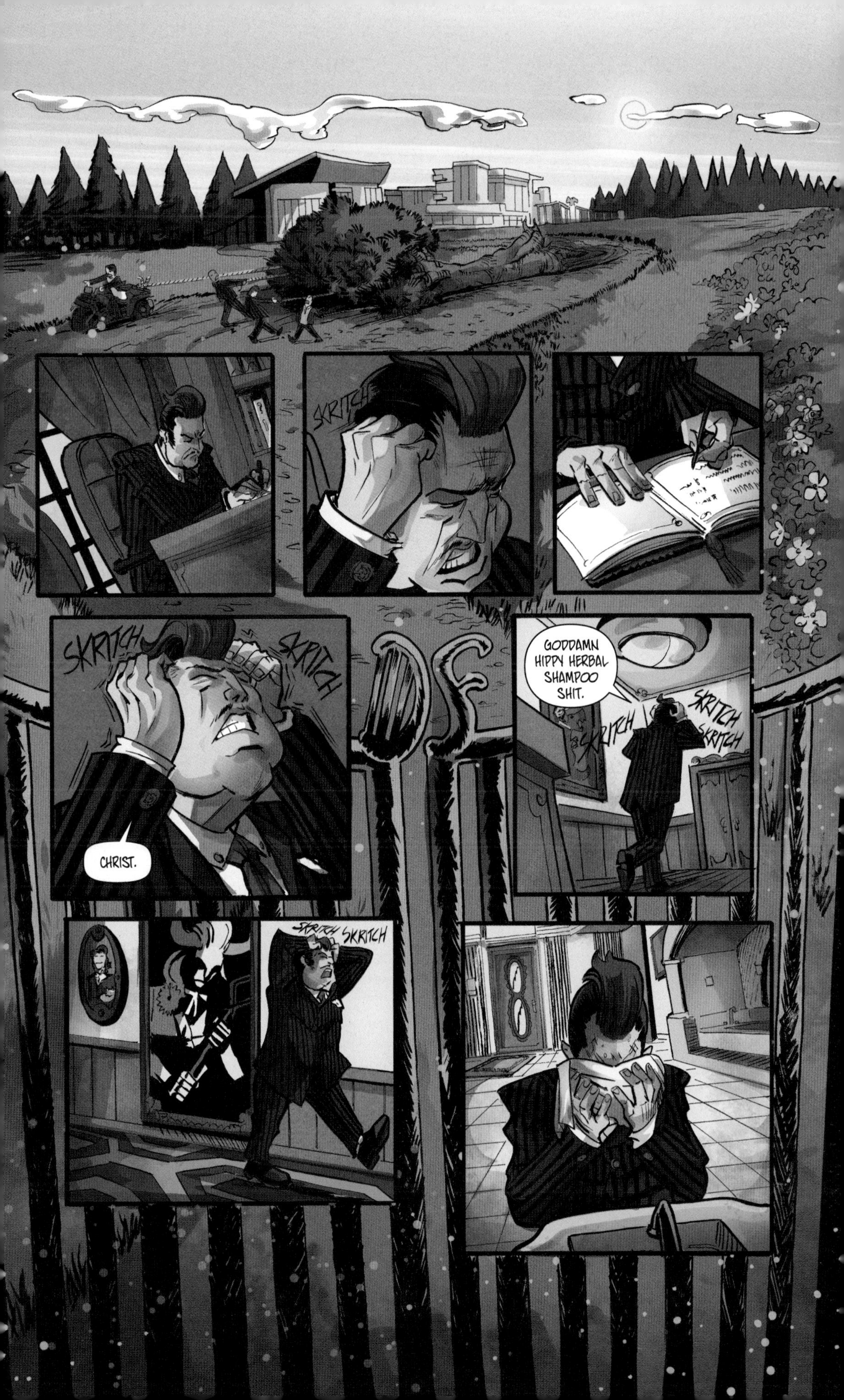
SKRITCH
SKRITCH
SKRITCH
CHRIST.
GODDAMN HIPPY HERBAL SHAMPOO SHIT.
SKRITCH
SKRITCH
SKRITCH
SKRITCH
SKRITCH

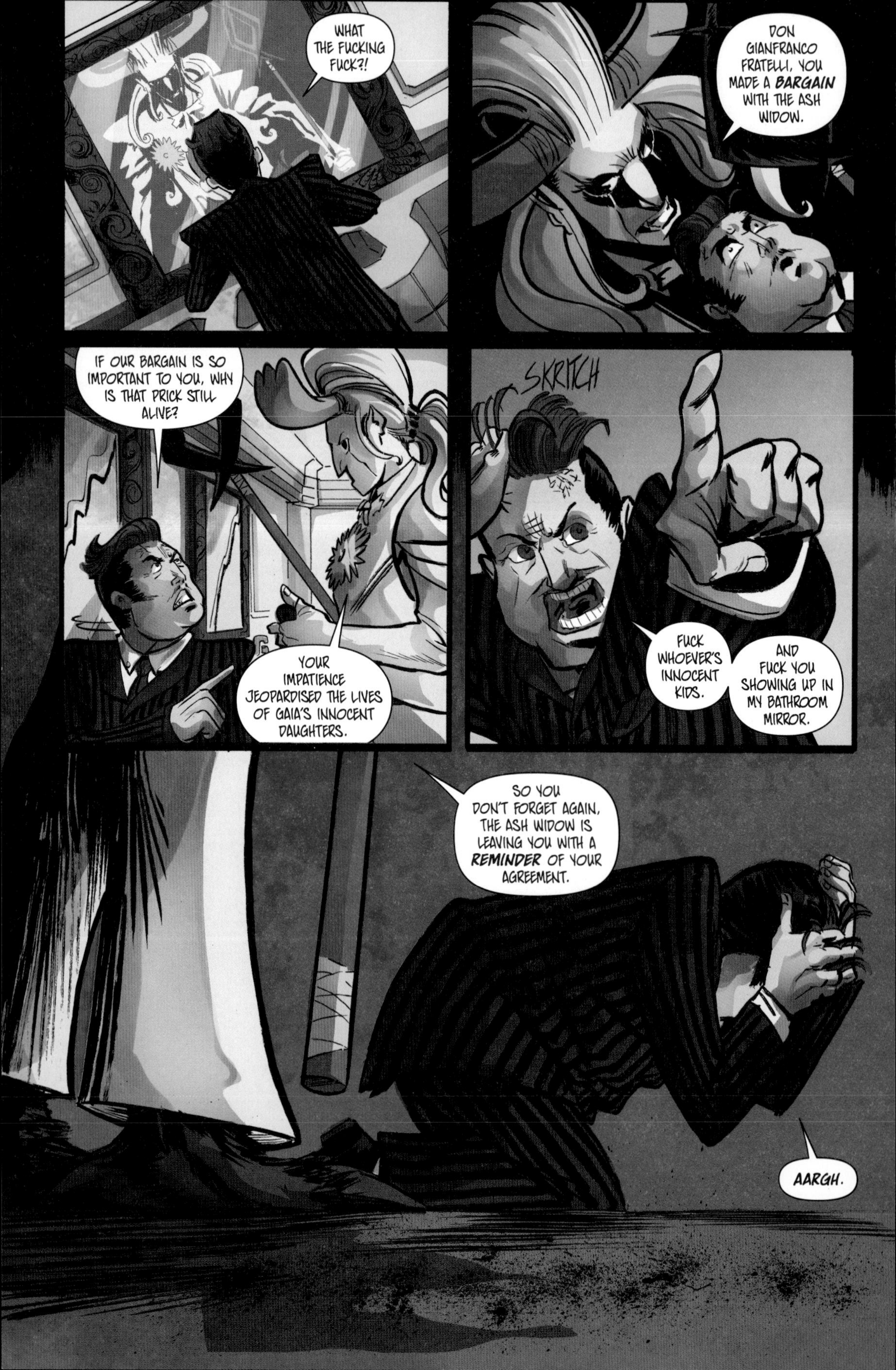
WHAT THE FUCKING FUCK?!
DON GIANFRANCO FRATELLI, YOU MADE A BARGAIN WITH THE ASH WIDOW.
IF OUR BARGAIN IS SO IMPORTANT TO YOU, WHY IS THAT PRICK STILL ALIVE?
YOUR IMPATIENCE JEOPARDISED THE LIVES OF GAIA'S INNOCENT DAUGHTERS.
SKRITCH
FUCK WHOEVER'S INNOCENT KIDS.
AND FUCK YOU SHOWING UP IN MY BATHROOM MIRROR.
SO YOU DON'T FORGET AGAIN, THE ASH WIDOW IS LEAVING YOU WITH A REMINDER OF YOUR AGREEMENT.
AARGH.

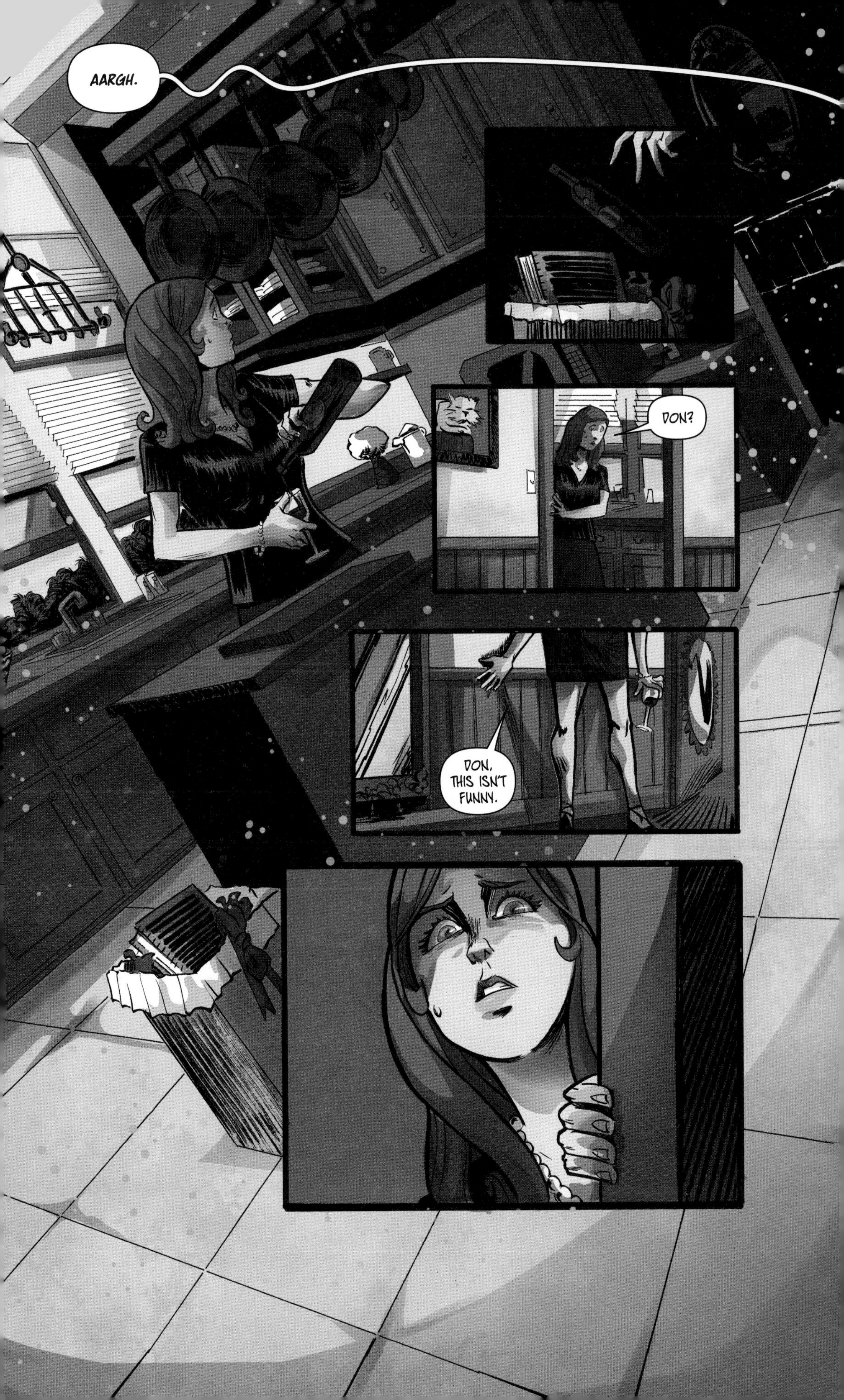
AARGH.
DON?
DON, THIS ISN'T FUNNY.

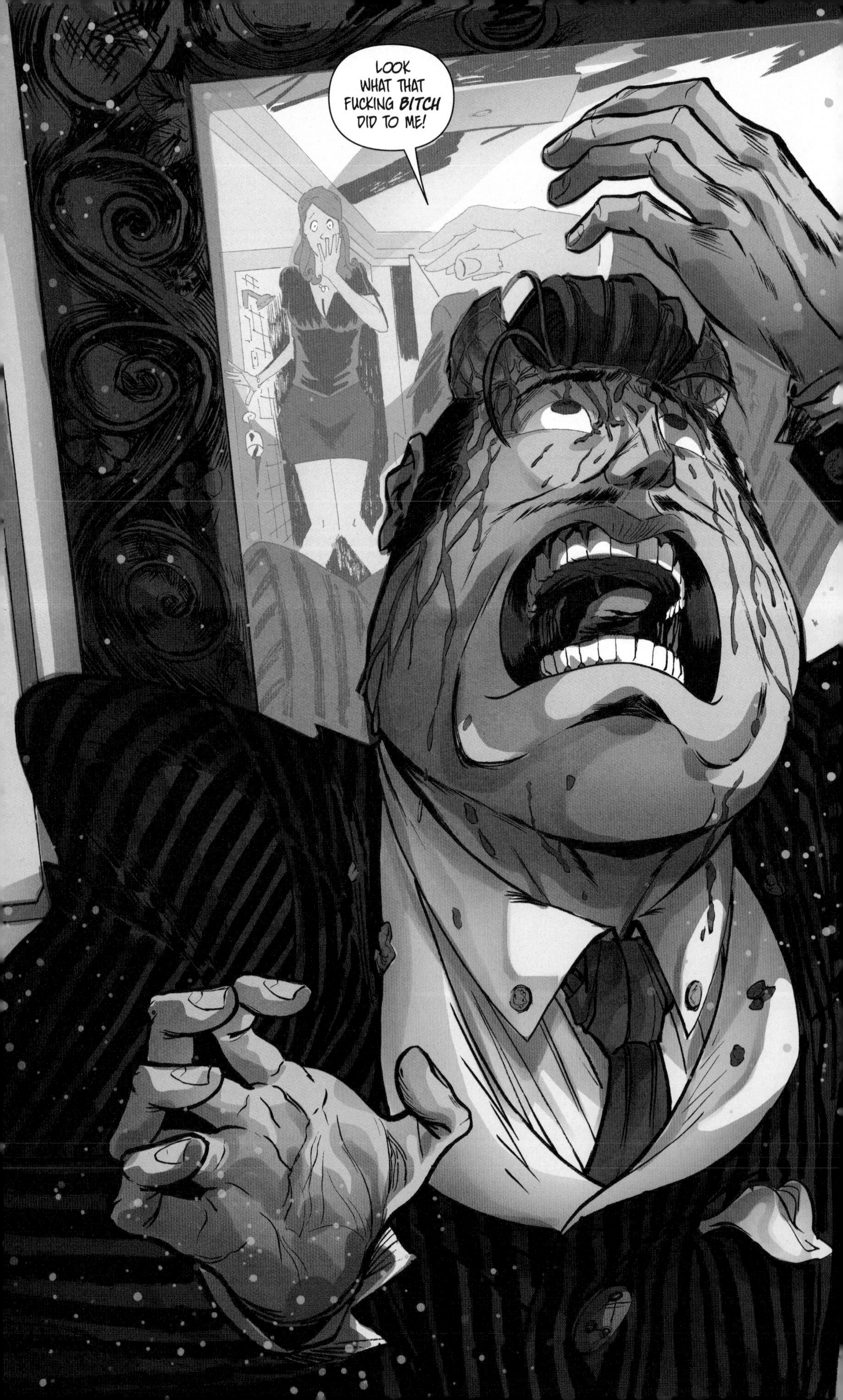
LOOK WHAT THAT FUCKING BITCH DID TO ME!

CHAPTER
4

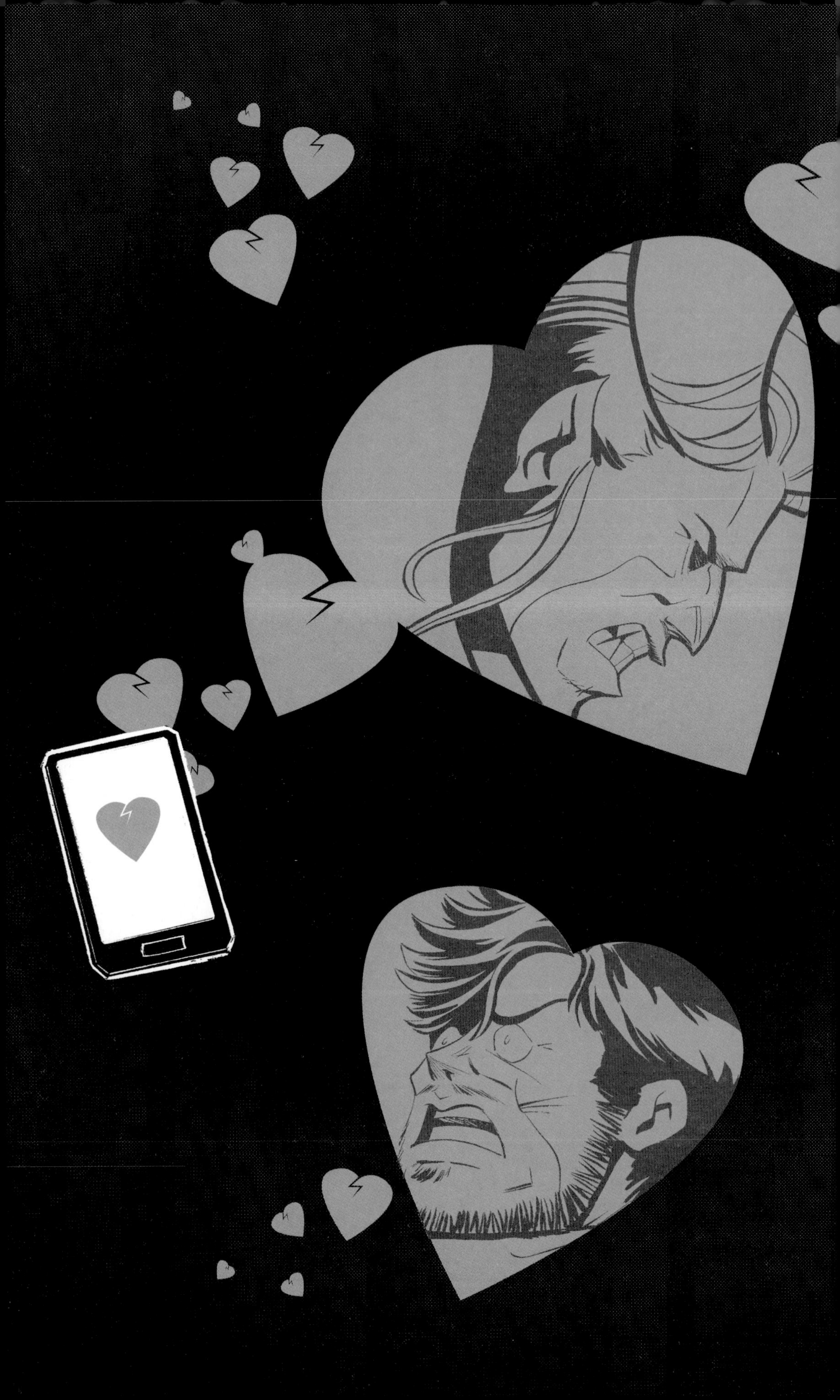

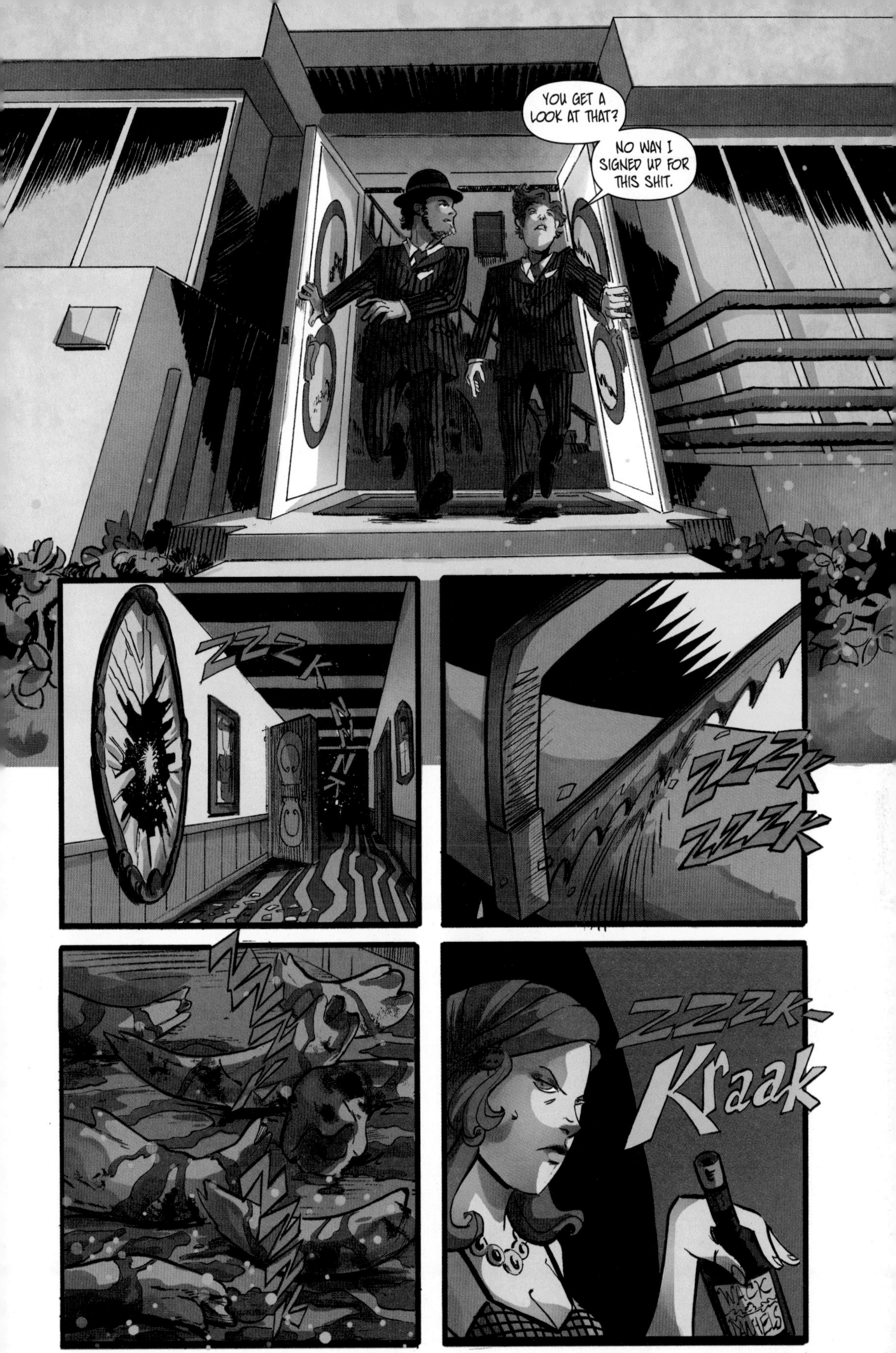
YOU GET A LOOK AT THAT?
NO WAY I SIGNED UP FOR THIS SHIT.
ZZZK
ZZZK
ZZZK-
Kraak

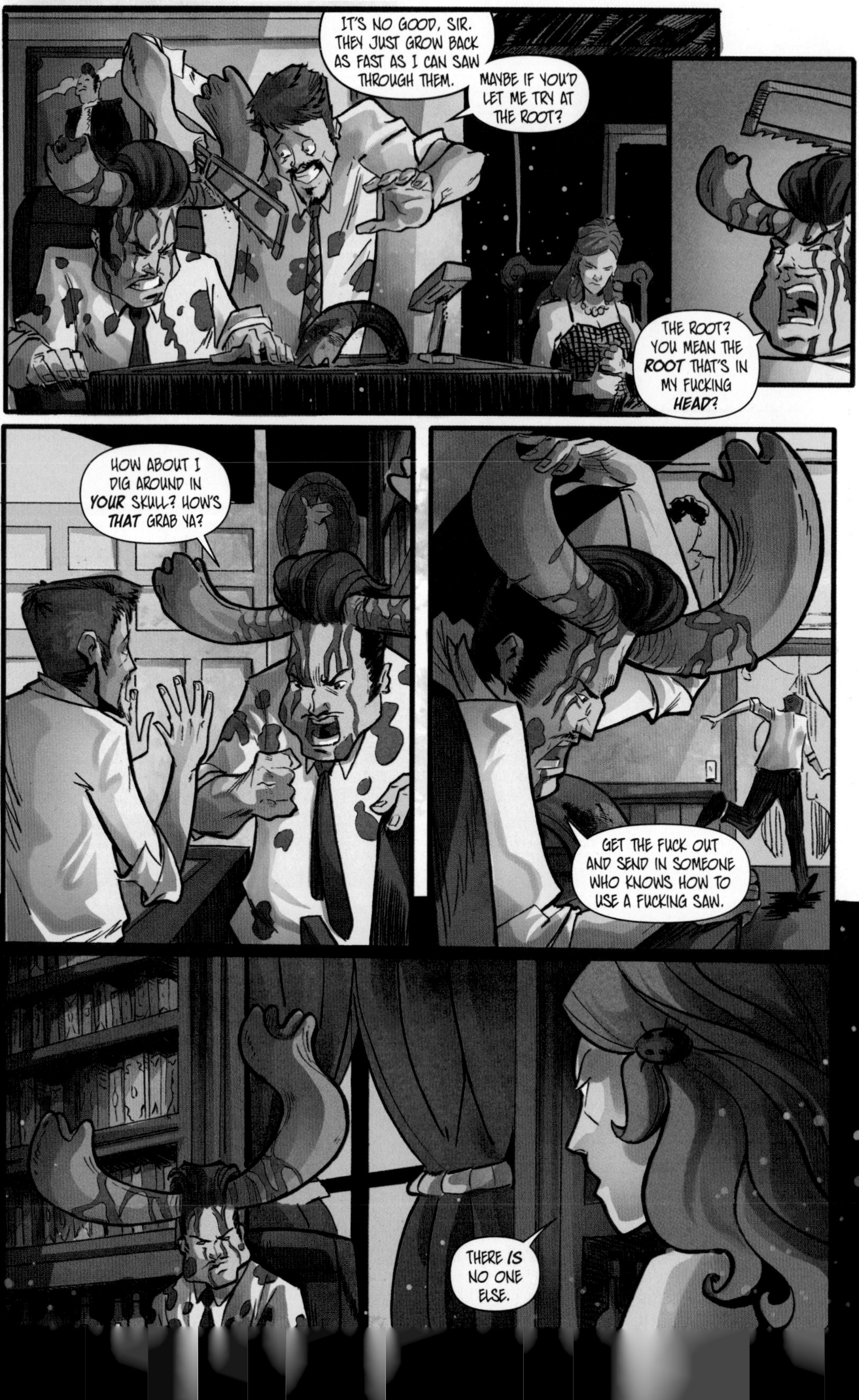
IT'S NO GOOD, SIR. THEY JUST GROW BACK AS FAST AS I CAN SAW THROUGH THEM.
MAYBE IF YOU'D LET ME TRY AT THE ROOT?
THE ROOT? YOU MEAN THE ROOT THAT'S IN MY FUCKING HEAD?
HOW ABOUT I DIG AROUND IN YOUR SKULL? HOW'S THAT GRAB YA?
GET THE FUCK OUT AND SEND IN SOMEONE WHO KNOWS HOW TO USE A FUCKING SAW.
THERE IS NO ONE ELSE.

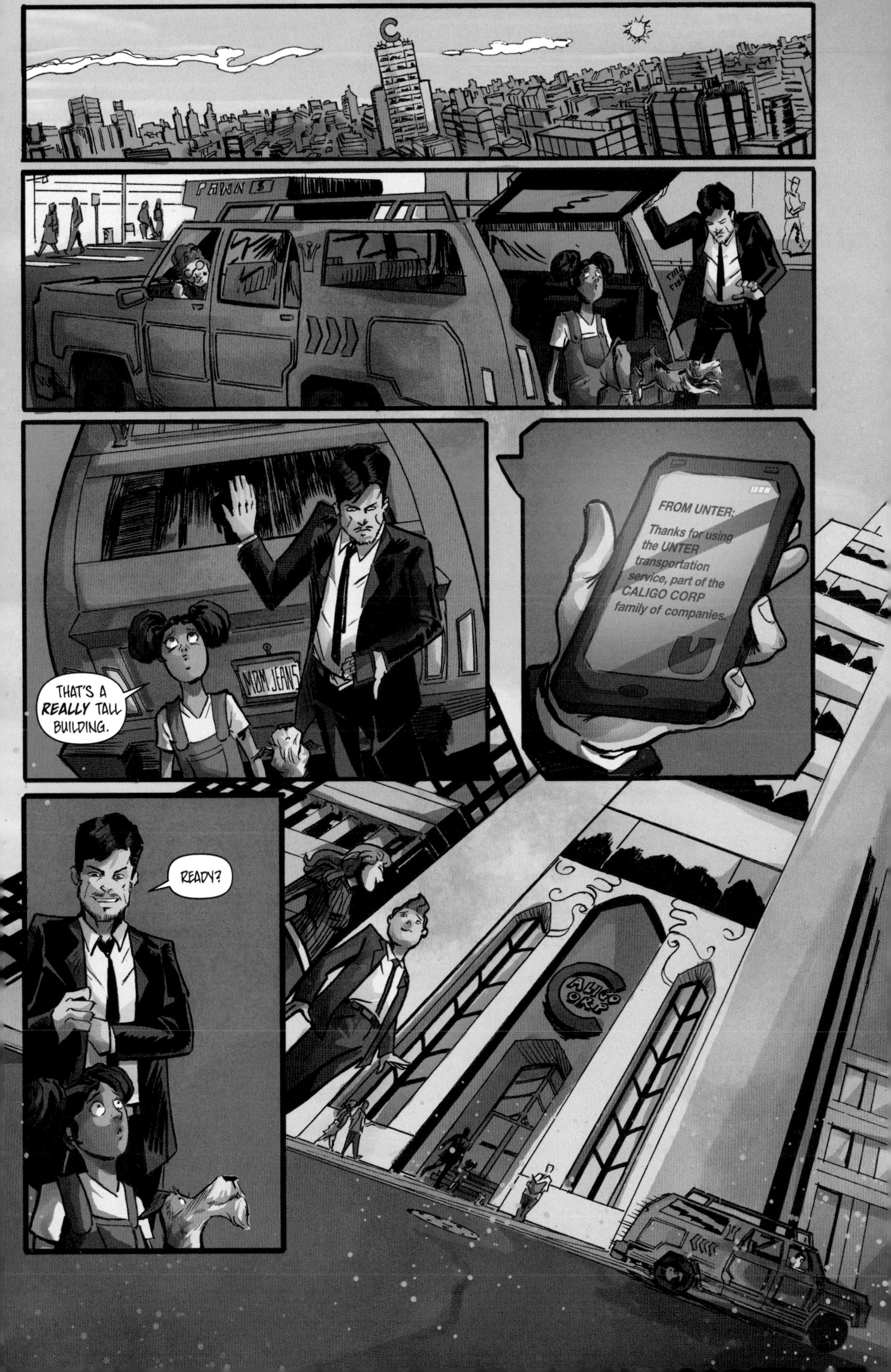

THAT'S A REALLY TALL BUILDING.
FROM UNTER:
Thanks for using the UNTER transportation service, part of the CALIGO CORP family of companies.
READY?
CALIGO CORP
MOM JEANS

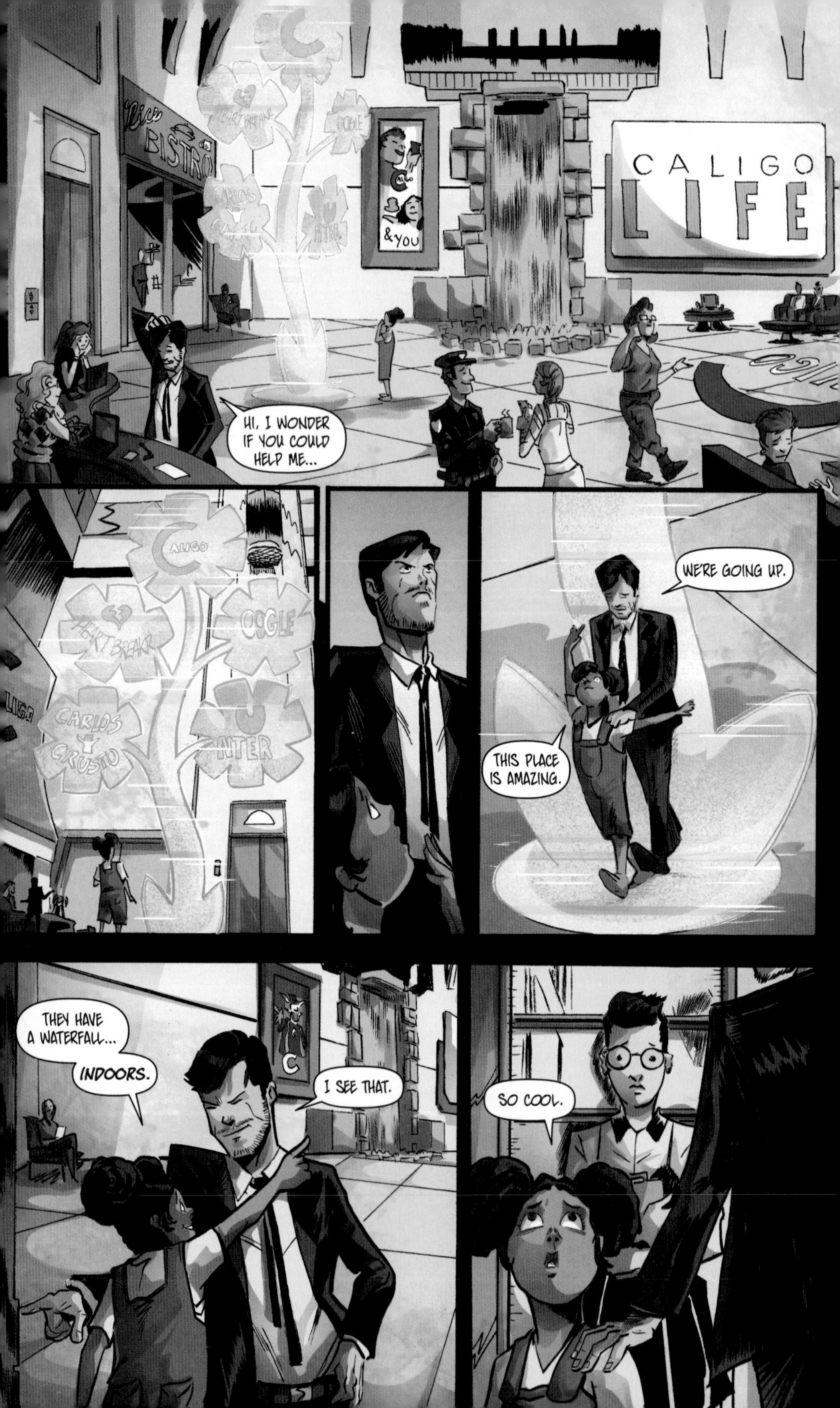
BISTRO
CALIGO
LIFE
HI, I WONDER IF YOU COULD HELP ME...
CALIGO
OOGLE
CARLOS CRUSTO
WE'RE GOING UP.
THIS PLACE IS AMAZING.
THEY HAVE A WATERFALL...
INDOORS.
I SEE THAT.
SO COOL.

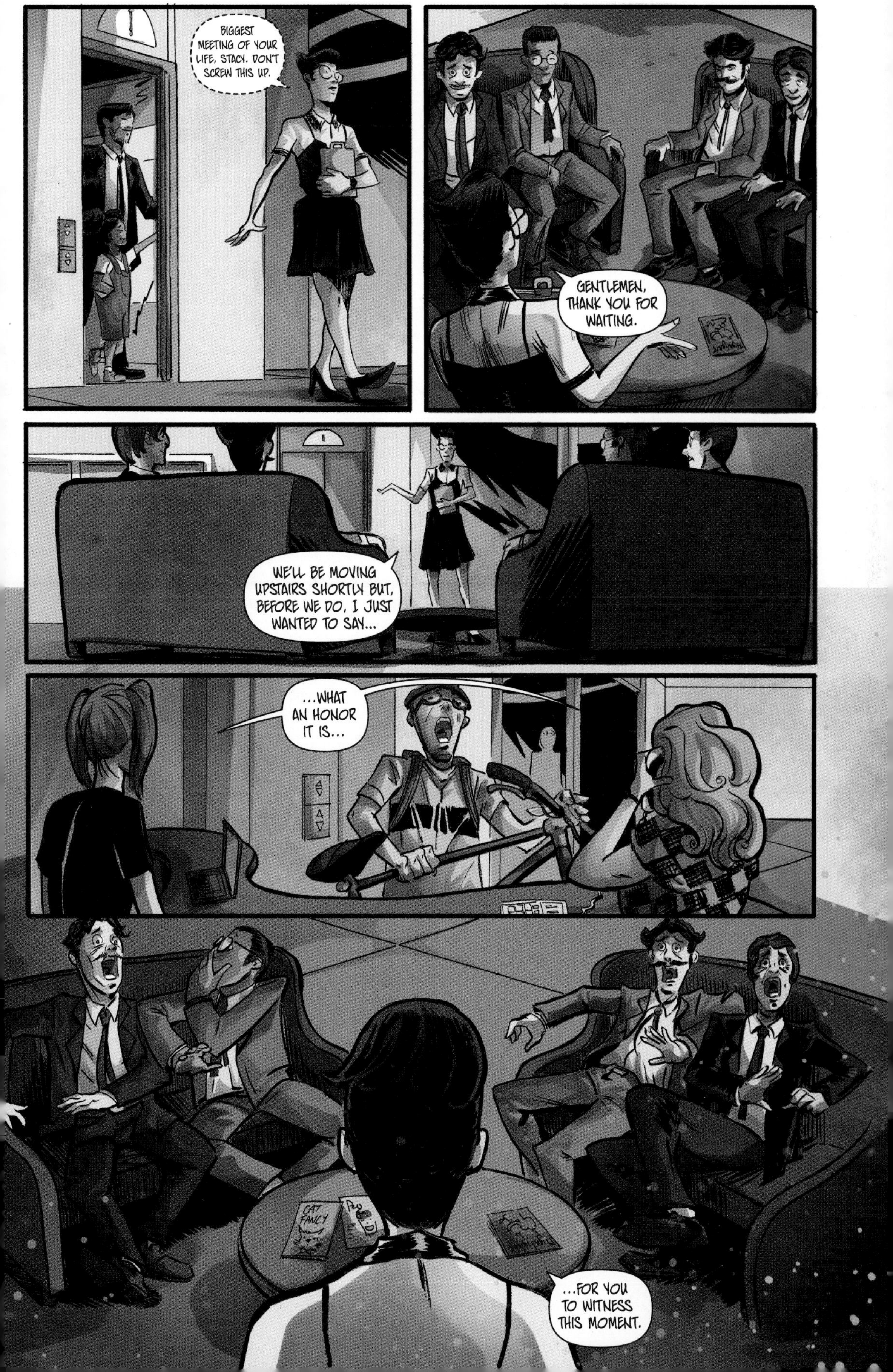
BIGGEST MEETING OF YOUR LIFE, STACY. DON'T SCREW THIS UP.
GENTLEMEN, THANK YOU FOR WAITING.
WE'LL BE MOVING UPSTAIRS SHORTLY BUT, BEFORE WE DO, I JUST WANTED TO SAY...
...WHAT AN HONOR IT IS...
CAT FANCY
...FOR YOU TO WITNESS THIS MOMENT.

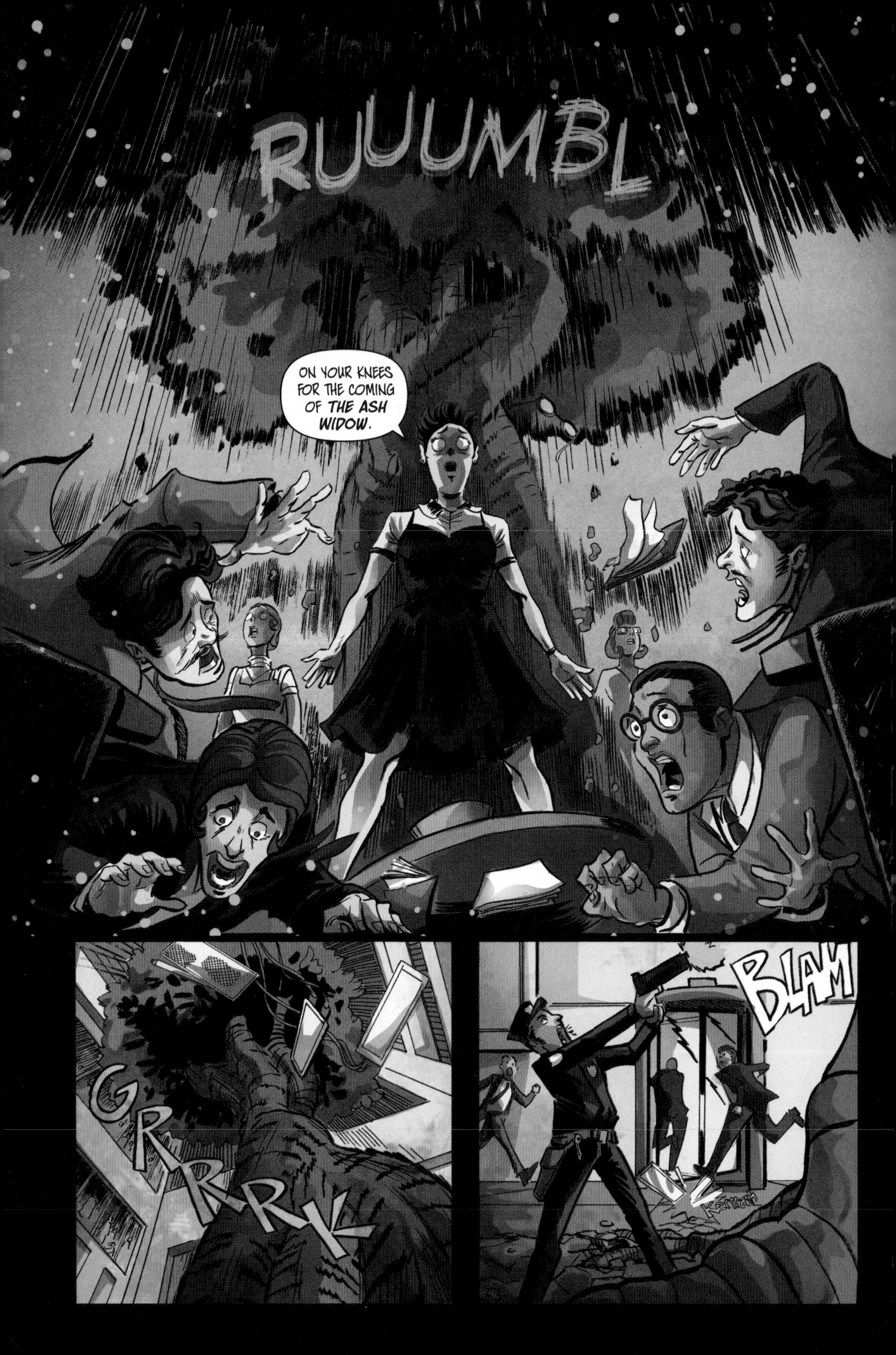
RUUUMBL
ON YOUR KNEES FOR THE COMING OF **THE ASH WIDOW**.
GRRRK
BLAM

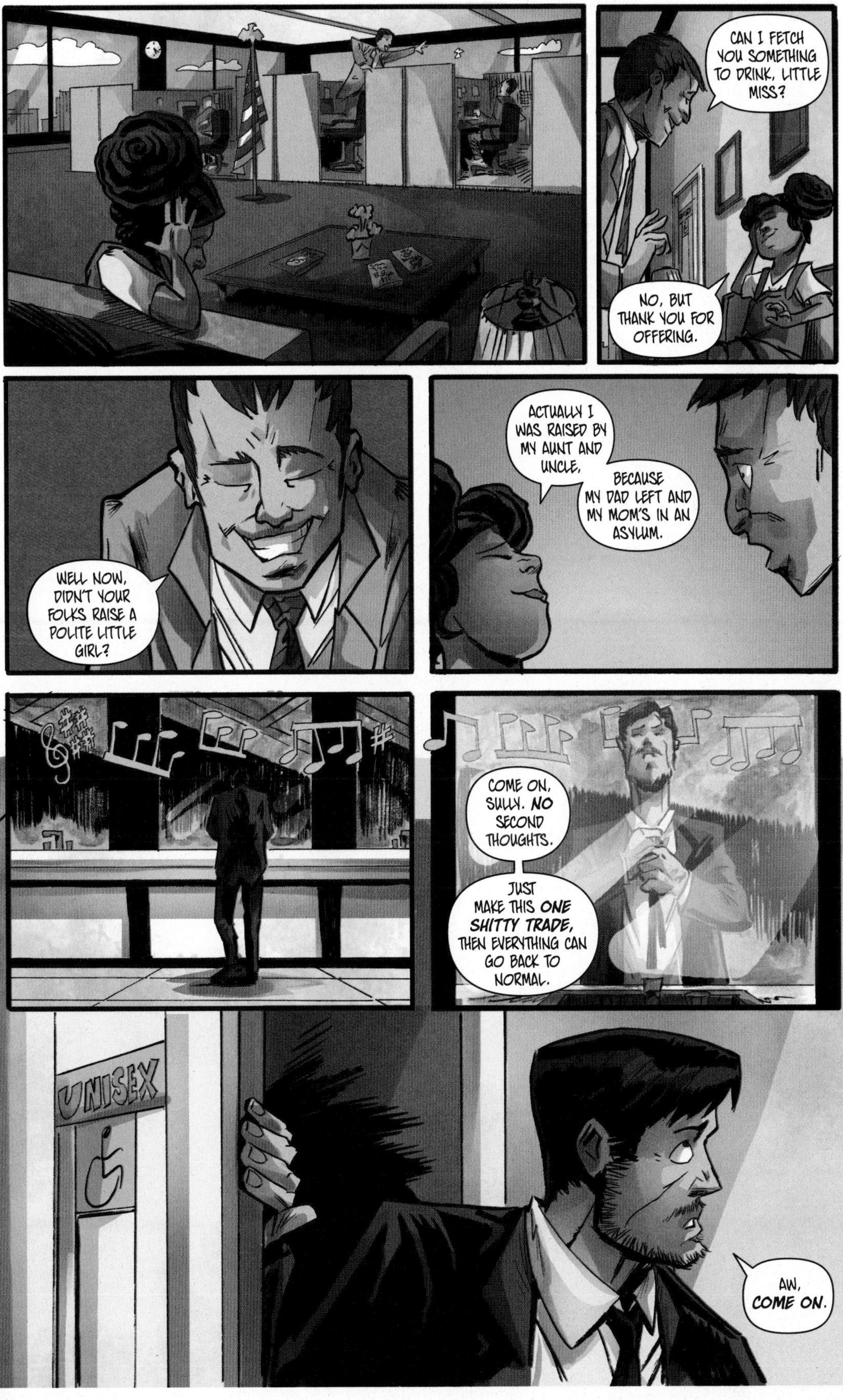
CAN I FETCH YOU SOMETHING TO DRINK, LITTLE MISS?
NO, BUT THANK YOU FOR OFFERING.
WELL NOW, DIDN'T YOUR FOLKS RAISE A POLITE LITTLE GIRL?
ACTUALLY I WAS RAISED BY MY AUNT AND UNCLE,
BECAUSE MY DAD LEFT AND MY MOM'S IN AN ASYLUM.
COME ON, SULLY. NO SECOND THOUGHTS.
JUST MAKE THIS ONE SHITTY TRADE, THEN EVERYTHING CAN GO BACK TO NORMAL.
UNISEX
AW, COME ON.

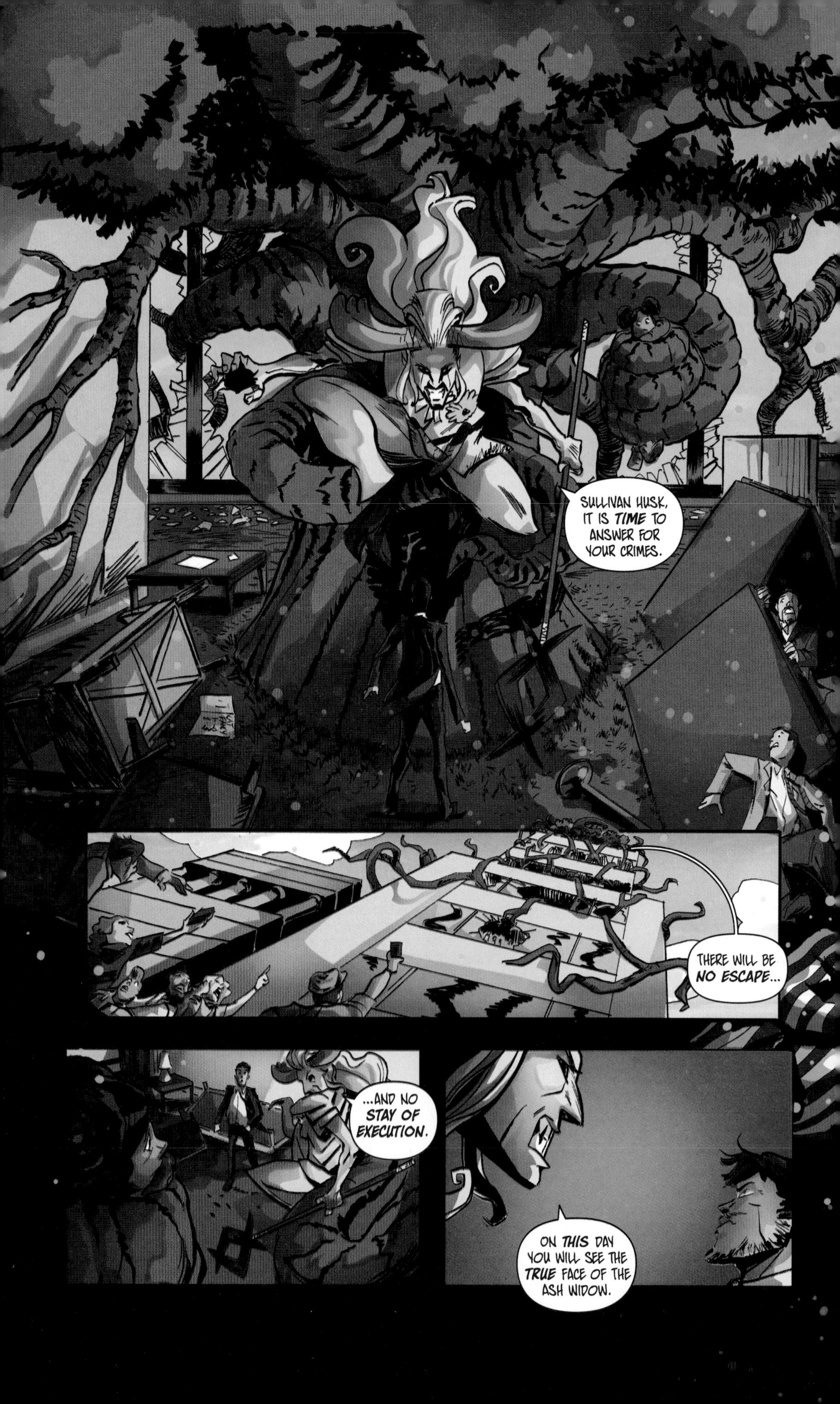
SULLIVAN HUSK, IT IS TIME TO ANSWER FOR YOUR CRIMES.
THERE WILL BE NO ESCAPE...
...AND NO STAY OF EXECUTION.
ON THIS DAY YOU WILL SEE THE TRUE FACE OF THE ASH WIDOW.

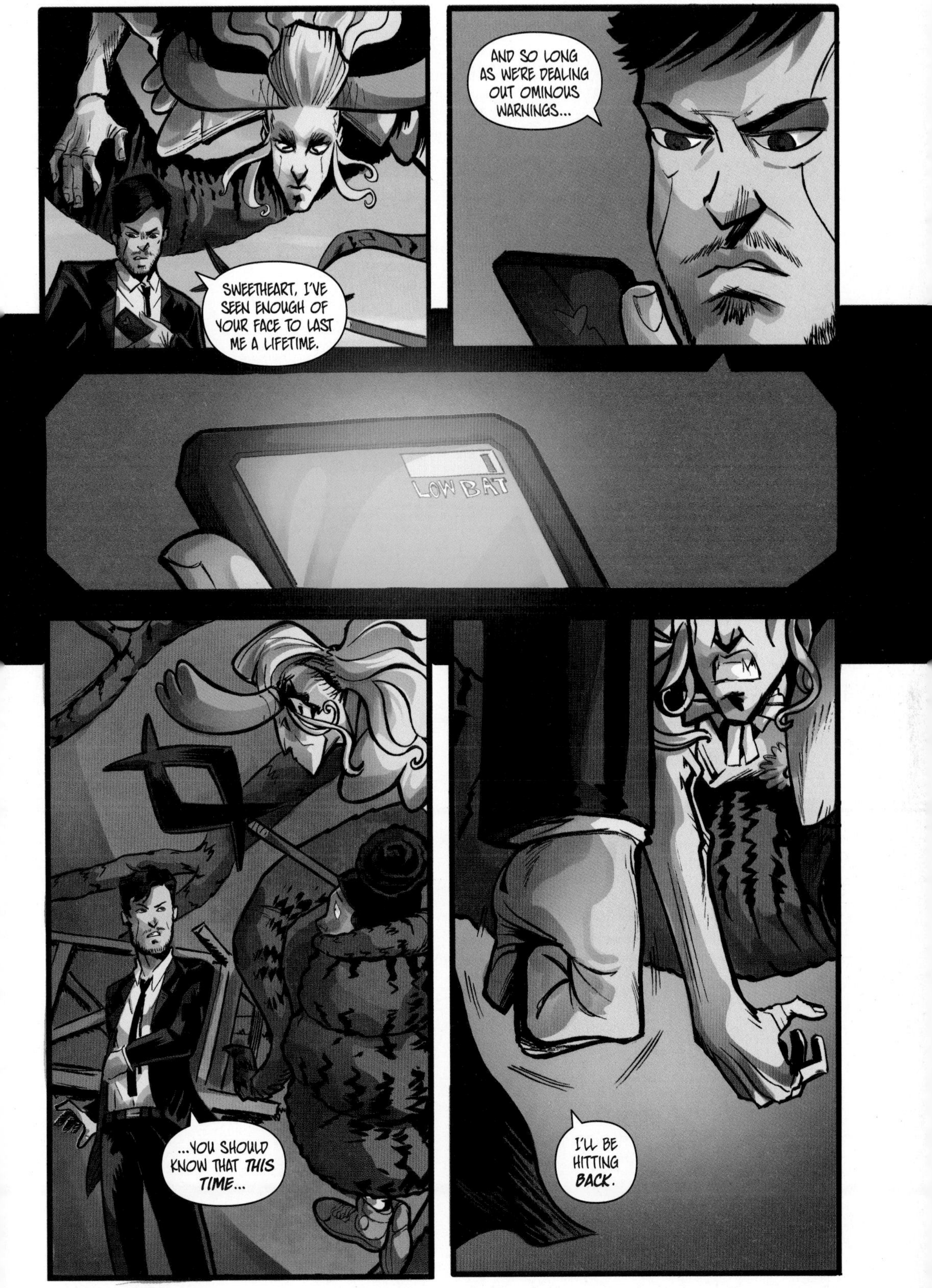
SWEETHEART, I'VE SEEN ENOUGH OF YOUR FACE TO LAST ME A LIFETIME.
AND SO LONG AS WE'RE DEALING OUT OMINOUS WARNINGS...
LOW BAT
...YOU SHOULD KNOW THAT THIS TIME...
I'LL BE HITTING BACK.

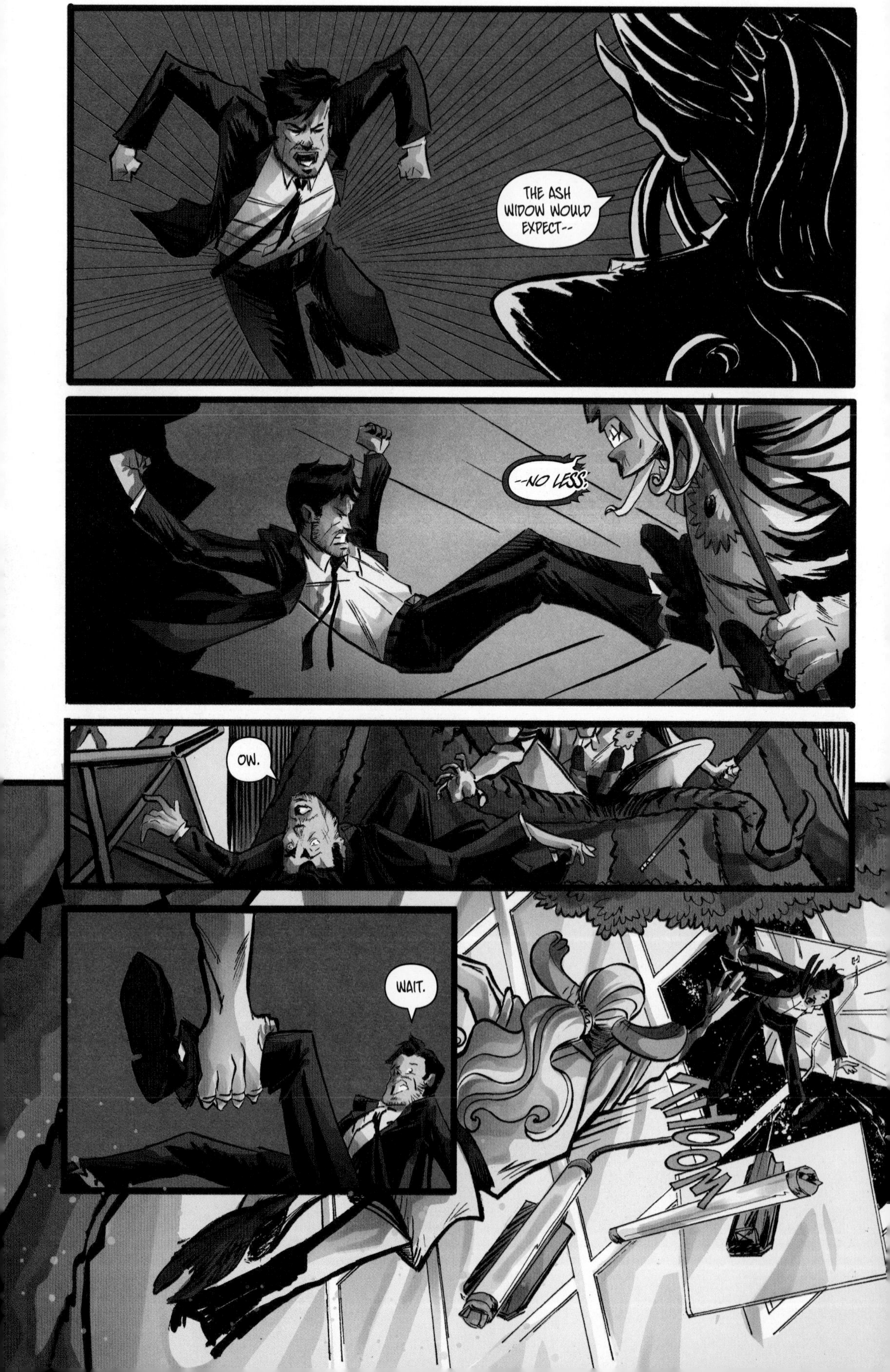

THE ASH WIDOW WOULD EXPECT--
--NO LESS.
OW.
WAIT.
WHOOM

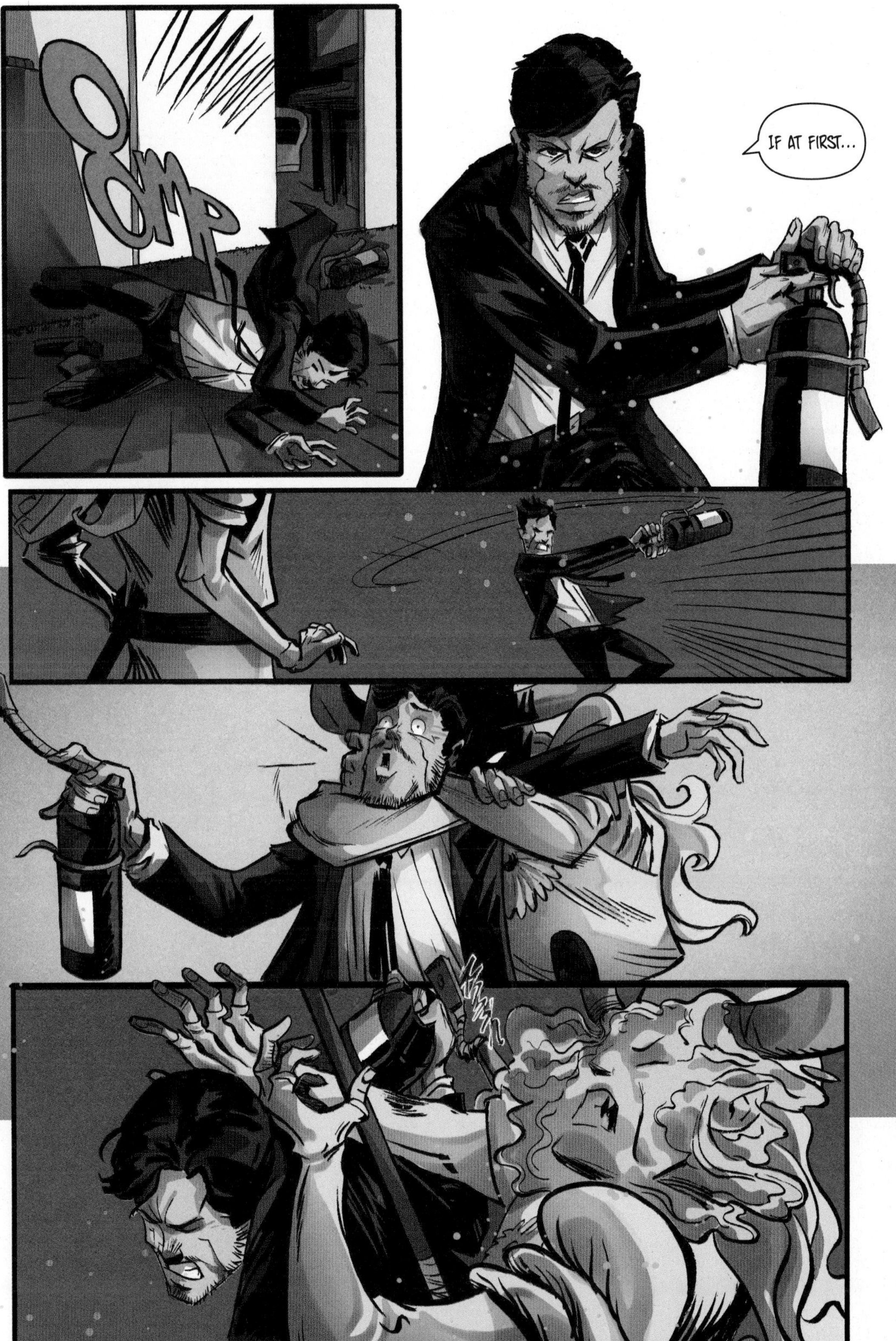
OOMP
IF AT FIRST...

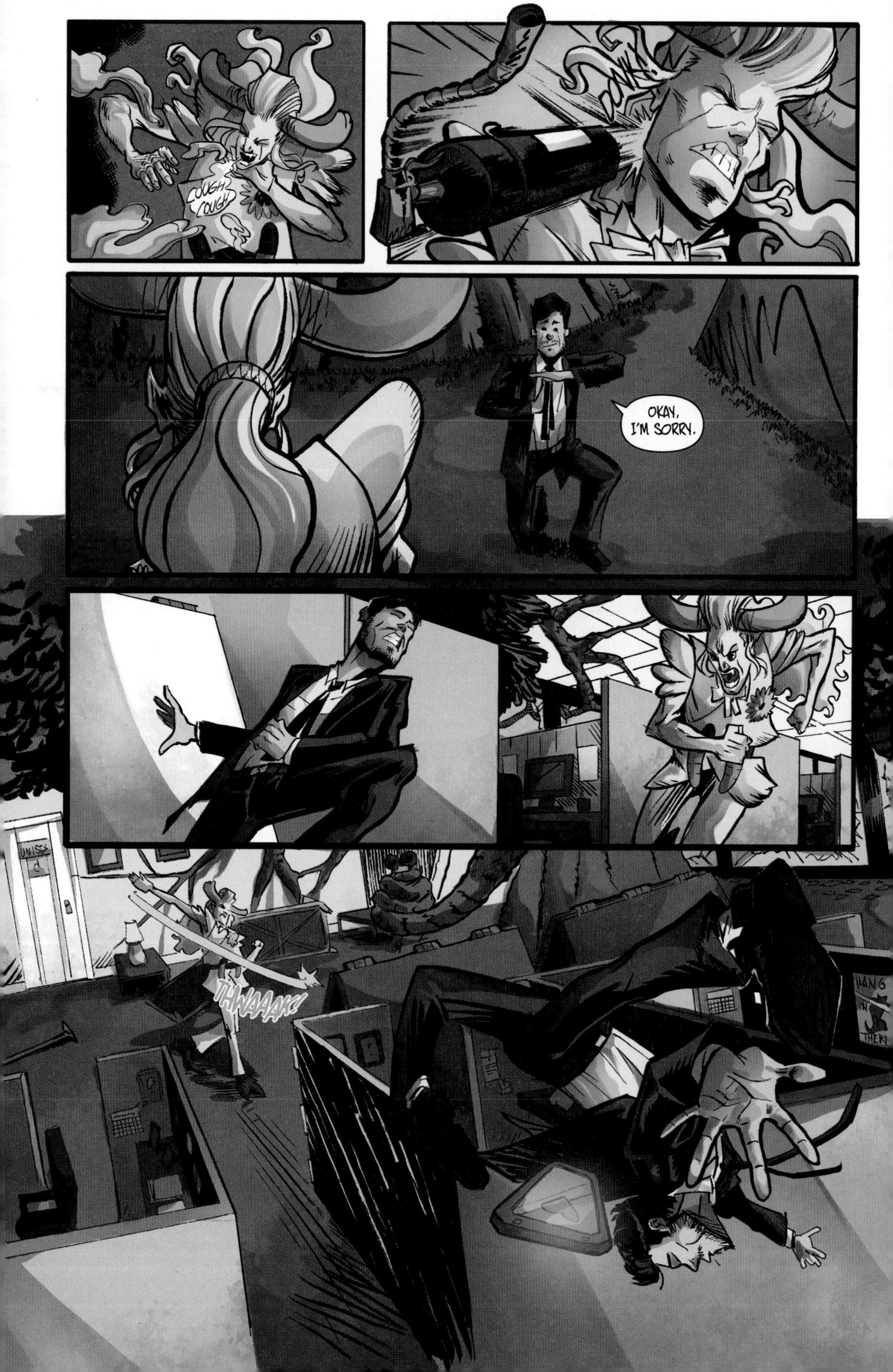
COUGH COUGH
CONK!
OKAY, I'M SORRY.
THWAAAK!
HANG IN THERE

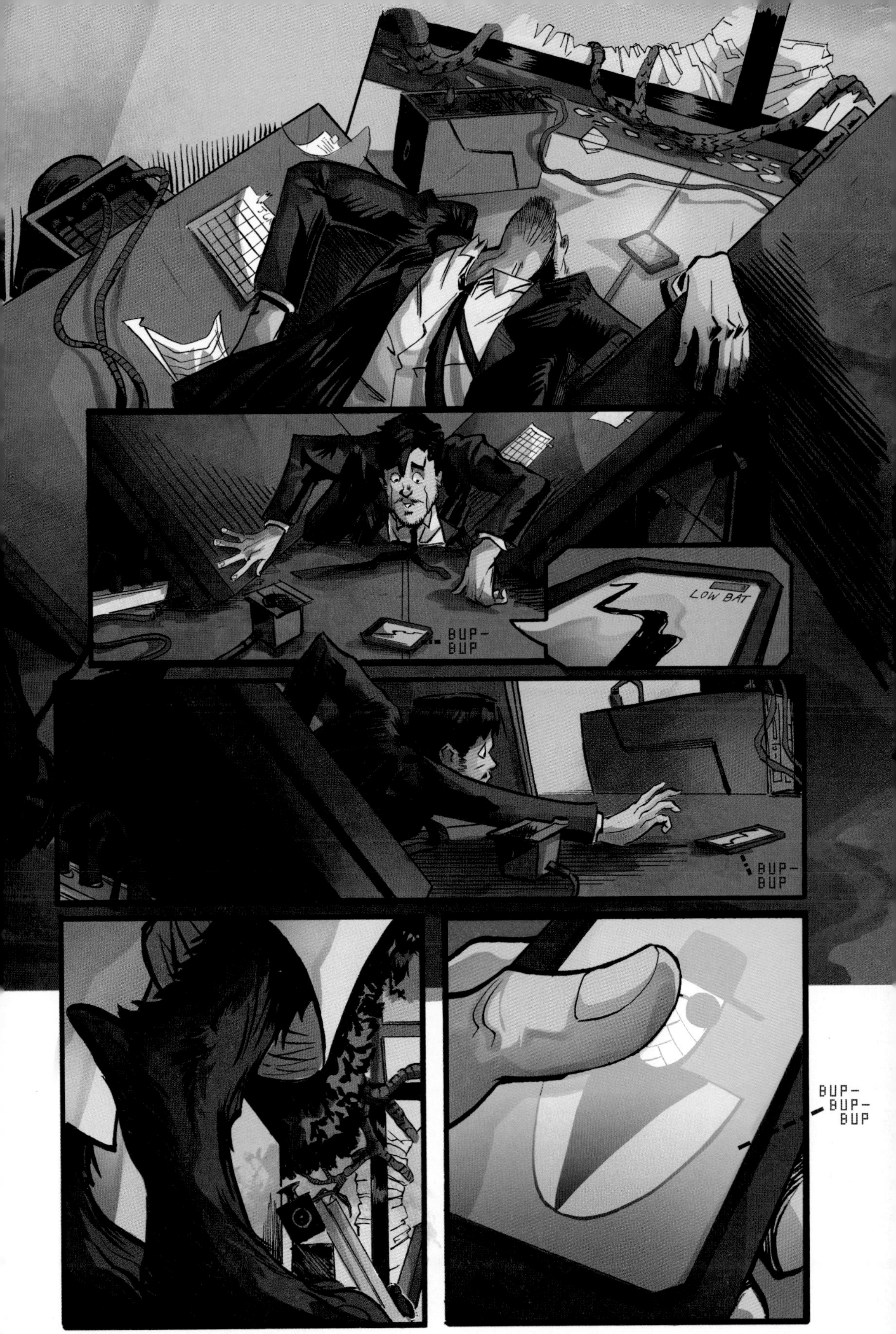

LOW BAT
BUP-BUP
BUP-BUP
BUP-BUP-BUP

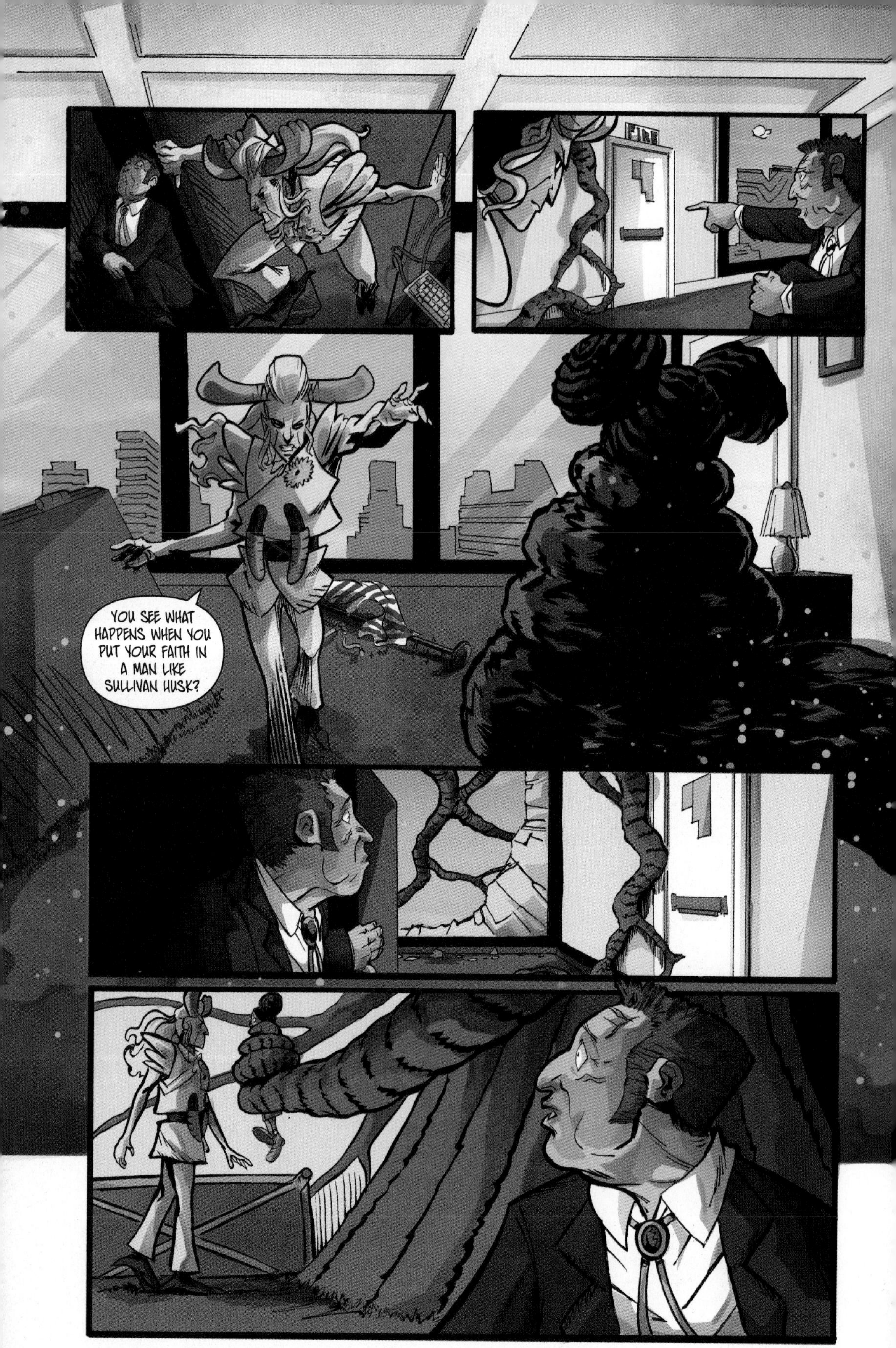
FIRE
YOU SEE WHAT HAPPENS WHEN YOU PUT YOUR FAITH IN A MAN LIKE SULLIVAN HUSK?

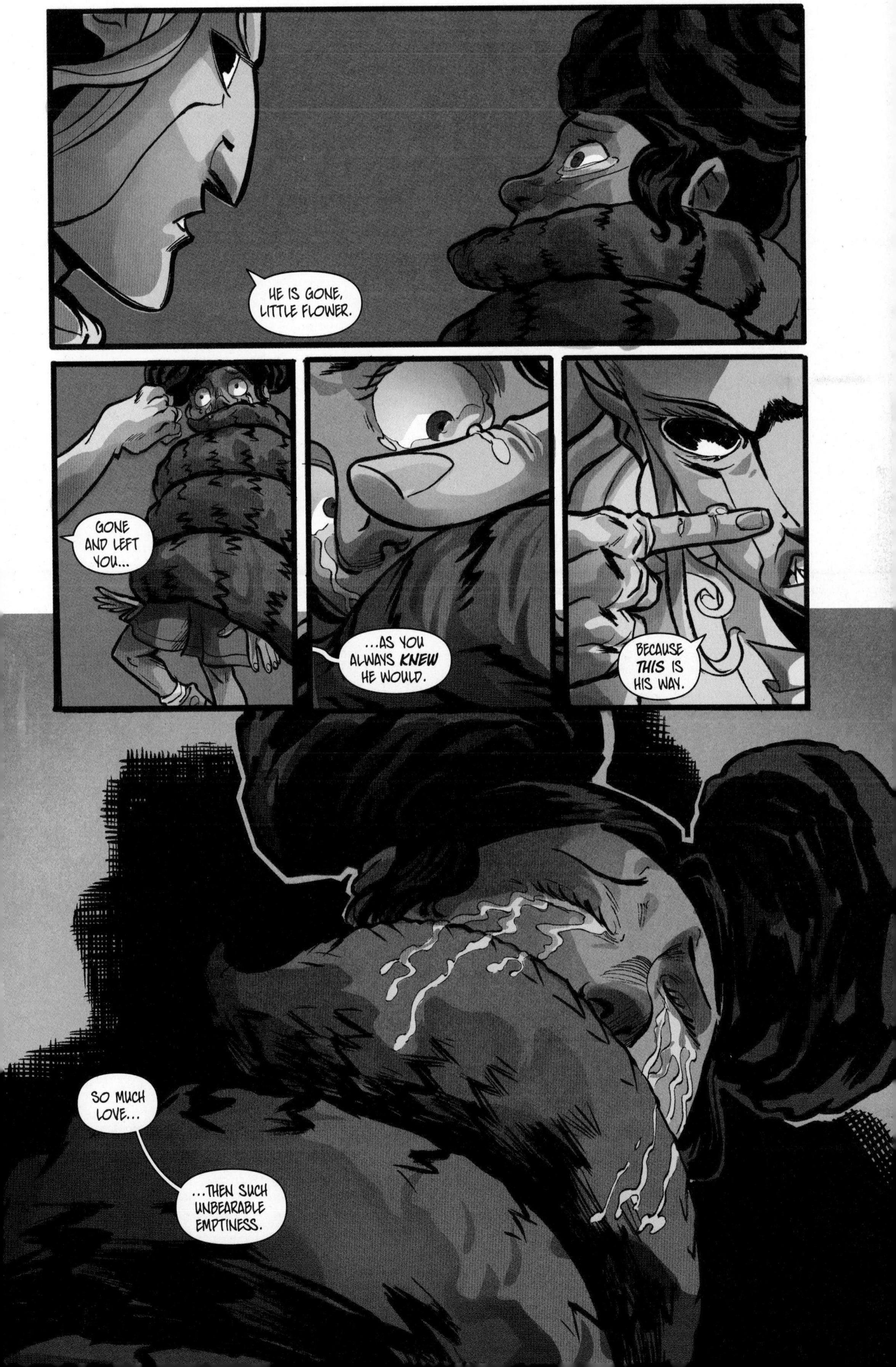
HE IS GONE, LITTLE FLOWER.
GONE AND LEFT YOU...
...AS YOU ALWAYS KNEW HE WOULD.
BECAUSE THIS IS HIS WAY.
SO MUCH LOVE...
...THEN SUCH UNBEARABLE EMPTINESS.

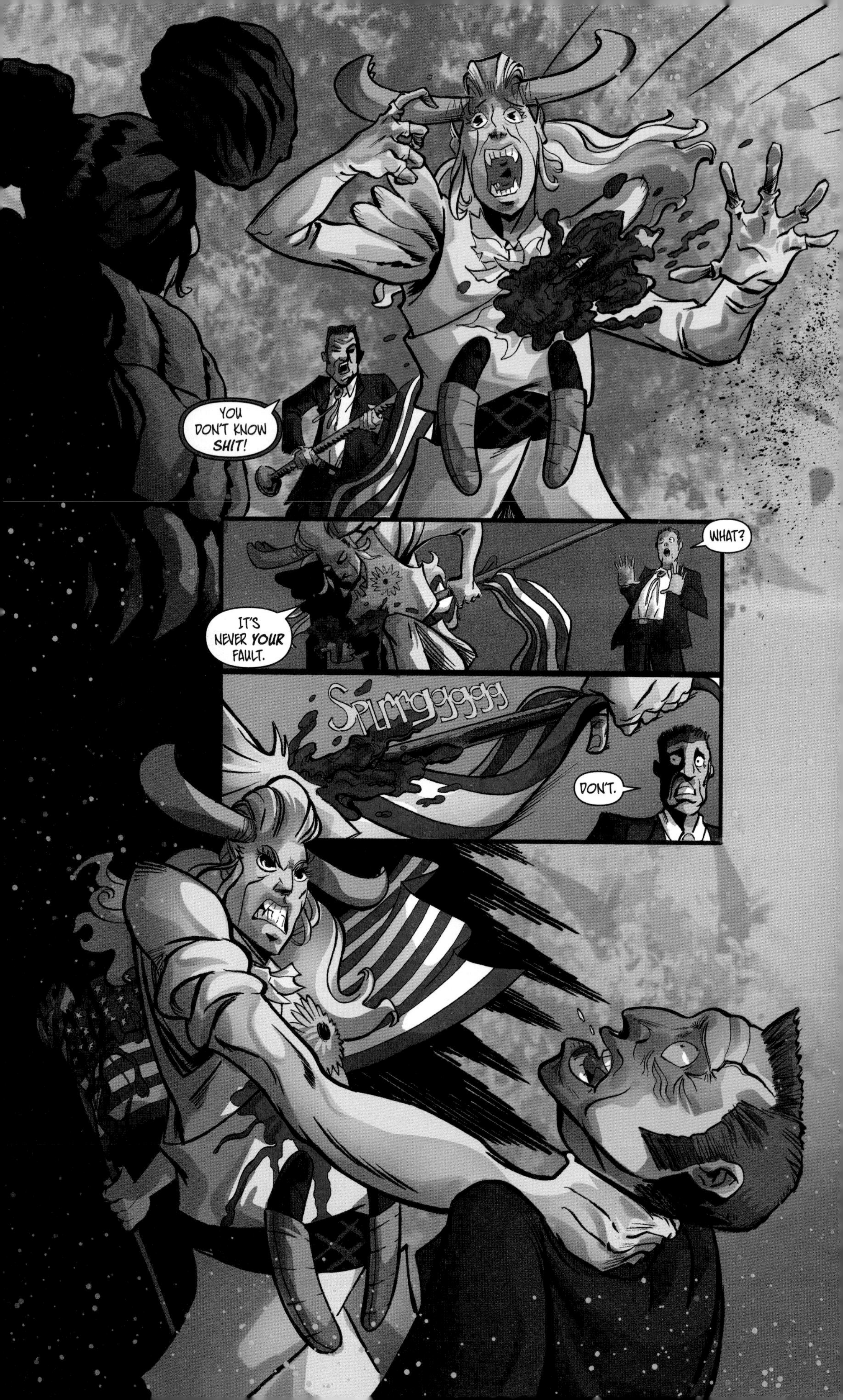

YOU DON'T KNOW SHIT!
WHAT?
IT'S NEVER YOUR FAULT.
SPLRRGGGGGG
DON'T.

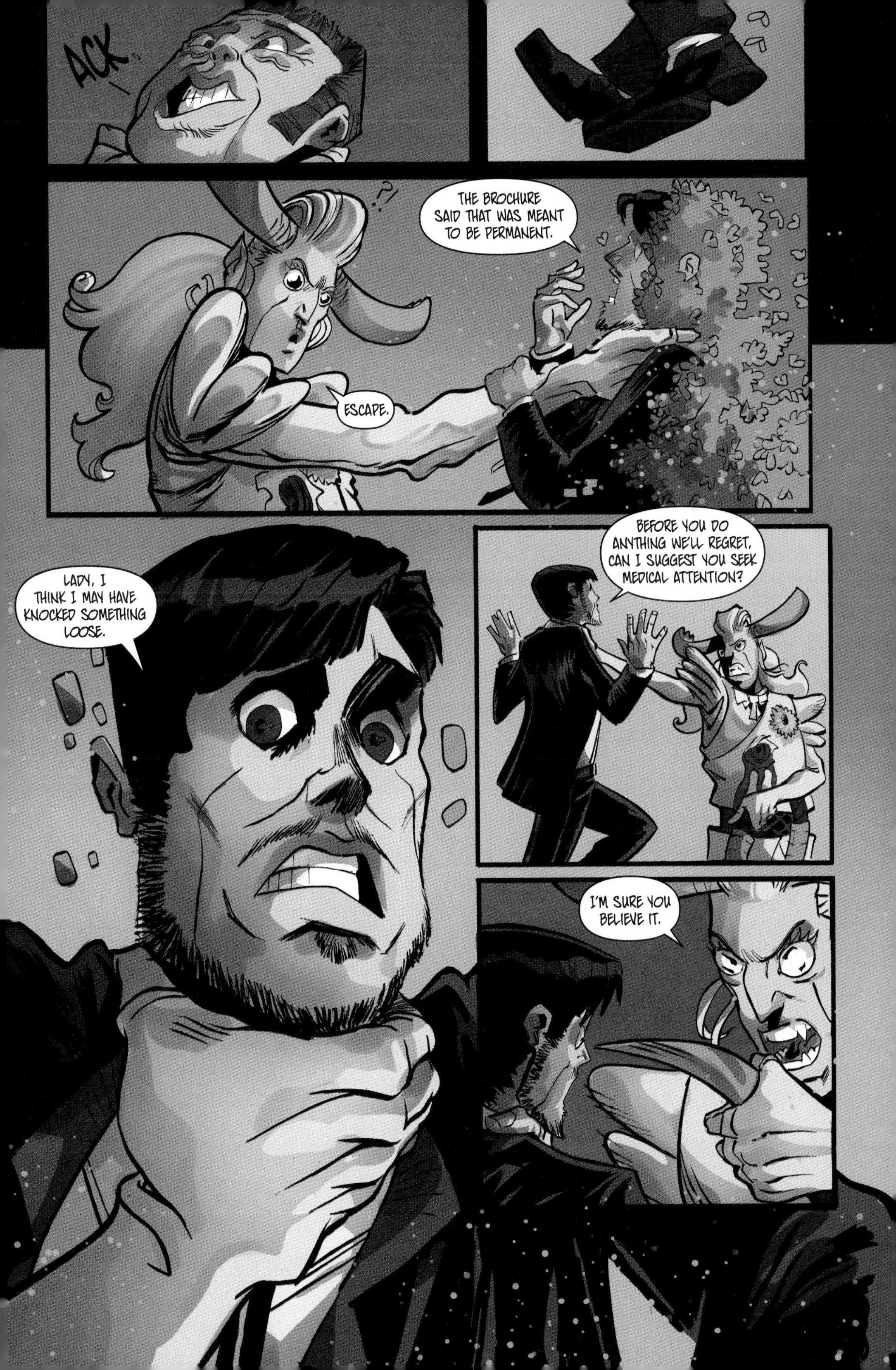
ACK
?!
THE BROCHURE SAID THAT WAS MEANT TO BE PERMANENT.
ESCAPE.
LADY, I THINK I MAY HAVE KNOCKED SOMETHING LOOSE.
BEFORE YOU DO ANYTHING WE'LL REGRET, CAN I SUGGEST YOU SEEK MEDICAL ATTENTION?
I'M SURE YOU BELIEVE IT.

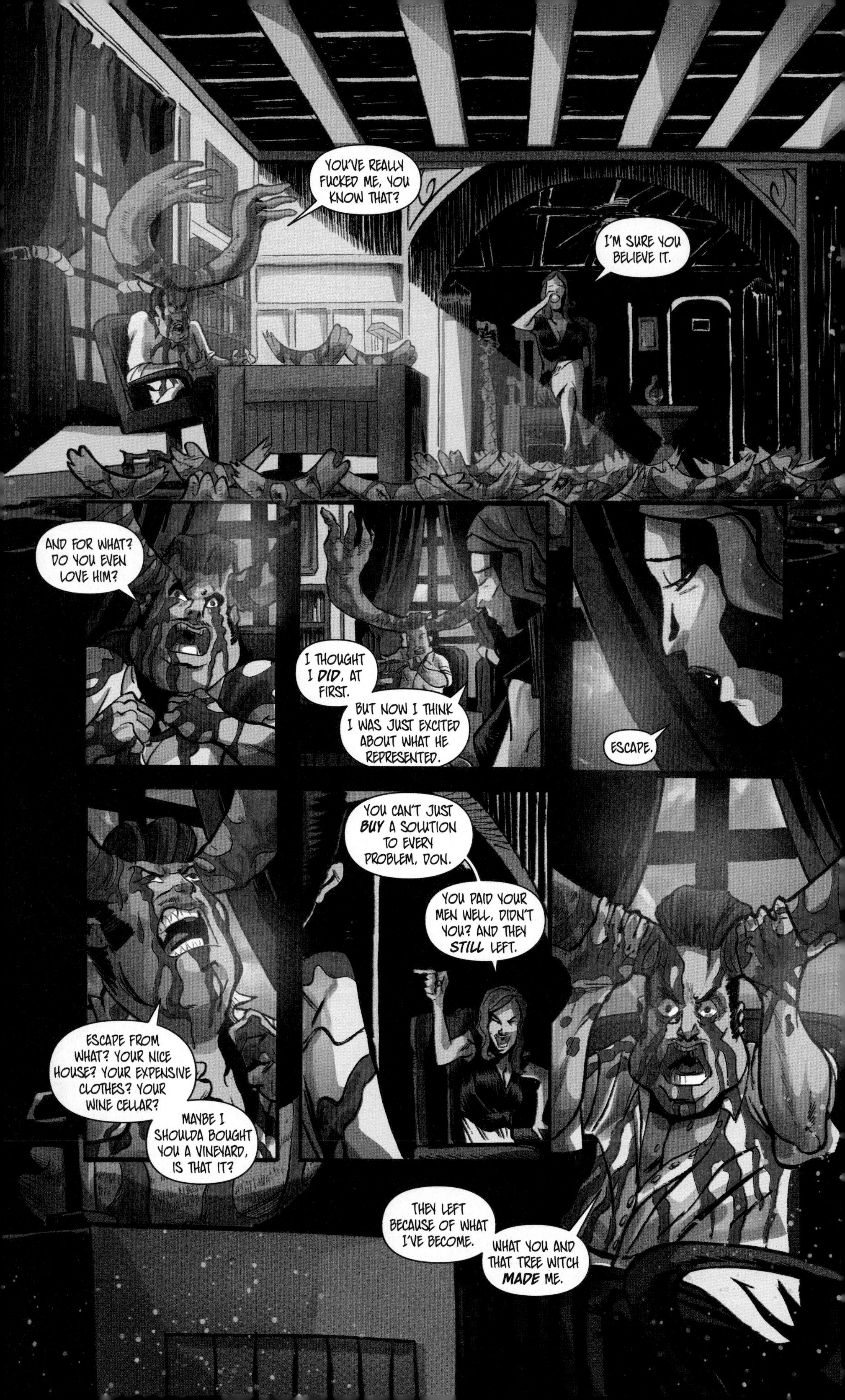
YOU'VE REALLY FUCKED ME, YOU KNOW THAT?
I'M SURE YOU BELIEVE IT.
AND FOR WHAT? DO YOU EVEN LOVE HIM?
I THOUGHT I *DID*, AT FIRST.
BUT NOW I THINK I WAS JUST EXCITED ABOUT WHAT HE REPRESENTED.
ESCAPE.
ESCAPE FROM WHAT? YOUR NICE HOUSE? YOUR EXPENSIVE CLOTHES? YOUR WINE CELLAR?
MAYBE I SHOULDA BOUGHT YOU A VINEYARD, IS THAT IT?
YOU CAN'T JUST *BUY* A SOLUTION TO EVERY PROBLEM, DON.
YOU PAID YOUR MEN WELL, DIDN'T YOU? AND THEY *STILL* LEFT.
THEY LEFT BECAUSE OF WHAT I'VE BECOME.
WHAT YOU AND THAT TREE WITCH *MADE* ME.

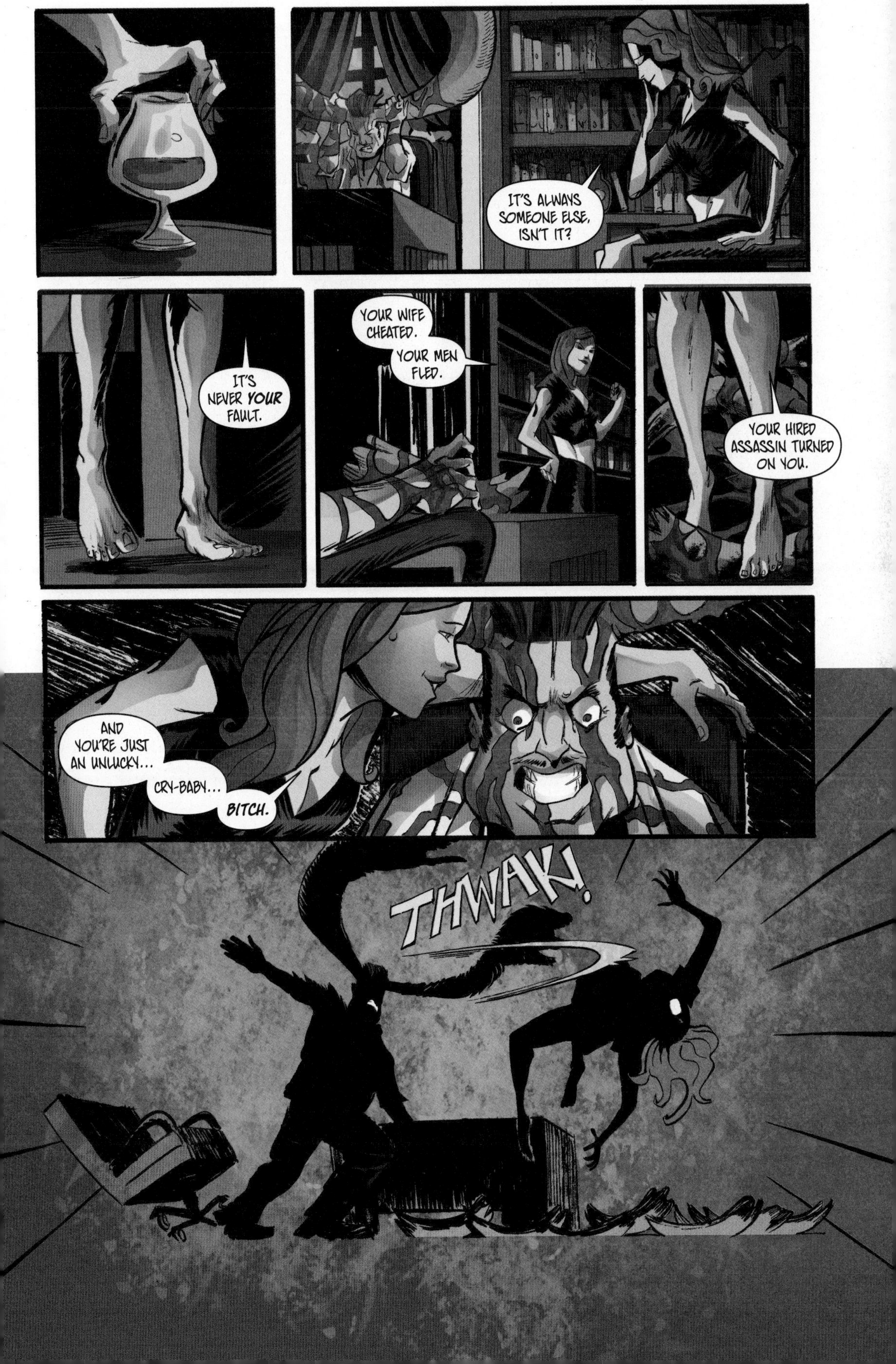

IT'S ALWAYS SOMEONE ELSE, ISN'T IT?
IT'S NEVER YOUR FAULT.
YOUR WIFE CHEATED.
YOUR MEN FLED.
YOUR HIRED ASSASSIN TURNED ON YOU.
AND YOU'RE JUST AN UNLUCKY...
CRY-BABY...
BITCH.
THWAK!

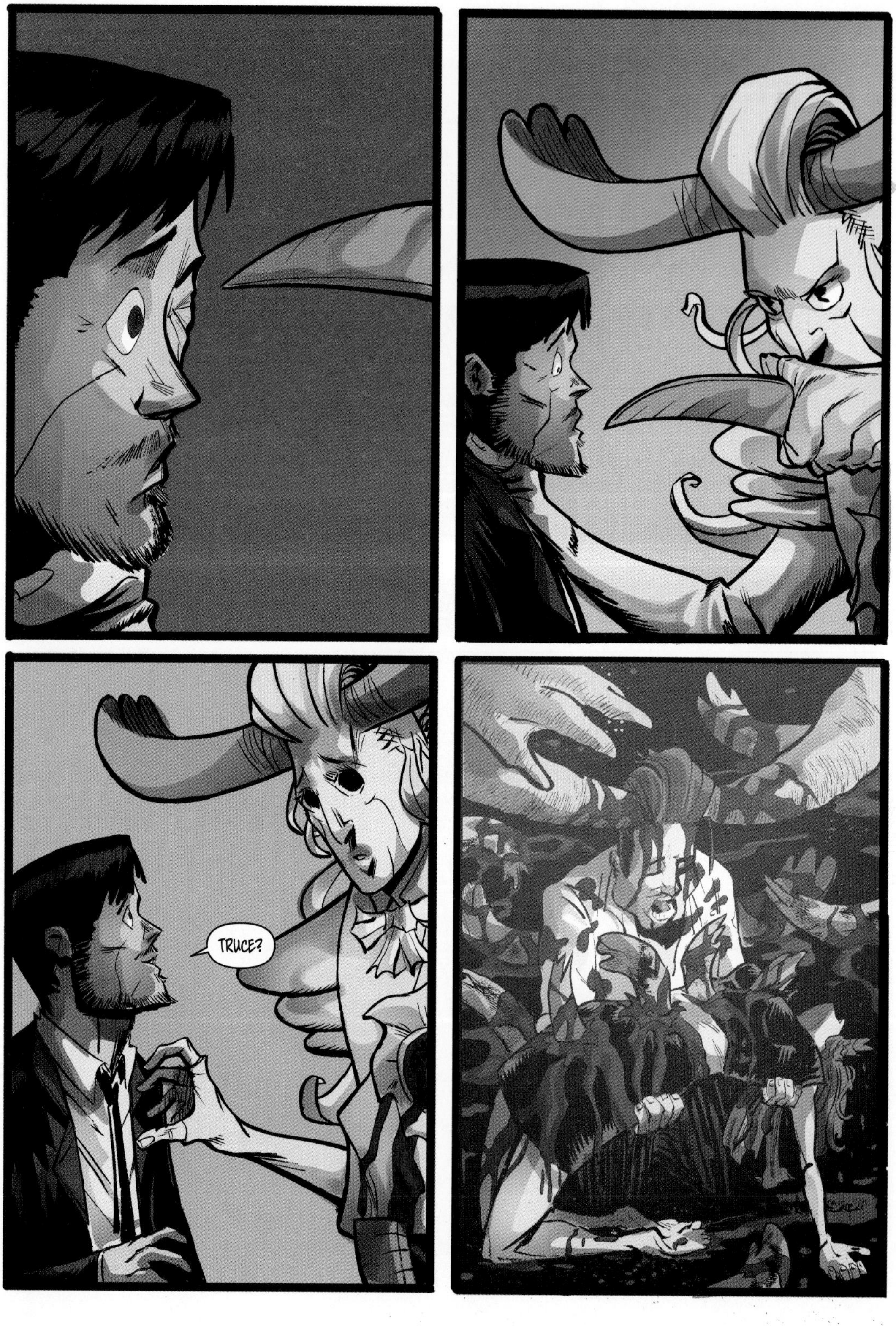
TRUCE?

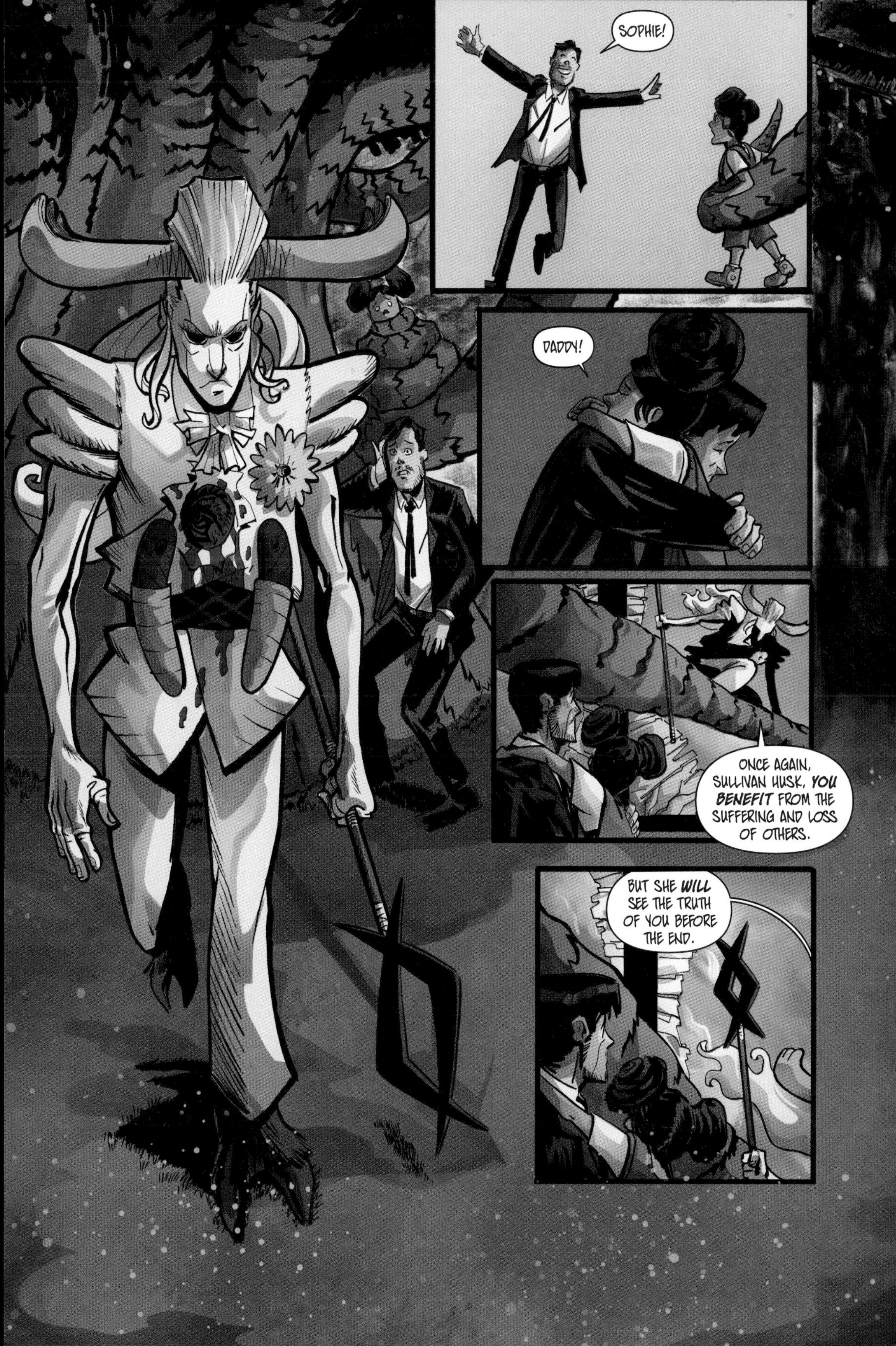
SOPHIE!
DADDY!
ONCE AGAIN, SULLIVAN HUSK, **YOU BENEFIT** FROM THE SUFFERING AND LOSS OF OTHERS.
BUT SHE **WILL** SEE THE TRUTH OF YOU BEFORE THE END.

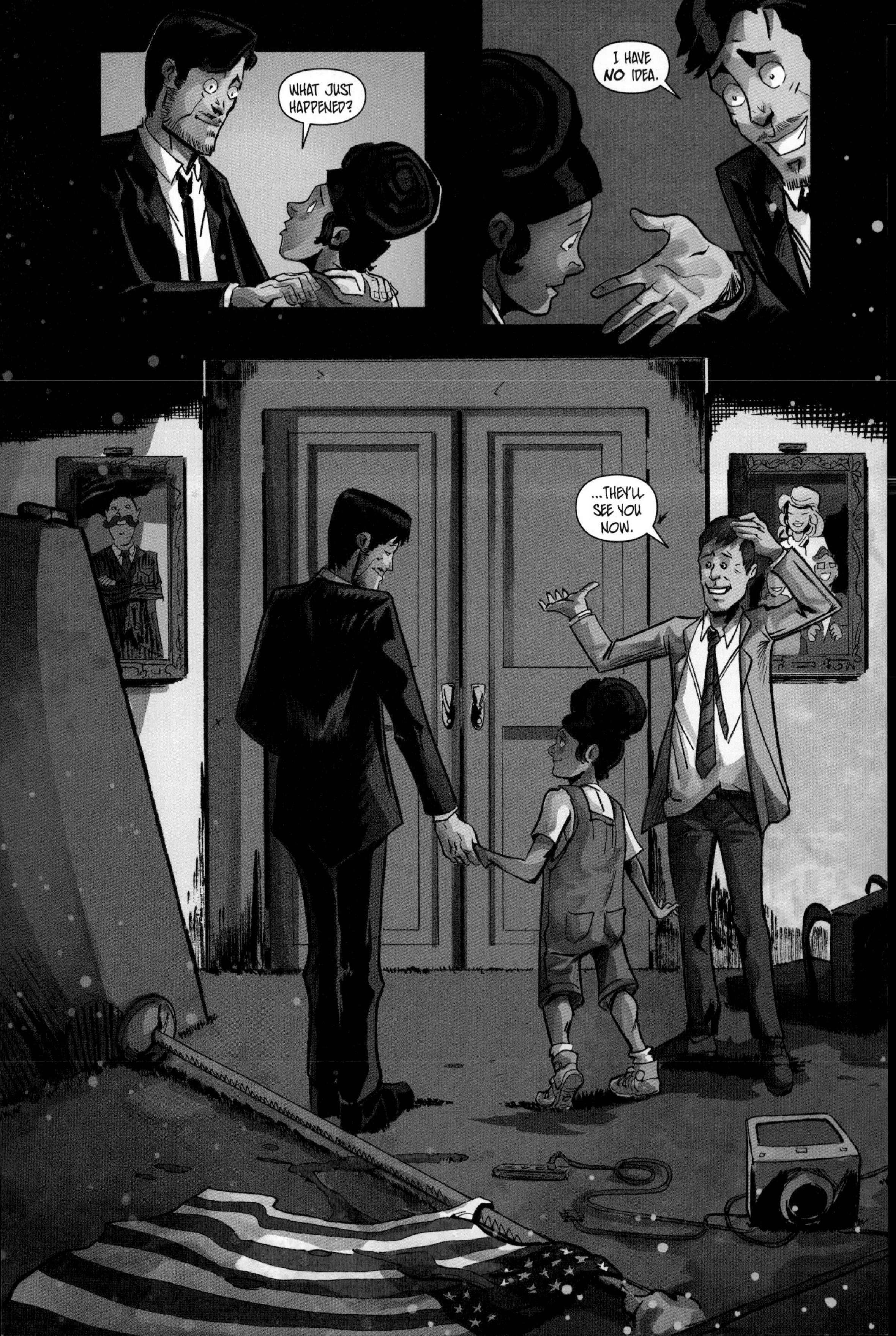
WHAT JUST HAPPENED?
I HAVE NO IDEA.
...THEY'LL SEE YOU NOW.

CHAPTER 5

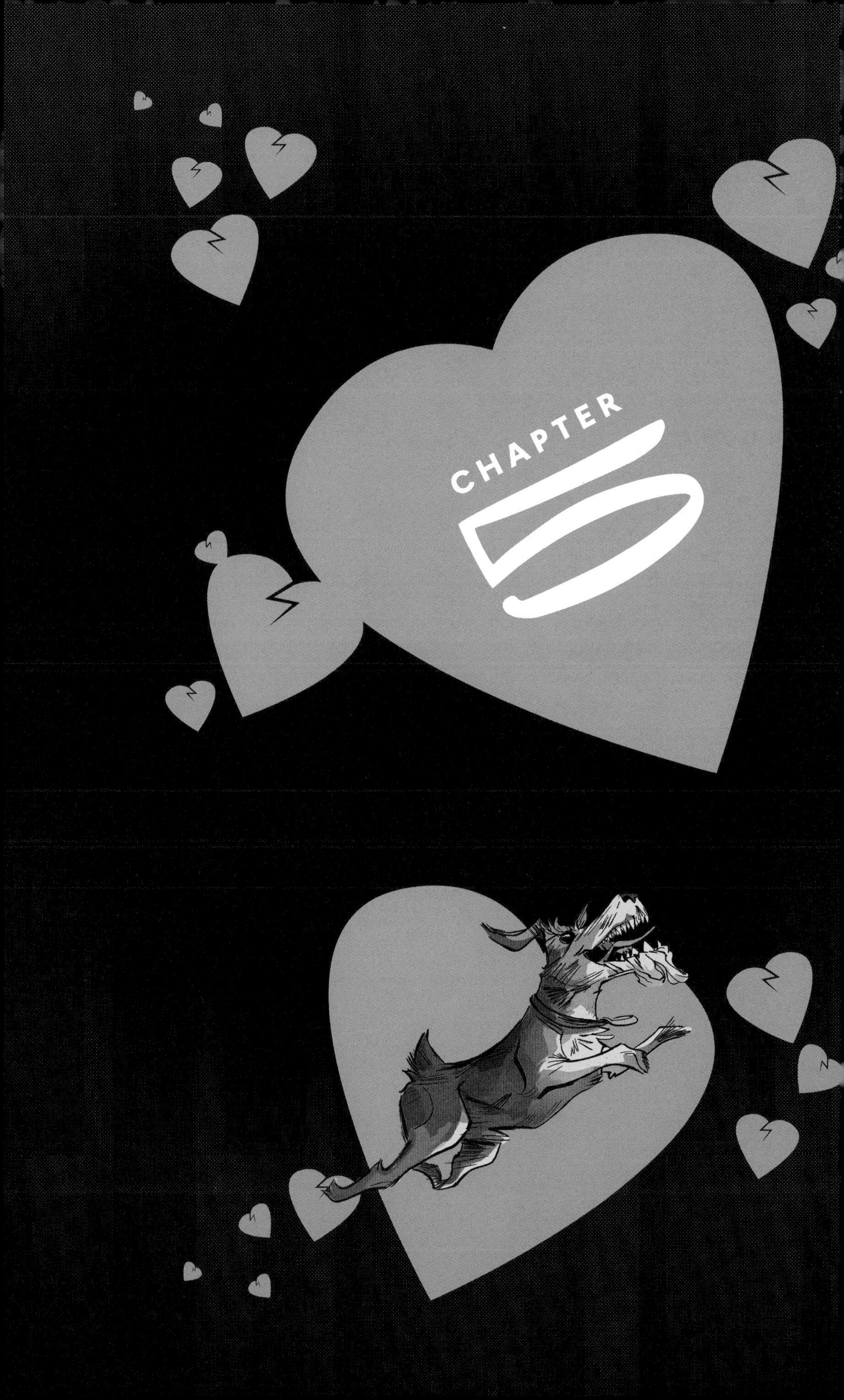

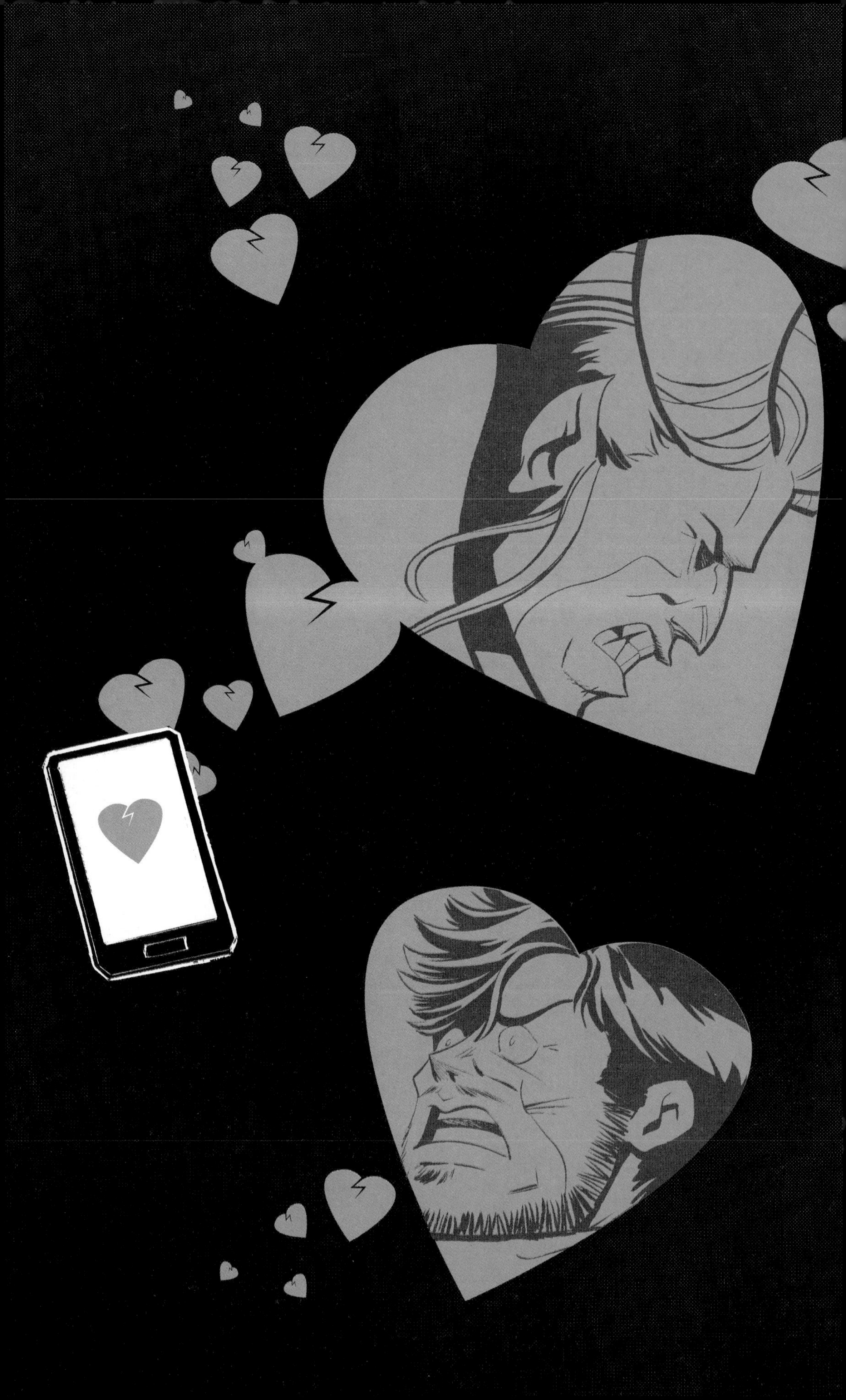

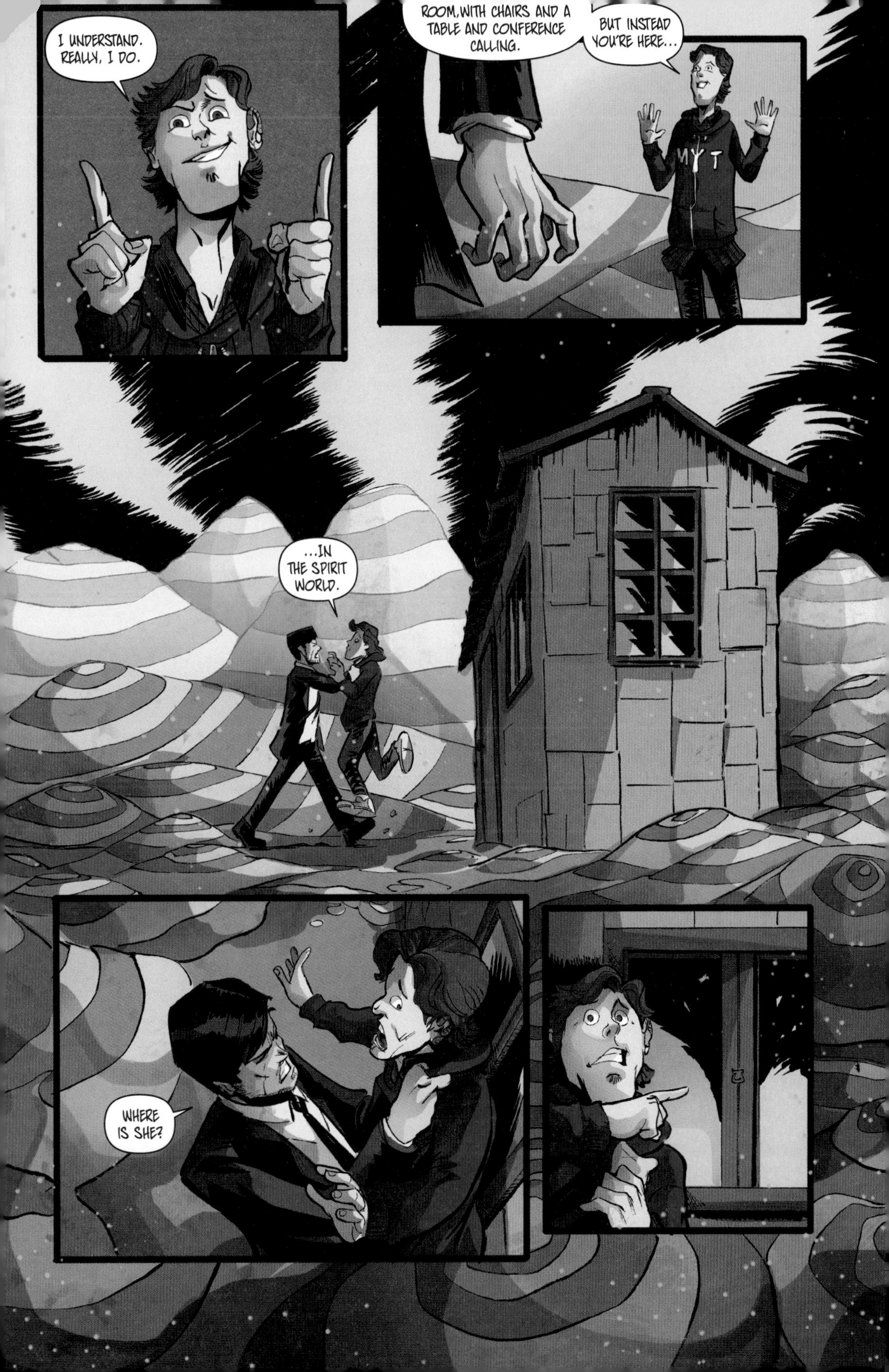
I UNDERSTAND. REALLY, I DO.
ROOM, WITH CHAIRS AND A TABLE AND CONFERENCE CALLING.
BUT INSTEAD YOU'RE HERE...
MYT
...IN THE SPIRIT WORLD.
WHERE IS SHE?

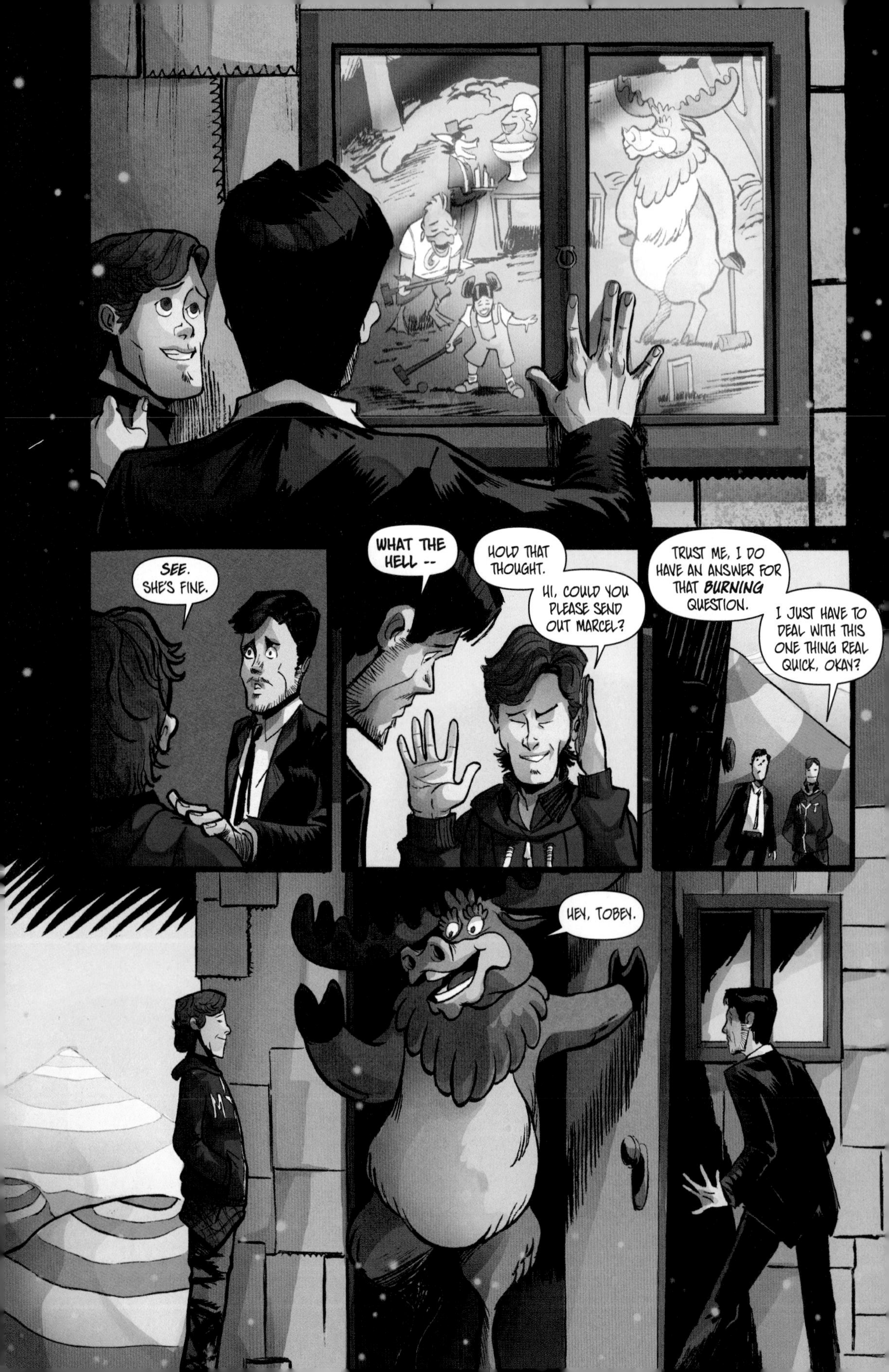
SEE. SHE'S FINE.
WHAT THE HELL --
HOLD THAT THOUGHT.
HI, COULD YOU PLEASE SEND OUT MARCEL?
TRUST ME, I DO HAVE AN ANSWER FOR THAT BURNING QUESTION.
I JUST HAVE TO DEAL WITH THIS ONE THING REAL QUICK, OKAY?
HEY, TOBEY.

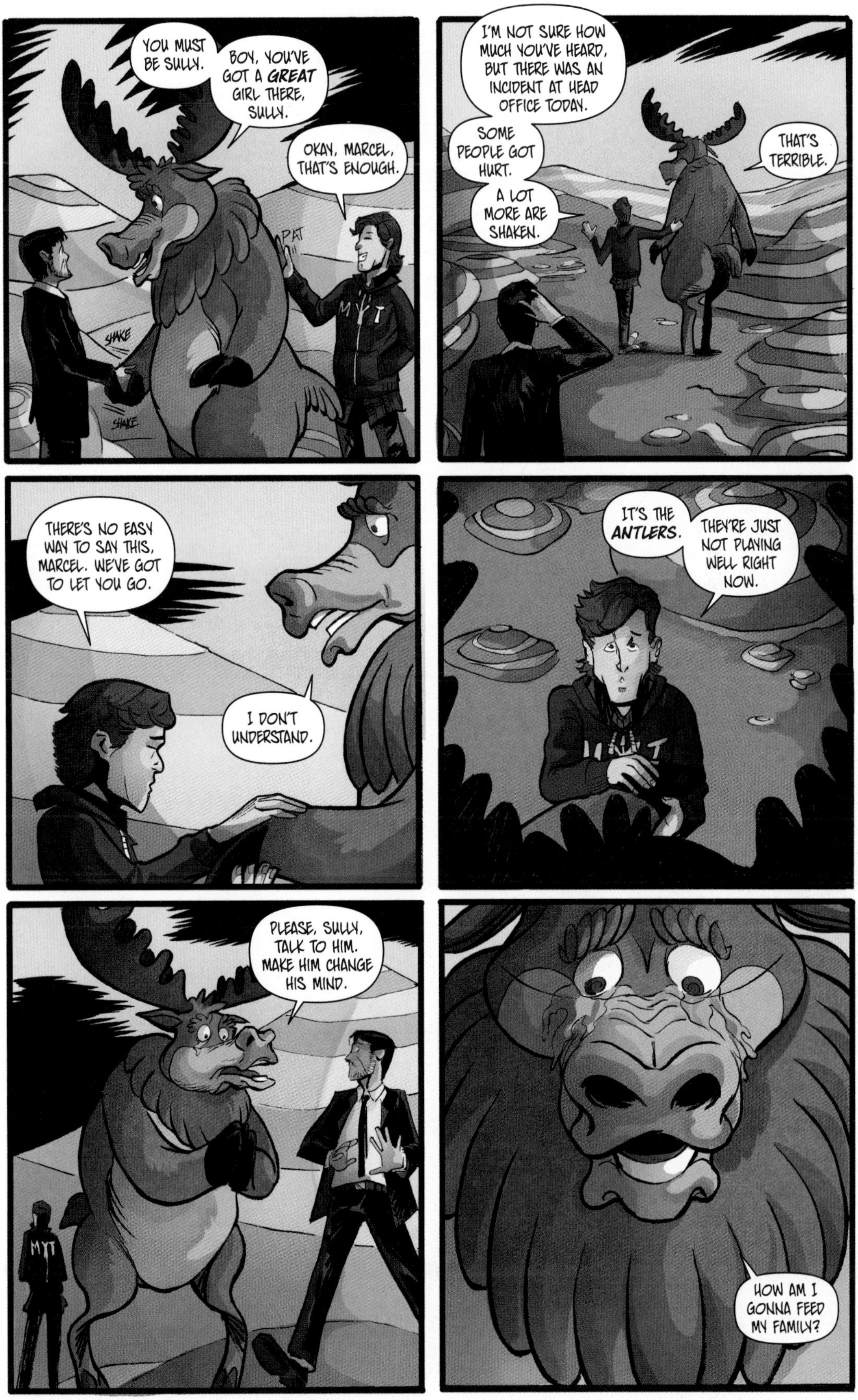

YOU MUST BE SULLY.
BOY, YOU'VE GOT A **GREAT** GIRL THERE, SULLY.
OKAY, MARCEL, THAT'S ENOUGH.
PAT
SHAKE
SHAKE
I'M NOT SURE HOW MUCH YOU'VE HEARD, BUT THERE WAS AN INCIDENT AT HEAD OFFICE TODAY.
SOME PEOPLE GOT HURT.
A LOT MORE ARE SHAKEN.
THAT'S TERRIBLE.
THERE'S NO EASY WAY TO SAY THIS, MARCEL. WE'VE GOT TO LET YOU GO.
I DON'T UNDERSTAND.
IT'S THE **ANTLERS**.
THEY'RE JUST NOT PLAYING WELL RIGHT NOW.
PLEASE, SULLY, TALK TO HIM. MAKE HIM CHANGE HIS MIND.
HOW AM I GONNA FEED MY FAMILY?

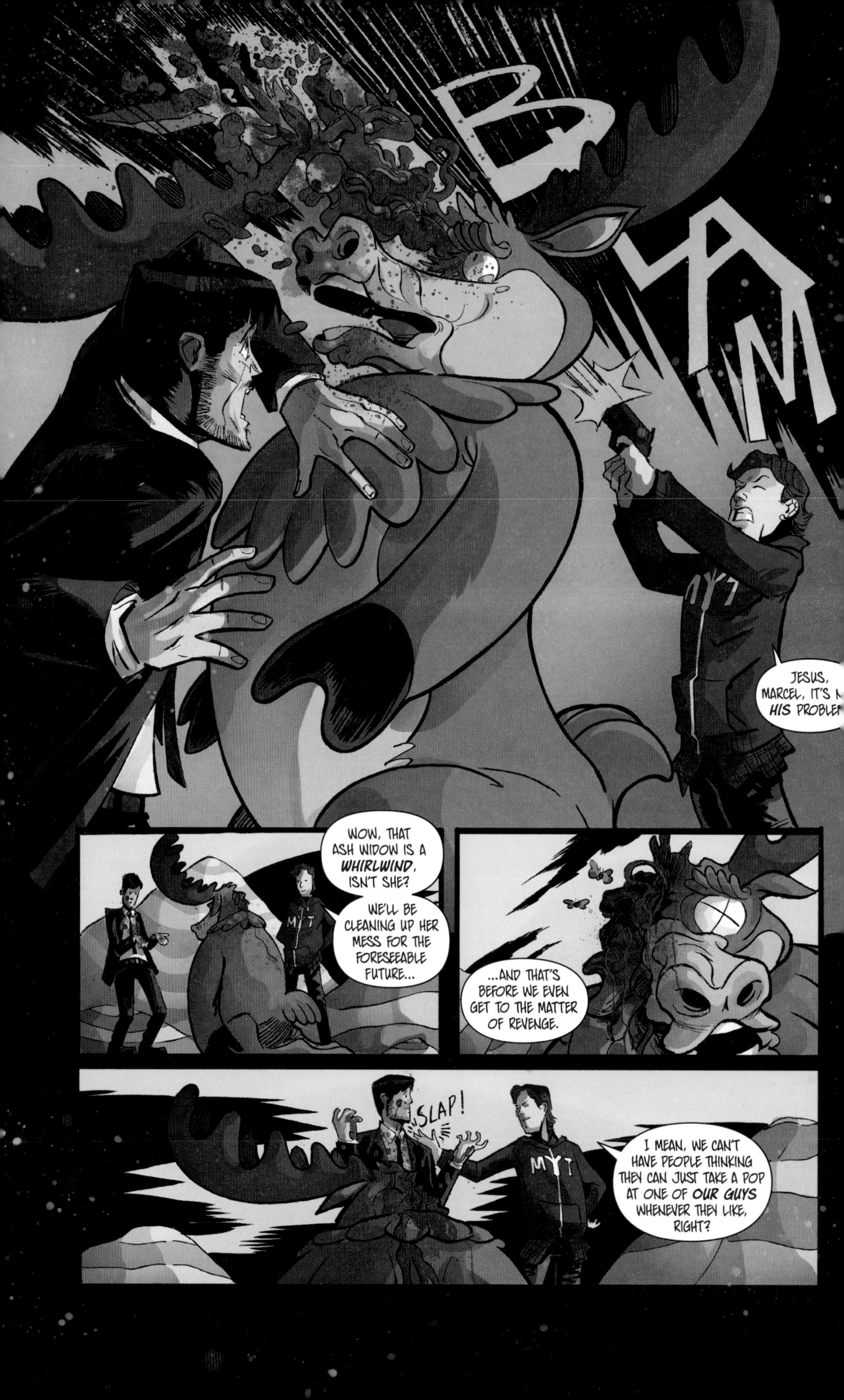
BLAM
JESUS, MARCEL, IT'S N
HIS PROBLEM
WOW, THAT ASH WIDOW IS A WHIRLWIND, ISN'T SHE?
WE'LL BE CLEANING UP HER MESS FOR THE FORESEEABLE FUTURE...
...AND THAT'S BEFORE WE EVEN GET TO THE MATTER OF REVENGE.
SLAP!
I MEAN, WE CAN'T HAVE PEOPLE THINKING THEY CAN JUST TAKE A POP AT ONE OF OUR GUYS WHENEVER THEY LIKE, RIGHT?

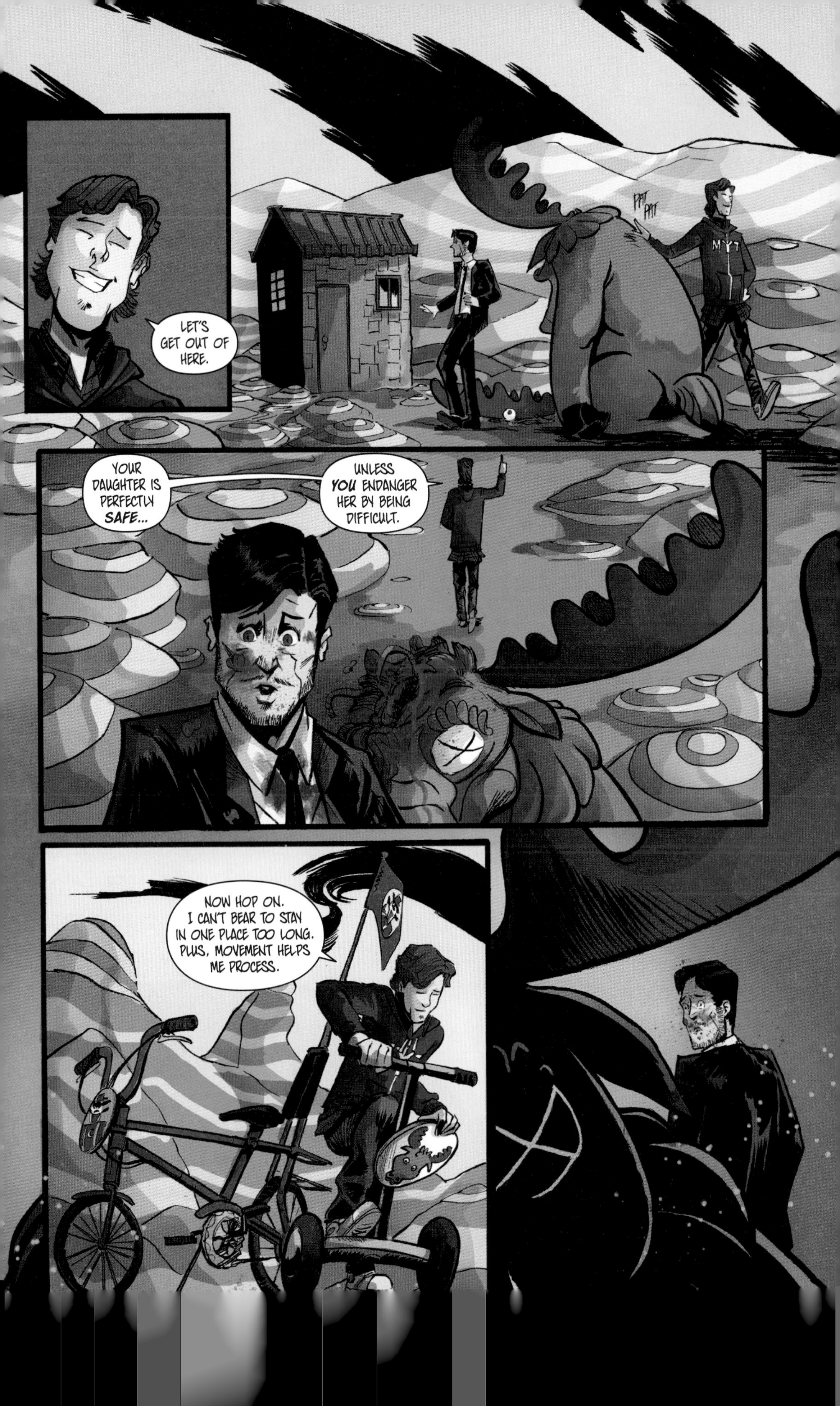
PAT PAT
LET'S GET OUT OF HERE.
YOUR DAUGHTER IS PERFECTLY SAFE...
UNLESS YOU ENDANGER HER BY BEING DIFFICULT.
NOW HOP ON. I CAN'T BEAR TO STAY IN ONE PLACE TOO LONG. PLUS, MOVEMENT HELPS ME PROCESS.

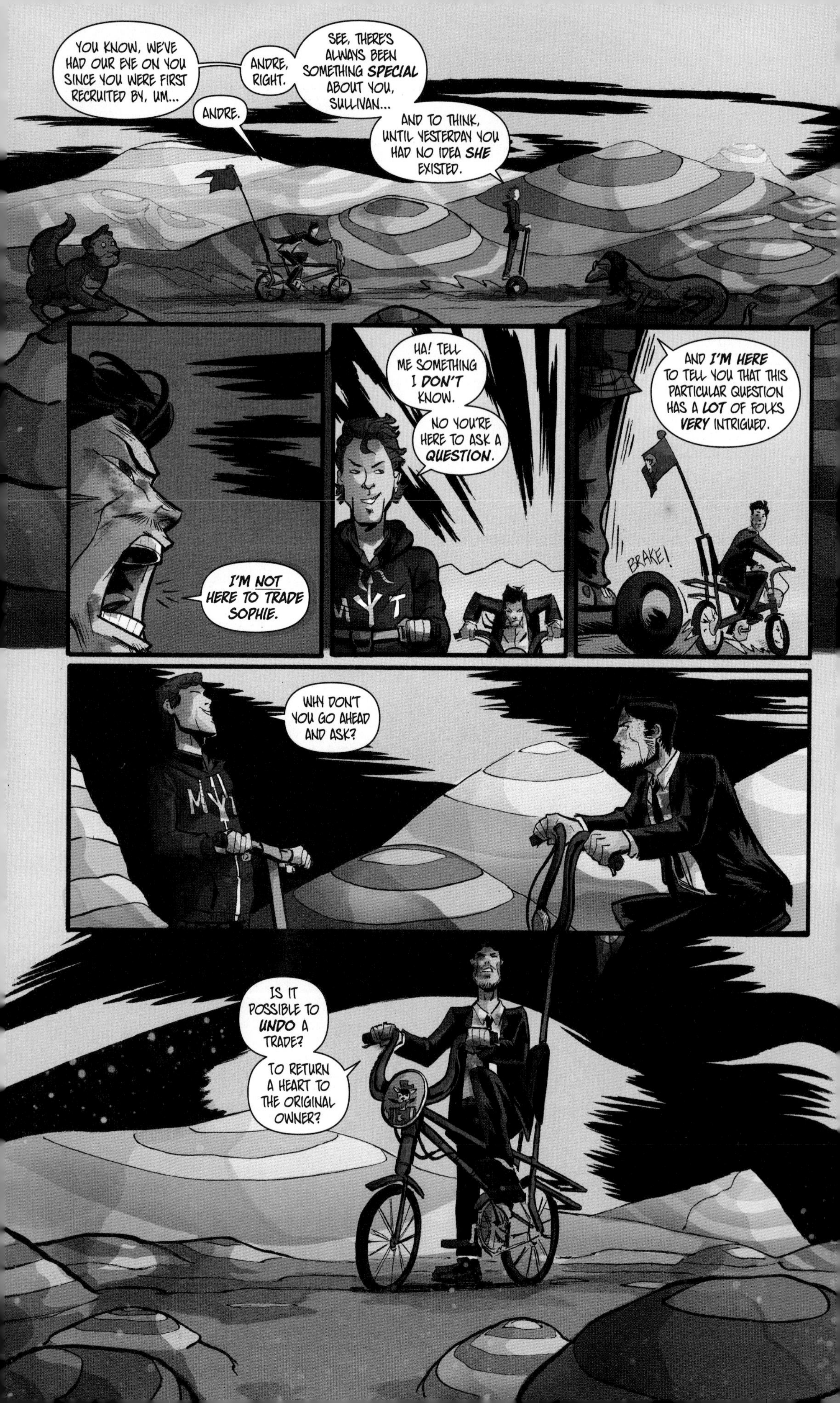

YOU KNOW, WE'VE HAD OUR EYE ON YOU SINCE YOU WERE FIRST RECRUITED BY, UM...
ANDRE.
ANDRE, RIGHT.
SEE, THERE'S ALWAYS BEEN SOMETHING SPECIAL ABOUT YOU, SULLIVAN...
AND TO THINK, UNTIL YESTERDAY YOU HAD NO IDEA SHE EXISTED.
I'M NOT HERE TO TRADE SOPHIE.
HA! TELL ME SOMETHING I DON'T KNOW.
NO YOU'RE HERE TO ASK A QUESTION.
BRAKE!
AND I'M HERE TO TELL YOU THAT THIS PARTICULAR QUESTION HAS A LOT OF FOLKS VERY INTRIGUED.
WHY DON'T YOU GO AHEAD AND ASK?
IS IT POSSIBLE TO UNDO A TRADE?
TO RETURN A HEART TO THE ORIGINAL OWNER?

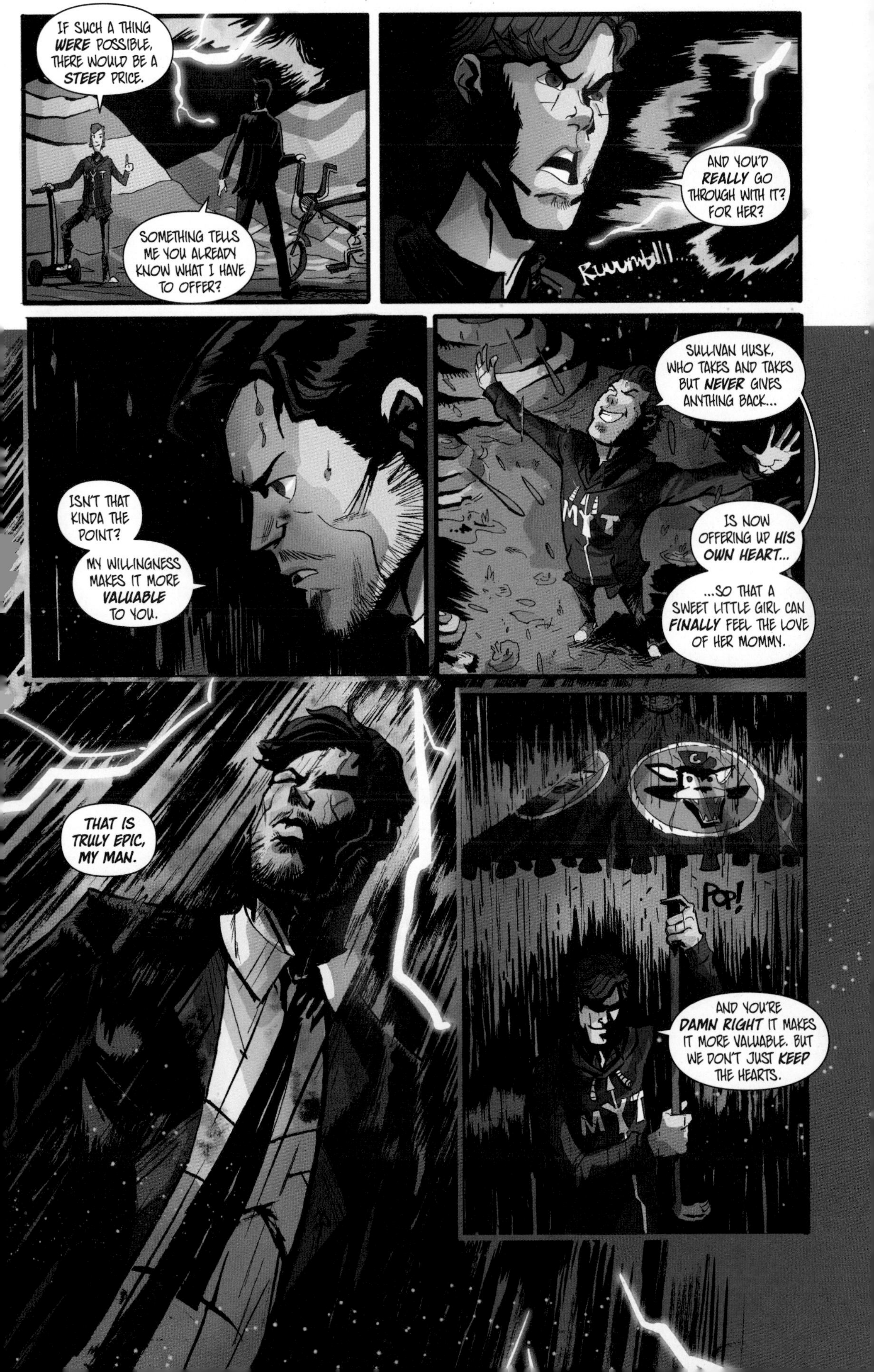
IF SUCH A THING WERE POSSIBLE, THERE WOULD BE A STEEP PRICE.
SOMETHING TELLS ME YOU ALREADY KNOW WHAT I HAVE TO OFFER?
AND YOU'D REALLY GO THROUGH WITH IT? FOR HER?
Ruuumblll...
ISN'T THAT KINDA THE POINT?
MY WILLINGNESS MAKES IT MORE VALUABLE TO YOU.
SULLIVAN HUSK, WHO TAKES AND TAKES BUT NEVER GIVES ANYTHING BACK...
IS NOW OFFERING UP HIS OWN HEART...
...SO THAT A SWEET LITTLE GIRL CAN FINALLY FEEL THE LOVE OF HER MOMMY.
THAT IS TRULY EPIC, MY MAN.
POP!
AND YOU'RE DAMN RIGHT IT MAKES IT MORE VALUABLE. BUT WE DON'T JUST KEEP THE HEARTS.

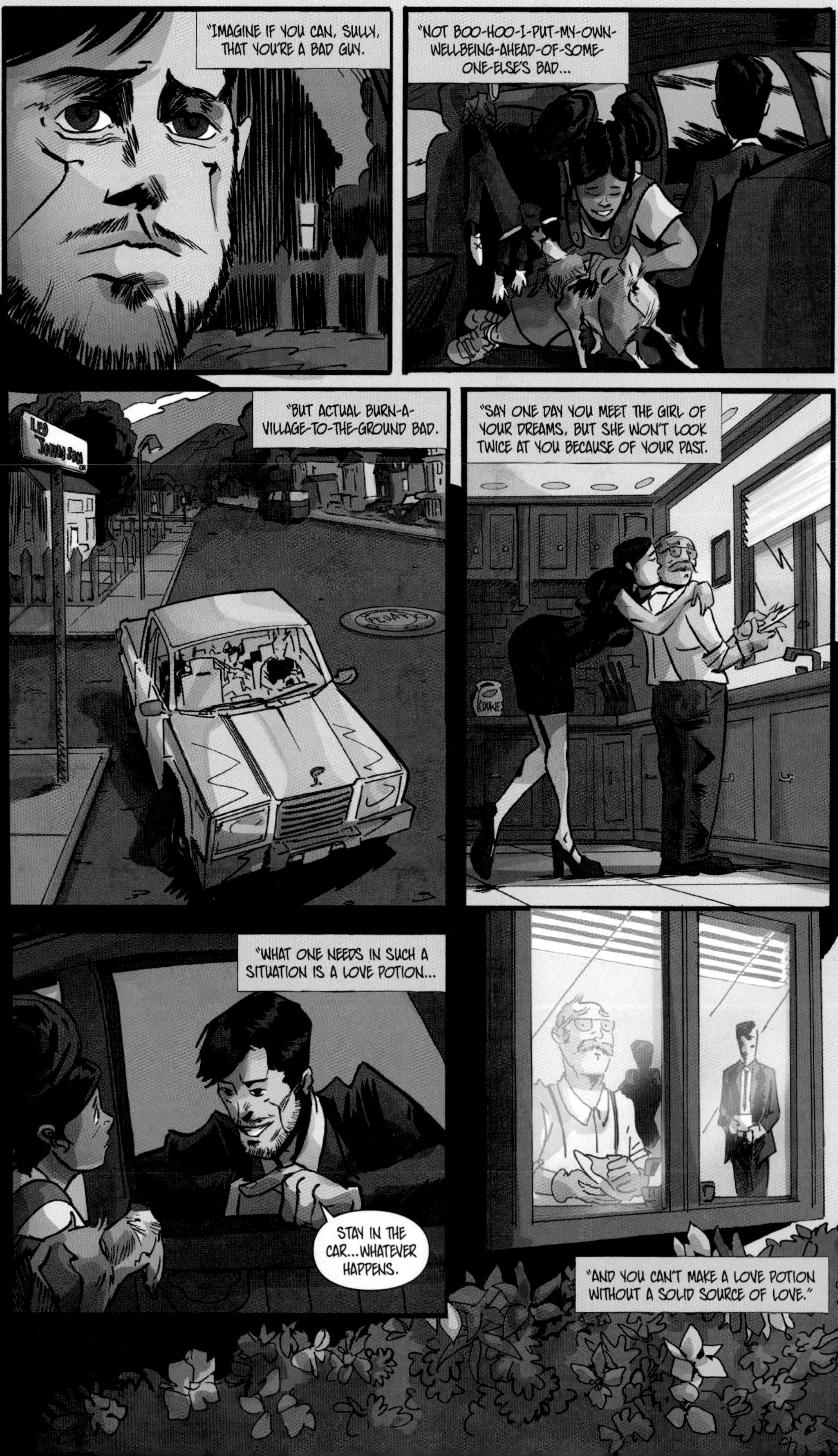
"IMAGINE IF YOU CAN, SULLY, THAT YOU'RE A BAD GUY.
"NOT BOO-HOO-I-PUT-MY-OWN-WELLBEING-AHEAD-OF-SOME-ONE-ELSE'S BAD...
"BUT ACTUAL BURN-A-VILLAGE-TO-THE-GROUND BAD.
"SAY ONE DAY YOU MEET THE GIRL OF YOUR DREAMS, BUT SHE WON'T LOOK TWICE AT YOU BECAUSE OF YOUR PAST.
COOKIES
"WHAT ONE NEEDS IN SUCH A SITUATION IS A LOVE POTION...
STAY IN THE CAR...WHATEVER HAPPENS.
"AND YOU CAN'T MAKE A LOVE POTION WITHOUT A SOLID SOURCE OF LOVE."

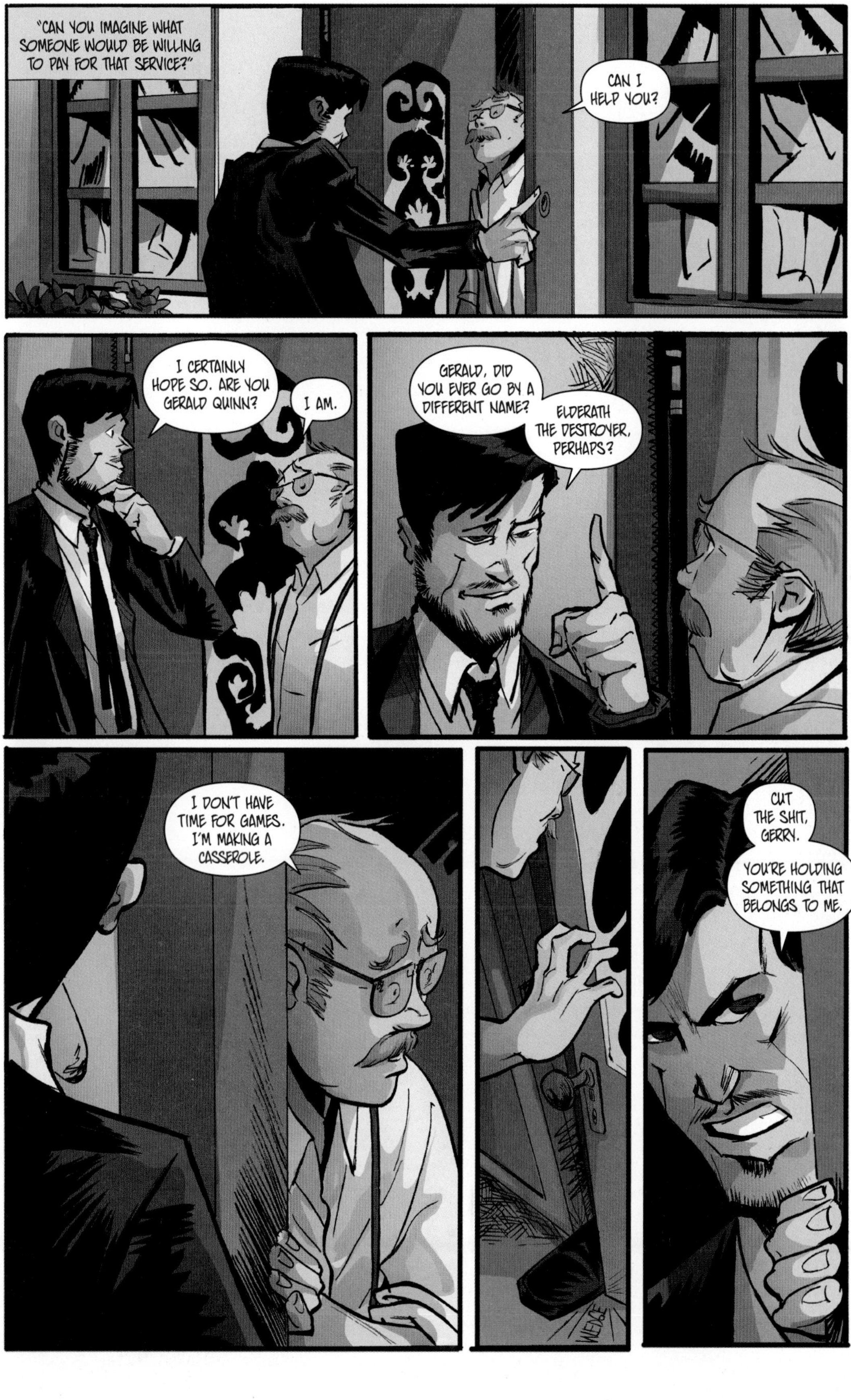
"CAN YOU IMAGINE WHAT SOMEONE WOULD BE WILLING TO PAY FOR THAT SERVICE?"
CAN I HELP YOU?
I CERTAINLY HOPE SO. ARE YOU GERALD QUINN?
I AM.
GERALD, DID YOU EVER GO BY A DIFFERENT NAME?
ELDERATH THE DESTROYER, PERHAPS?
I DON'T HAVE TIME FOR GAMES. I'M MAKING A CASSEROLE.
CUT THE SHIT, GERRY.
YOU'RE HOLDING SOMETHING THAT BELONGS TO ME.
WEIXE

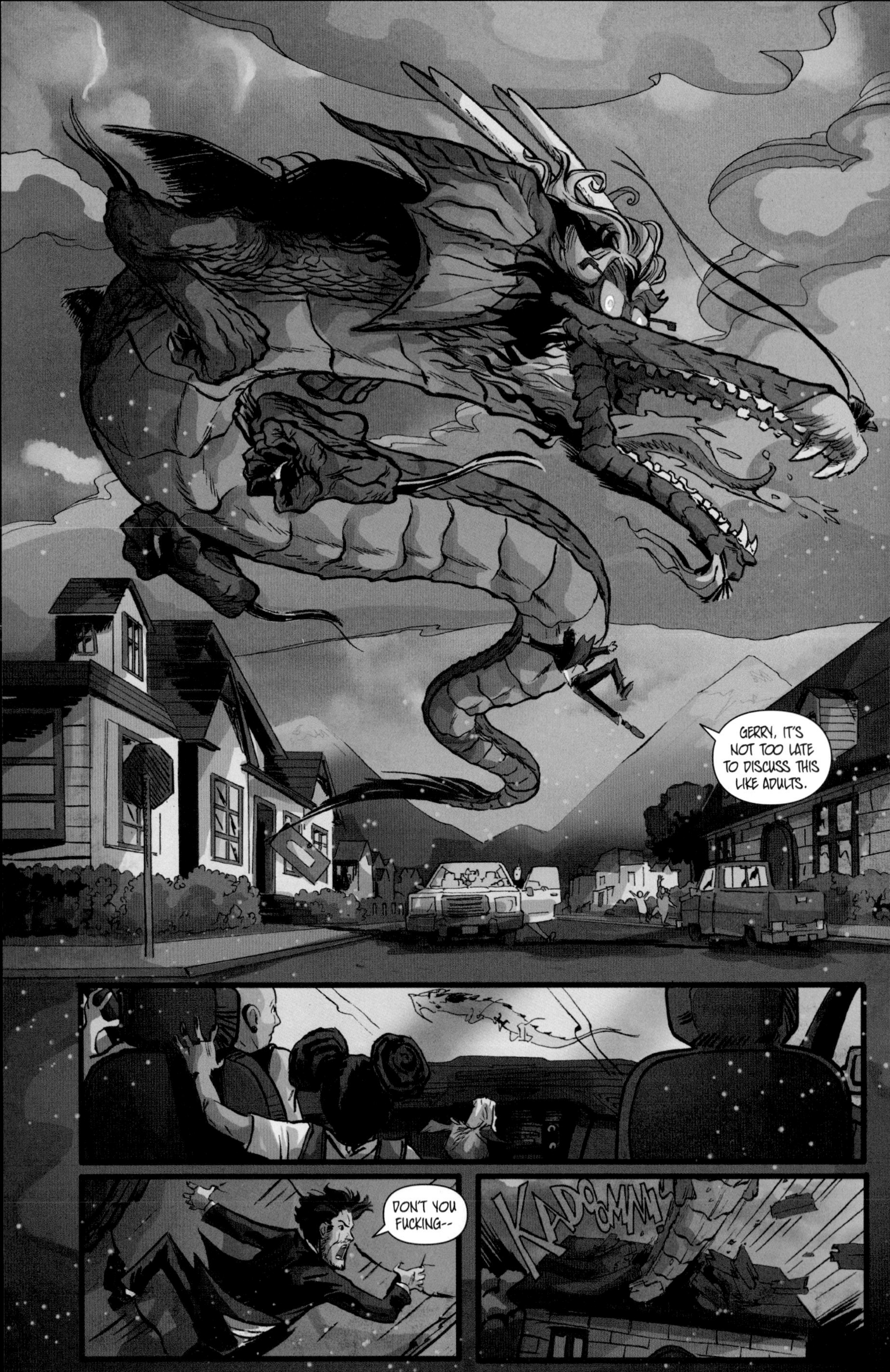
GERRY, IT'S NOT TOO LATE TO DISCUSS THIS LIKE ADULTS.
DON'T YOU FUCKING--
KADOOMM!

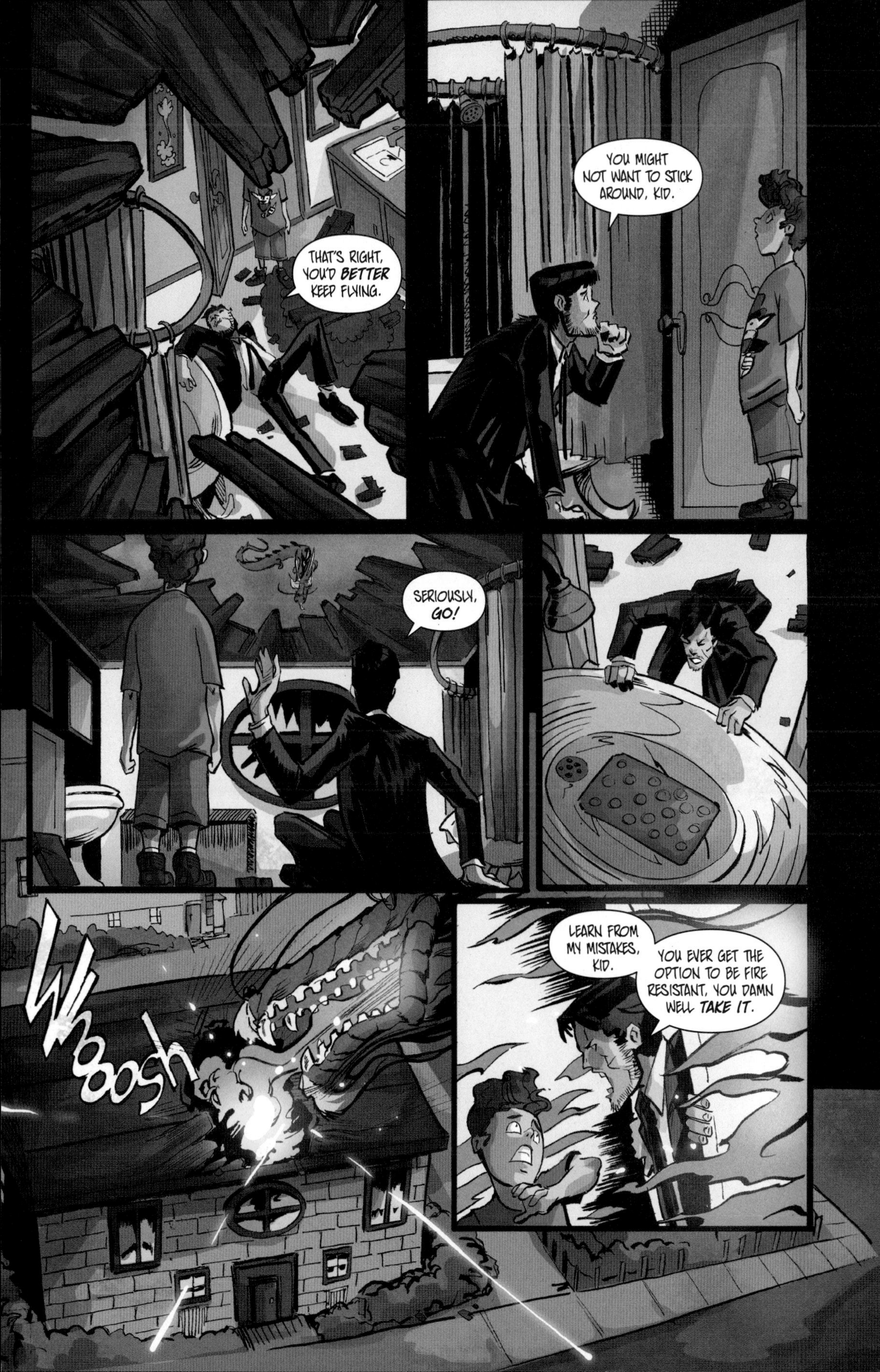
THAT'S RIGHT, YOU'D **BETTER** KEEP FLYING.
YOU MIGHT NOT WANT TO STICK AROUND, KID.
SERIOUSLY, **GO!**
WHOOSH
LEARN FROM MY MISTAKES, KID.
YOU EVER GET THE OPTION TO BE FIRE RESISTANT, YOU DAMN WELL ***TAKE IT***.

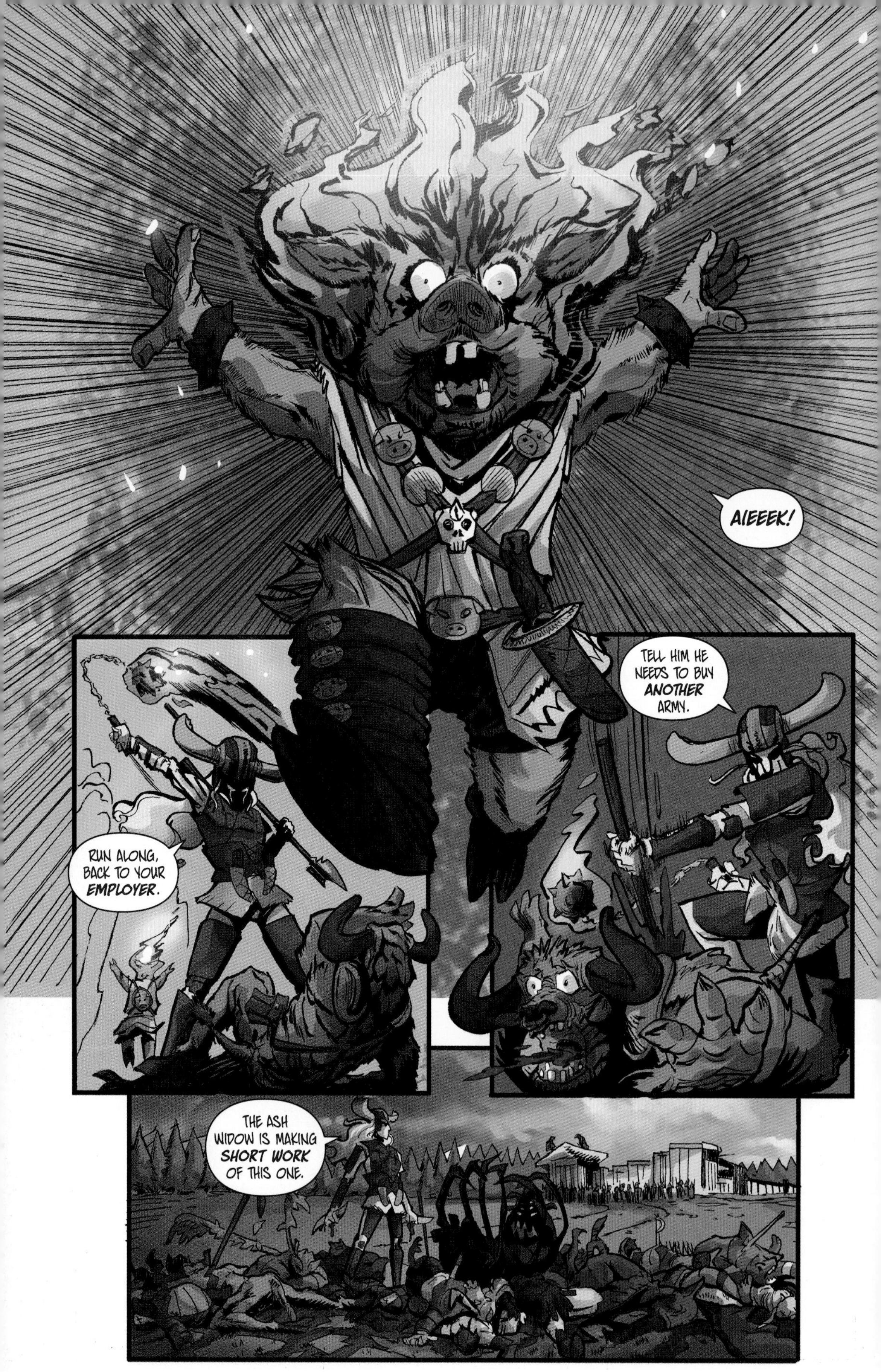
AIEEEK!
RUN ALONG, BACK TO YOUR EMPLOYER.
TELL HIM HE NEEDS TO BUY ANOTHER ARMY.
THE ASH WIDOW IS MAKING SHORT WORK OF THIS ONE.

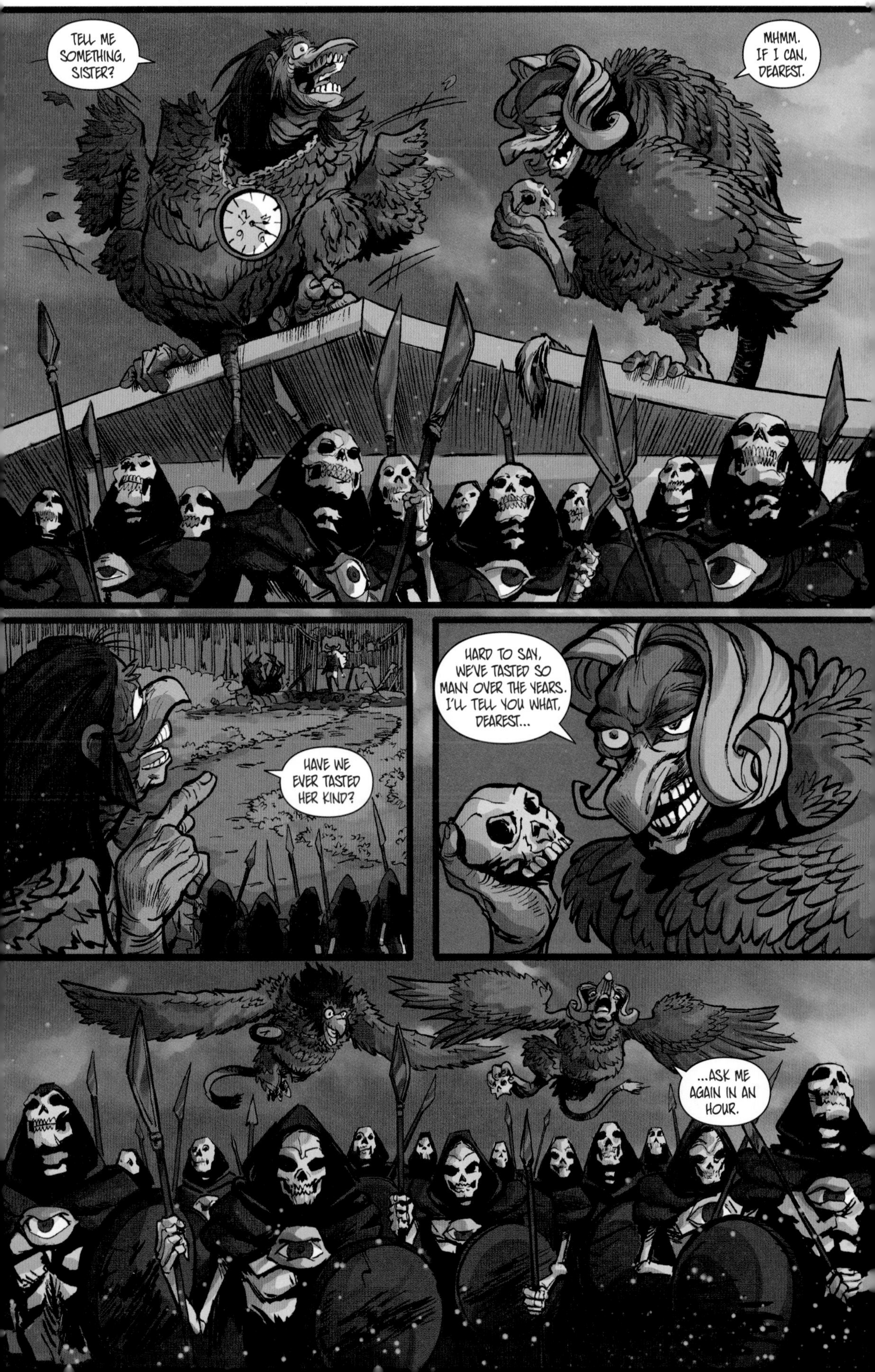
TELL ME SOMETHING, SISTER?
MHMM. IF I CAN, DEAREST.
HAVE WE EVER TASTED HER KIND?
HARD TO SAY, WE'VE TASTED SO MANY OVER THE YEARS. I'LL TELL YOU WHAT, DEAREST...
...ASK ME AGAIN IN AN HOUR.

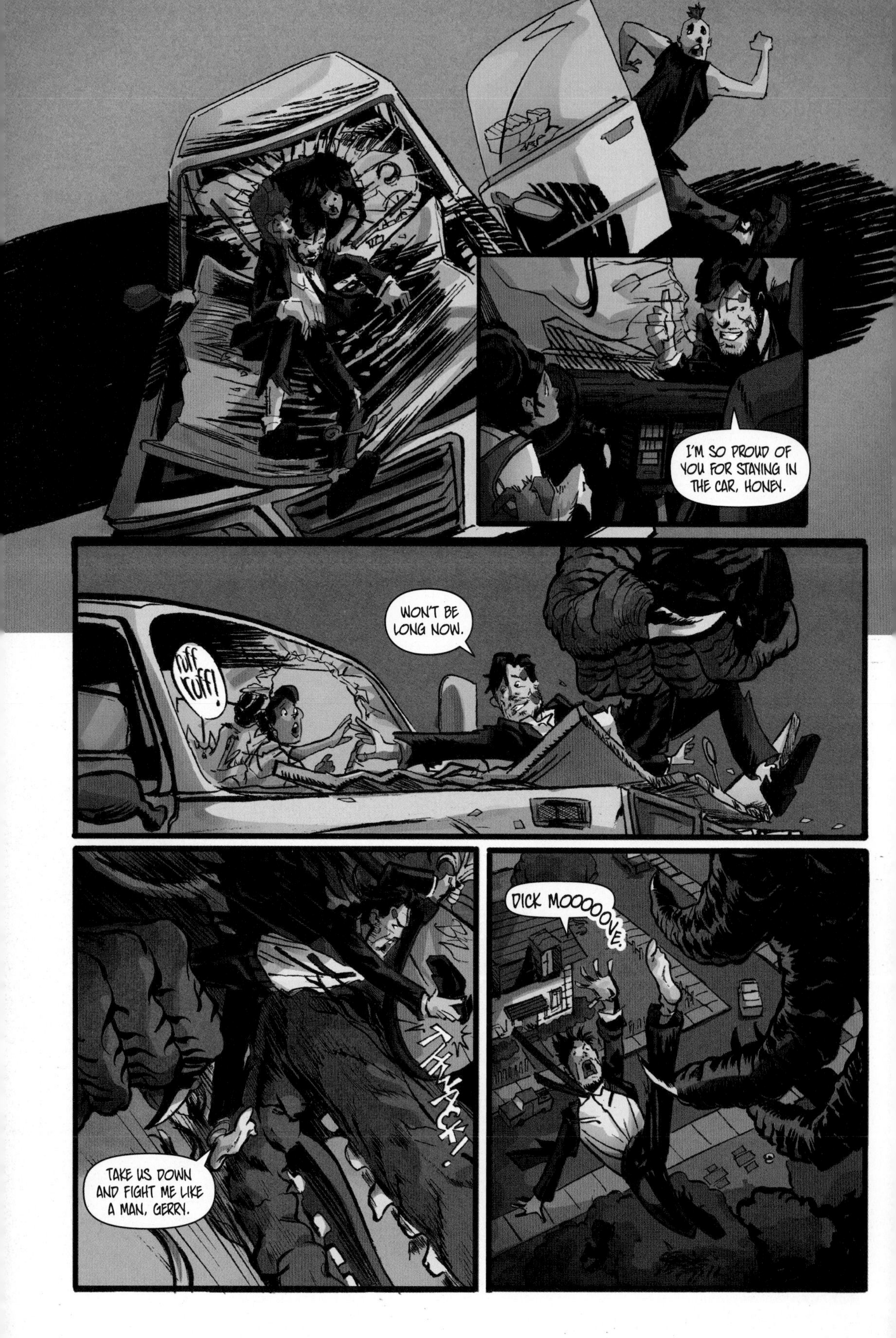
I'M SO PROUD OF YOU FOR STAYING IN THE CAR, HONEY.
WON'T BE LONG NOW.
ruff ruff!
TAKE US DOWN AND FIGHT ME LIKE A MAN, GERRY.
THWACK!
DICK MOOOOOOVE.

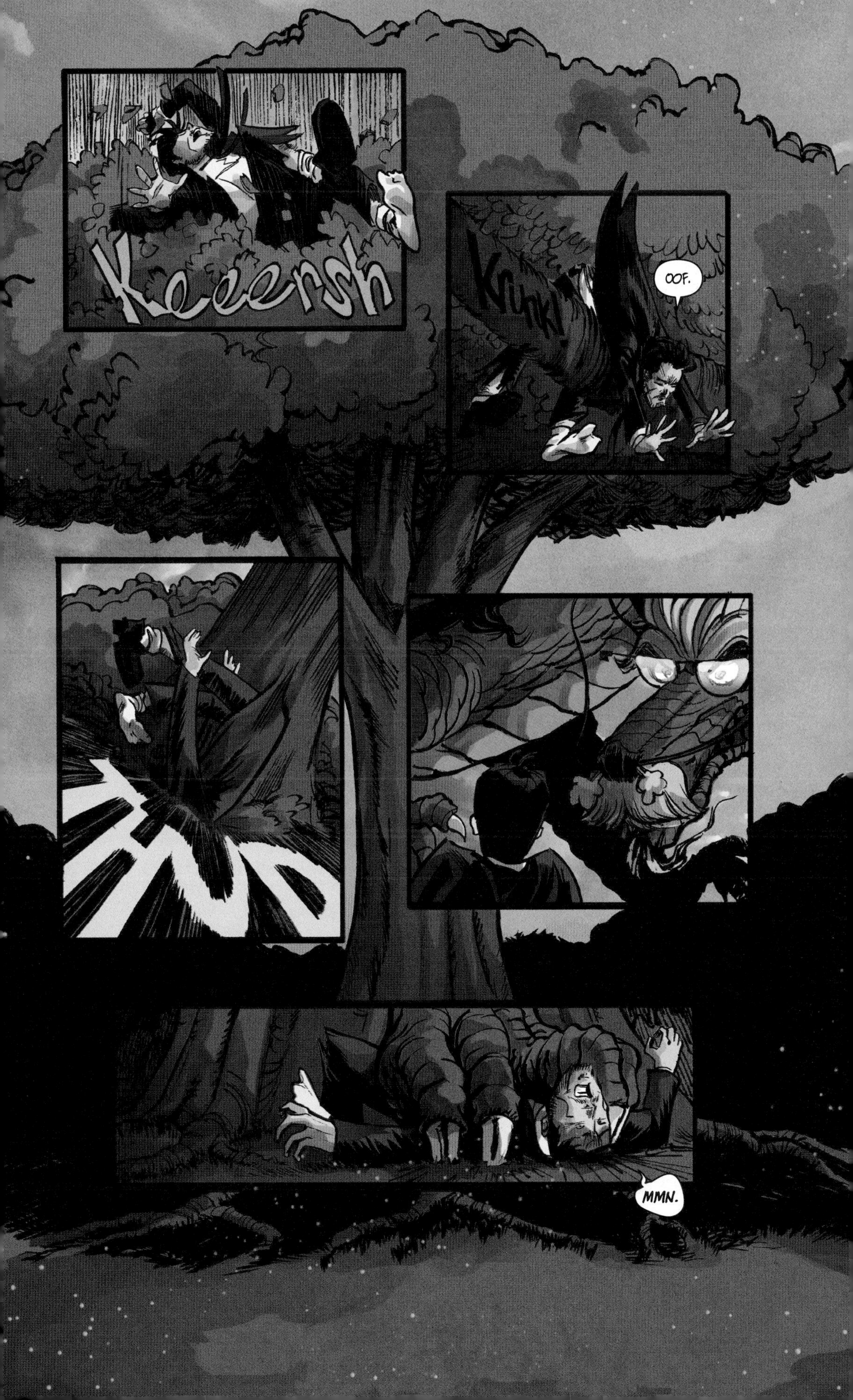
Keeersh
Krunk!
OOF.
MMN.

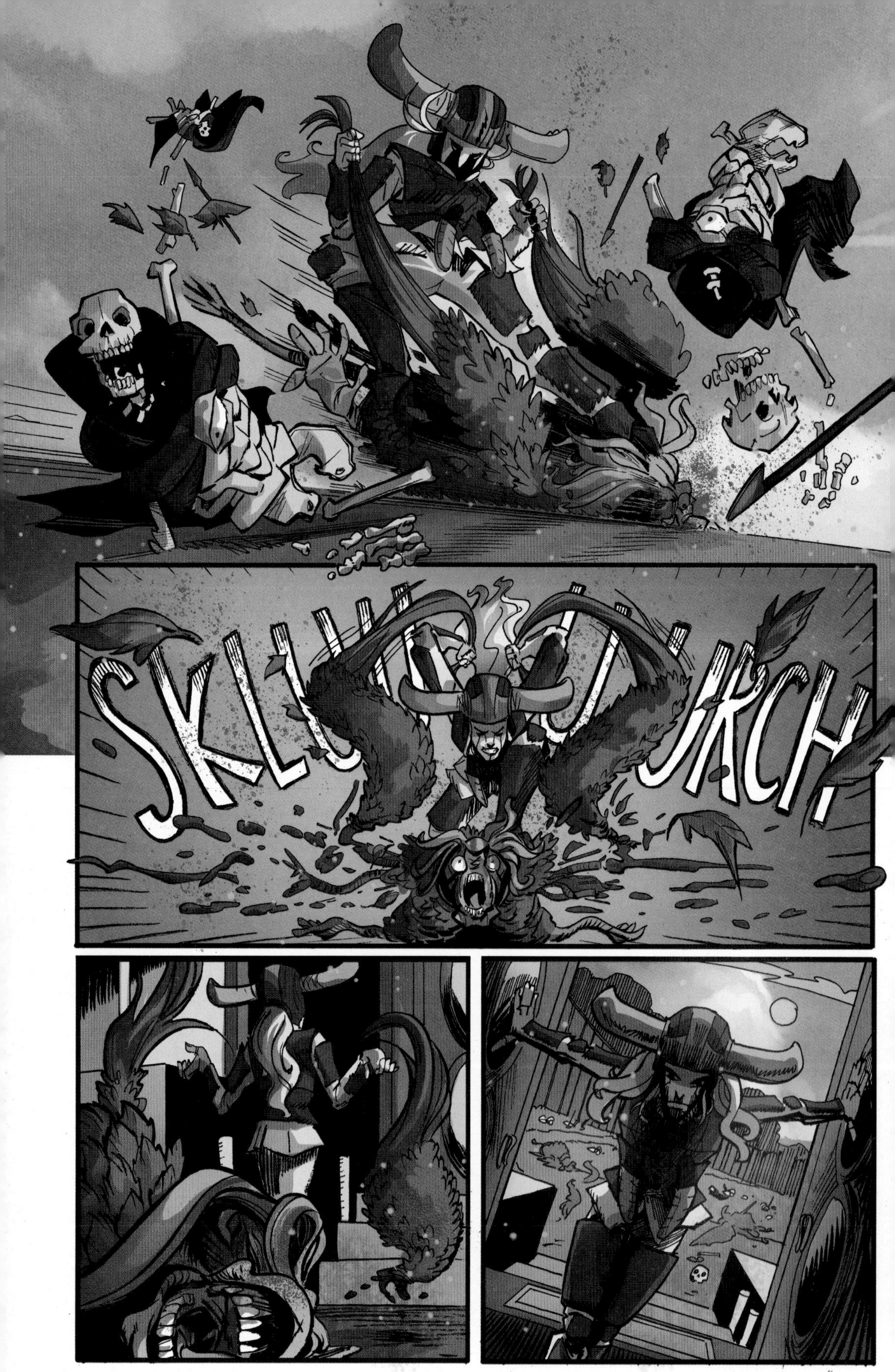
SKLU URCH

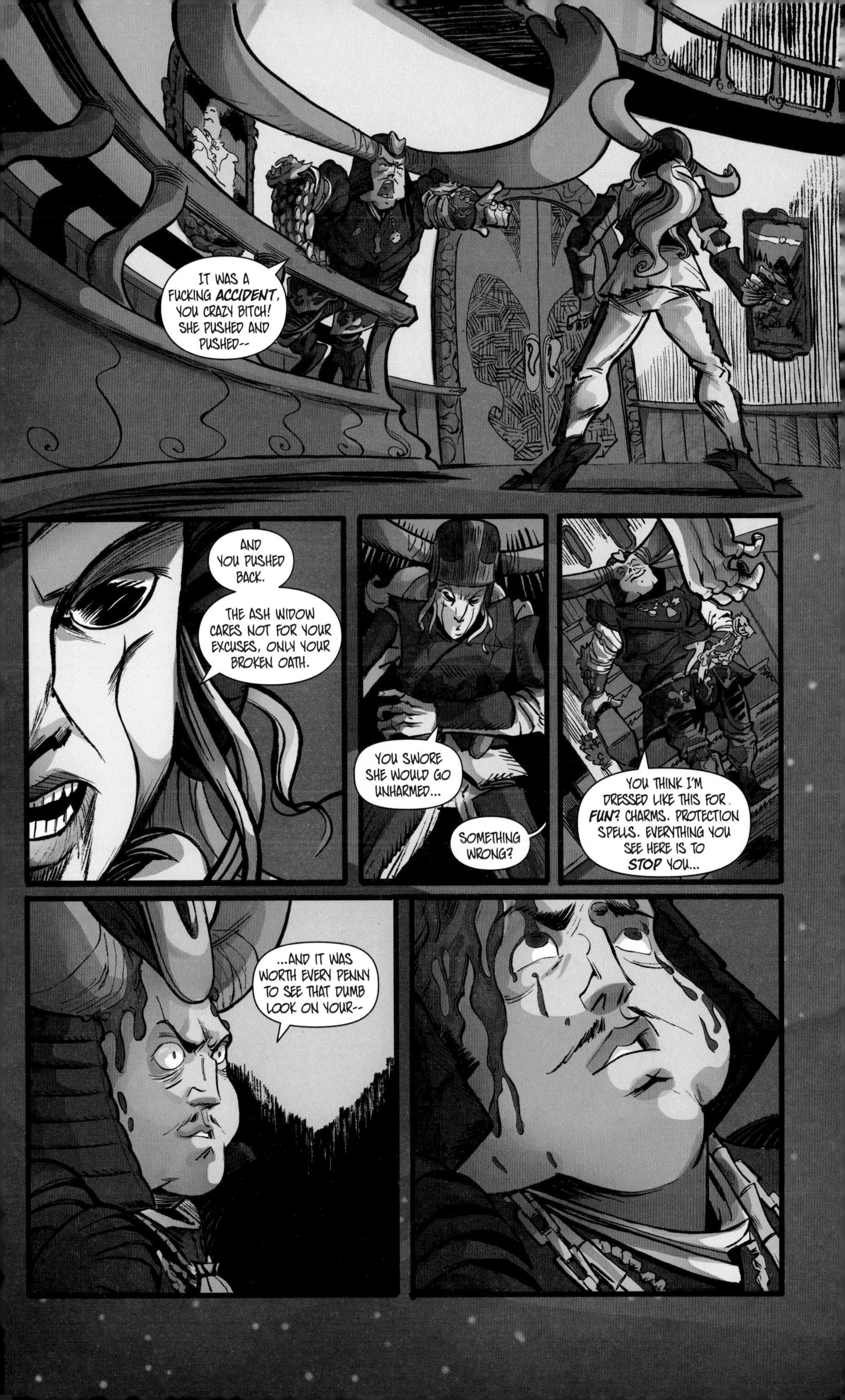
IT WAS A FUCKING **ACCIDENT**, YOU CRAZY BITCH! SHE PUSHED AND PUSHED--
AND YOU PUSHED BACK.
THE ASH WIDOW CARES NOT FOR YOUR EXCUSES, ONLY YOUR BROKEN OATH.
YOU SWORE SHE WOULD GO UNHARMED...
SOMETHING WRONG?
YOU THINK I'M DRESSED LIKE THIS FOR **FUN**? CHARMS. PROTECTION SPELLS. EVERYTHING YOU SEE HERE IS TO **STOP** YOU...
...AND IT WAS WORTH EVERY PENNY TO SEE THAT DUMB LOOK ON YOUR--

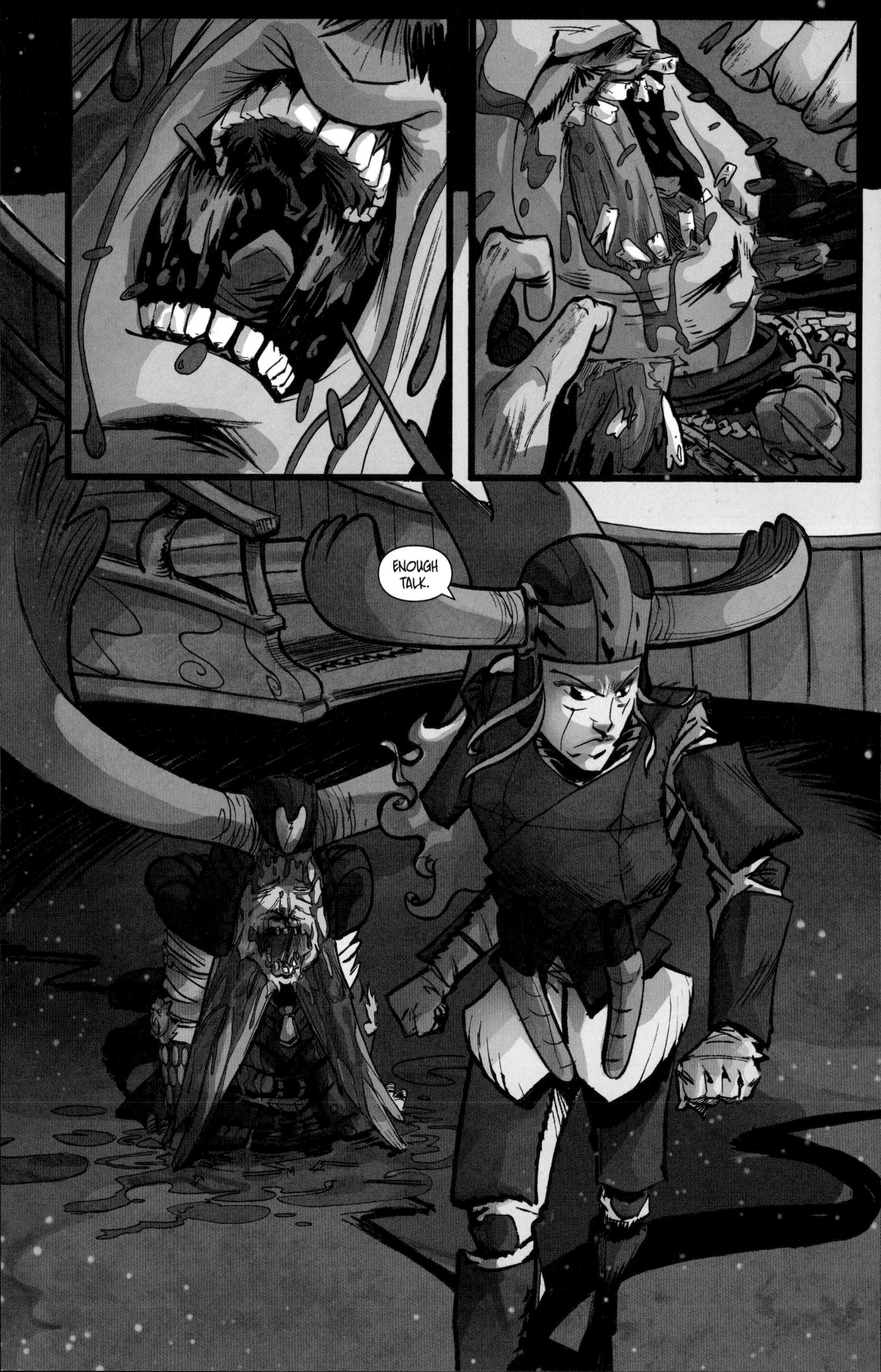
ENOUGH TALK.

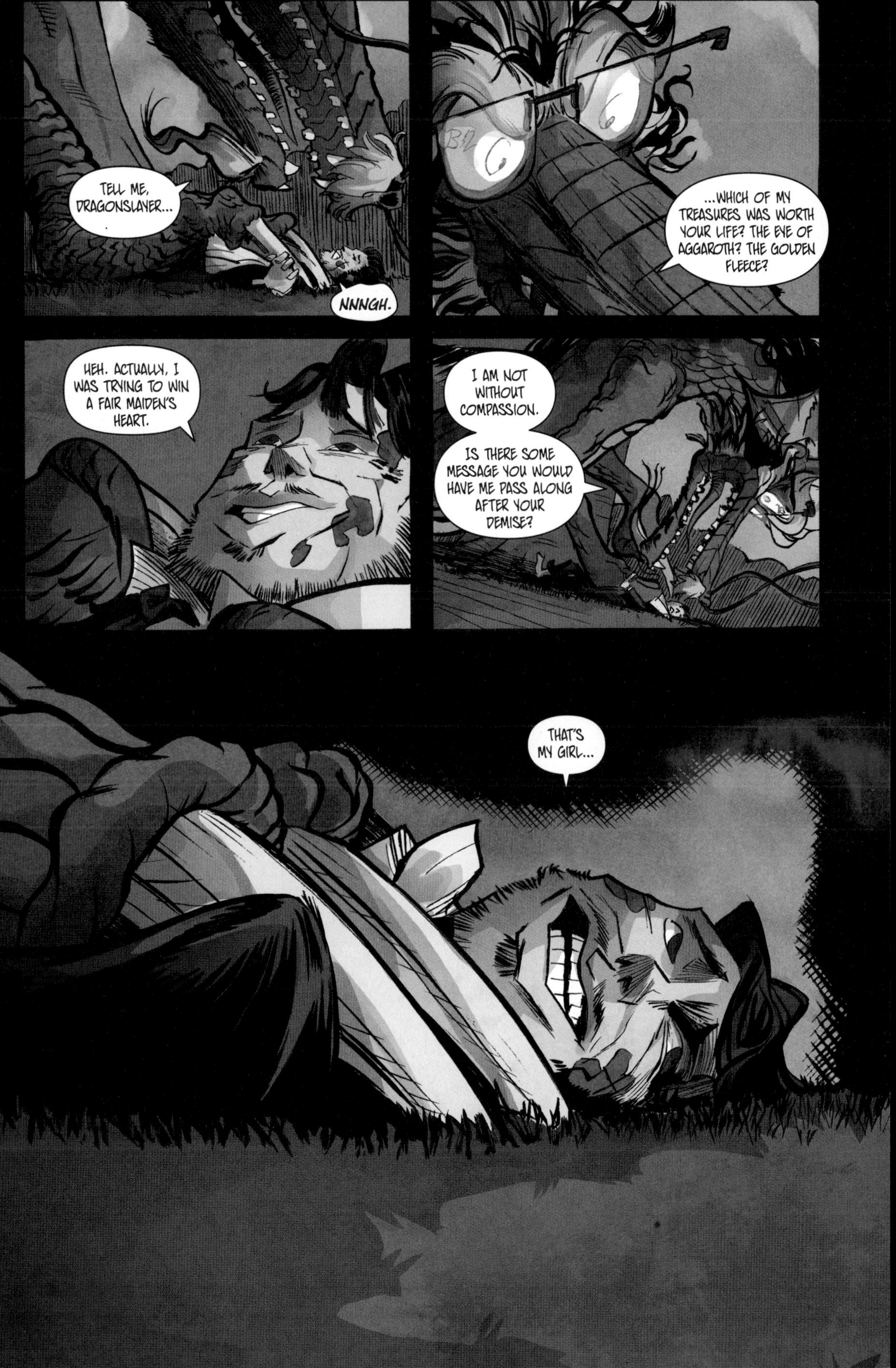

TELL ME, DRAGONSLAYER...
NNNGH.
...WHICH OF MY TREASURES WAS WORTH YOUR LIFE? THE EYE OF AGGAROTH? THE GOLDEN FLEECE?
HEH. ACTUALLY, I WAS TRYING TO WIN A FAIR MAIDEN'S HEART.
I AM NOT WITHOUT COMPASSION.
IS THERE SOME MESSAGE YOU WOULD HAVE ME PASS ALONG AFTER YOUR DEMISE?
THAT'S MY GIRL...

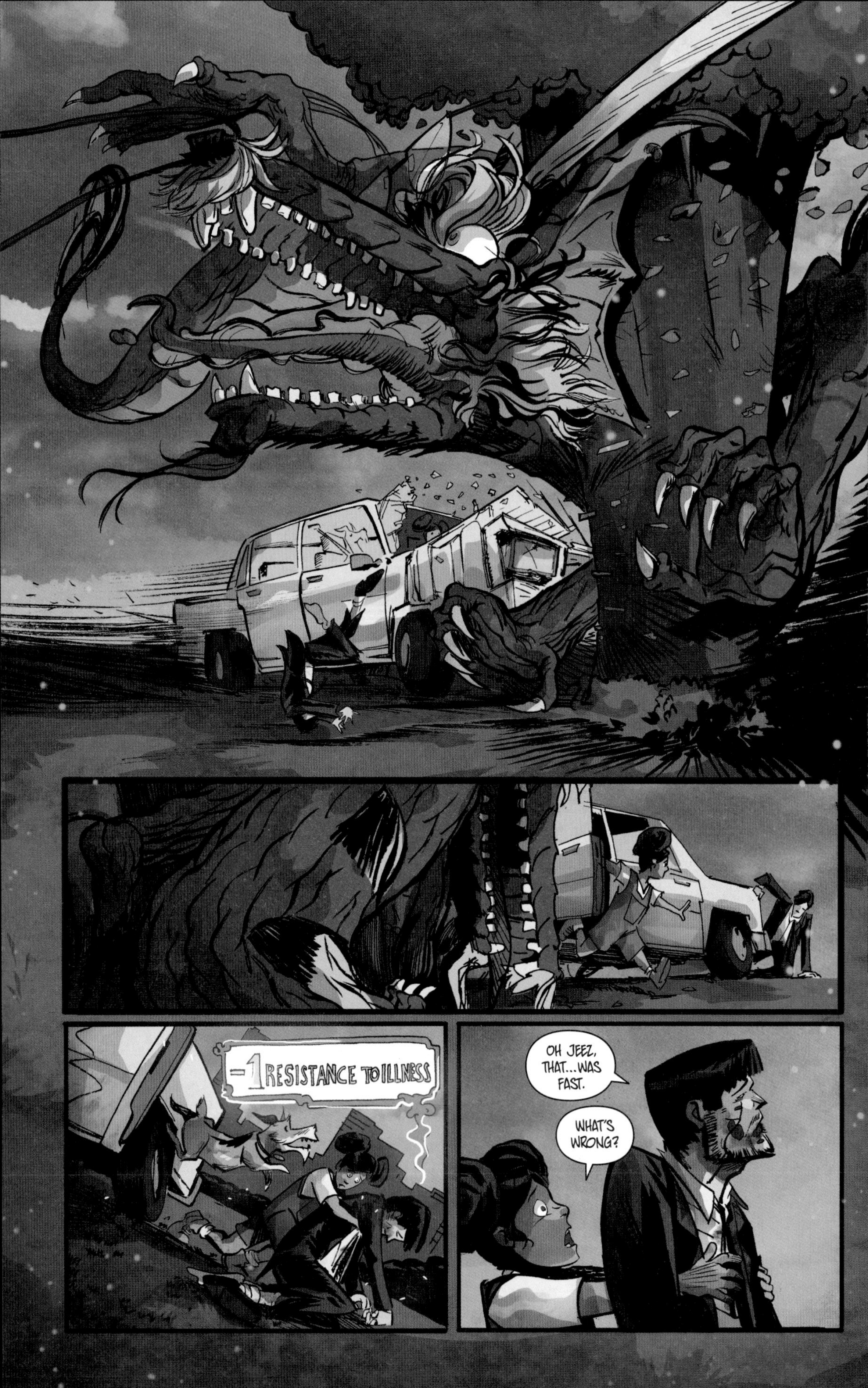
-1 RESISTANCE TO ILLNESS
OH JEEZ, THAT...WAS FAST.
WHAT'S WRONG?

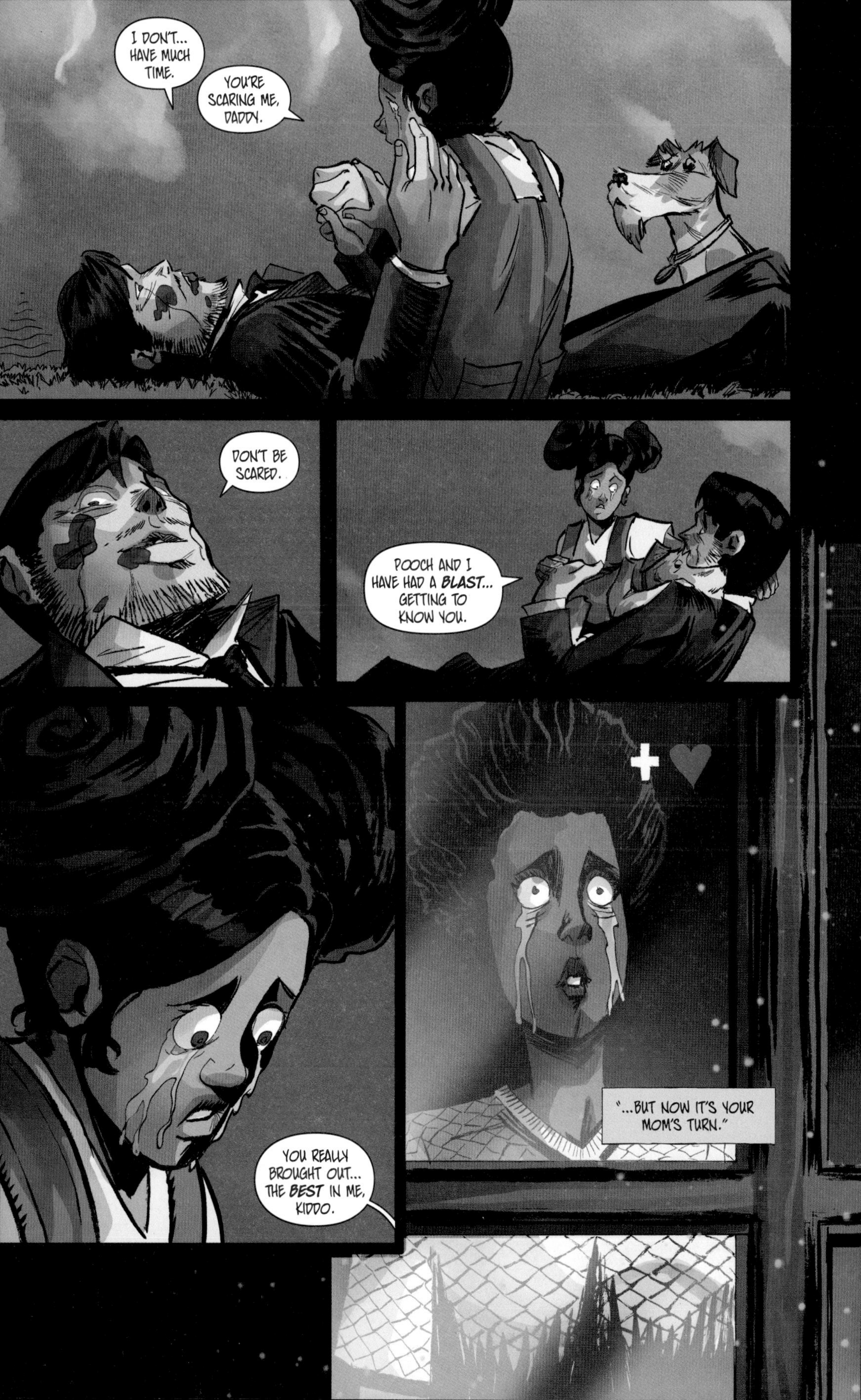
I DON'T... HAVE MUCH TIME.
YOU'RE SCARING ME, DADDY.
DON'T BE SCARED.
POOCH AND I HAVE HAD A **BLAST**... GETTING TO KNOW YOU.
YOU REALLY BROUGHT OUT... THE **BEST** IN ME, KIDDO.
"...BUT NOW IT'S YOUR MOM'S TURN."

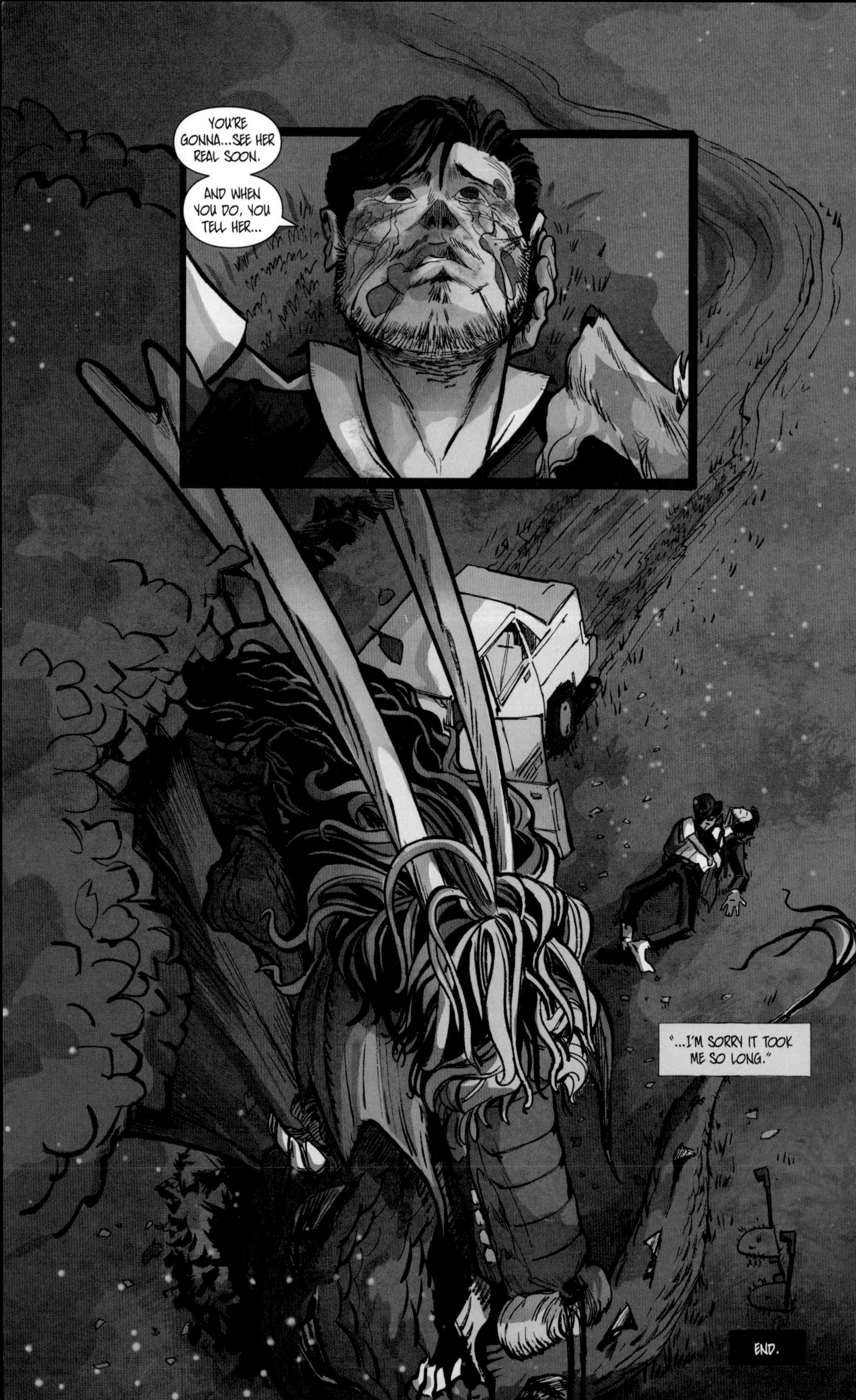
YOU'RE GONNA...SEE HER REAL SOON.
AND WHEN YOU DO, YOU TELL HER...
"...I'M SORRY IT TOOK ME SO LONG."
END.

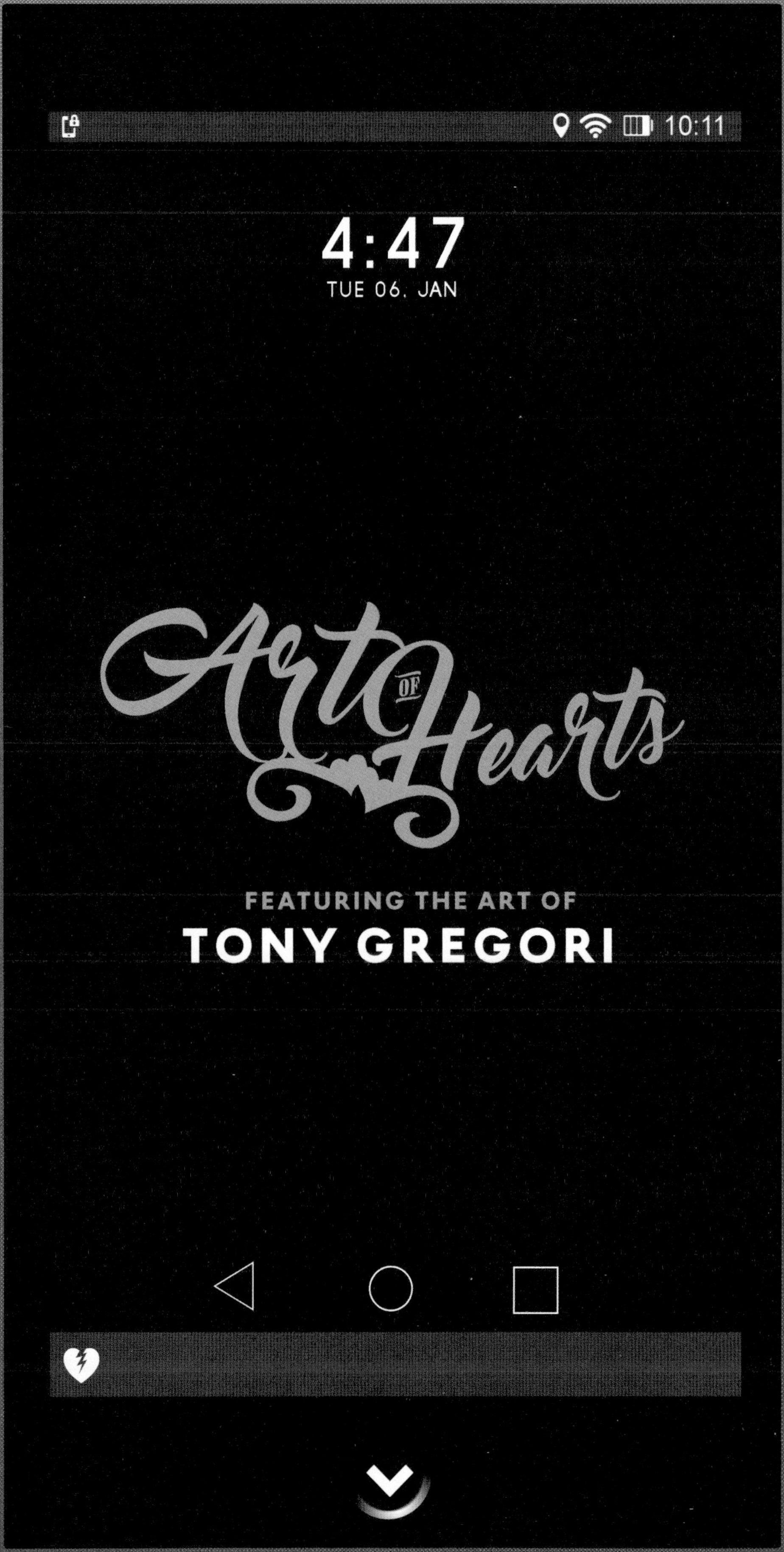
10:11
4:47
TUE 06. JAN
Art of Hearts
FEATURING THE ART OF
TONY GREGORI

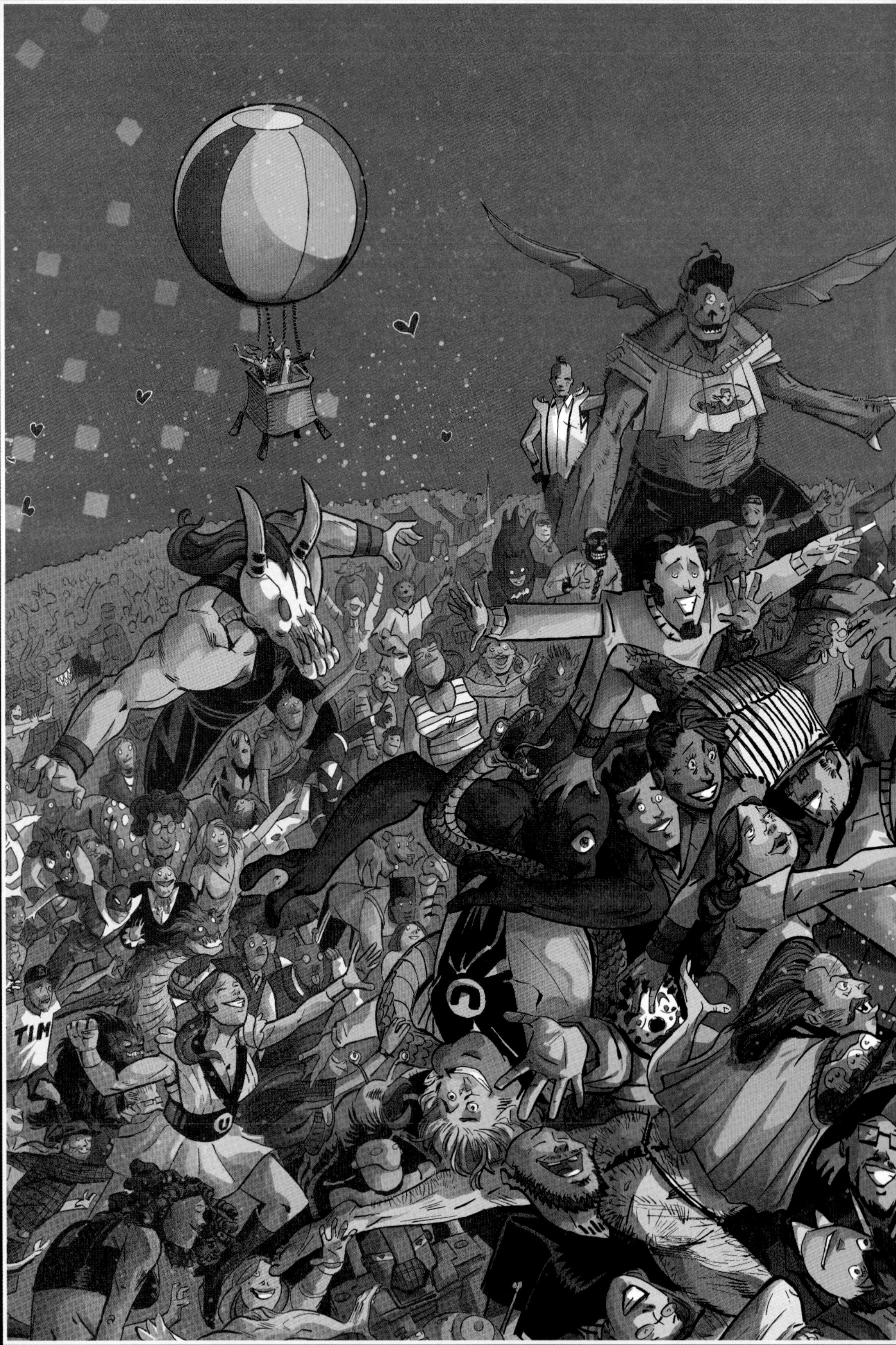
TIM

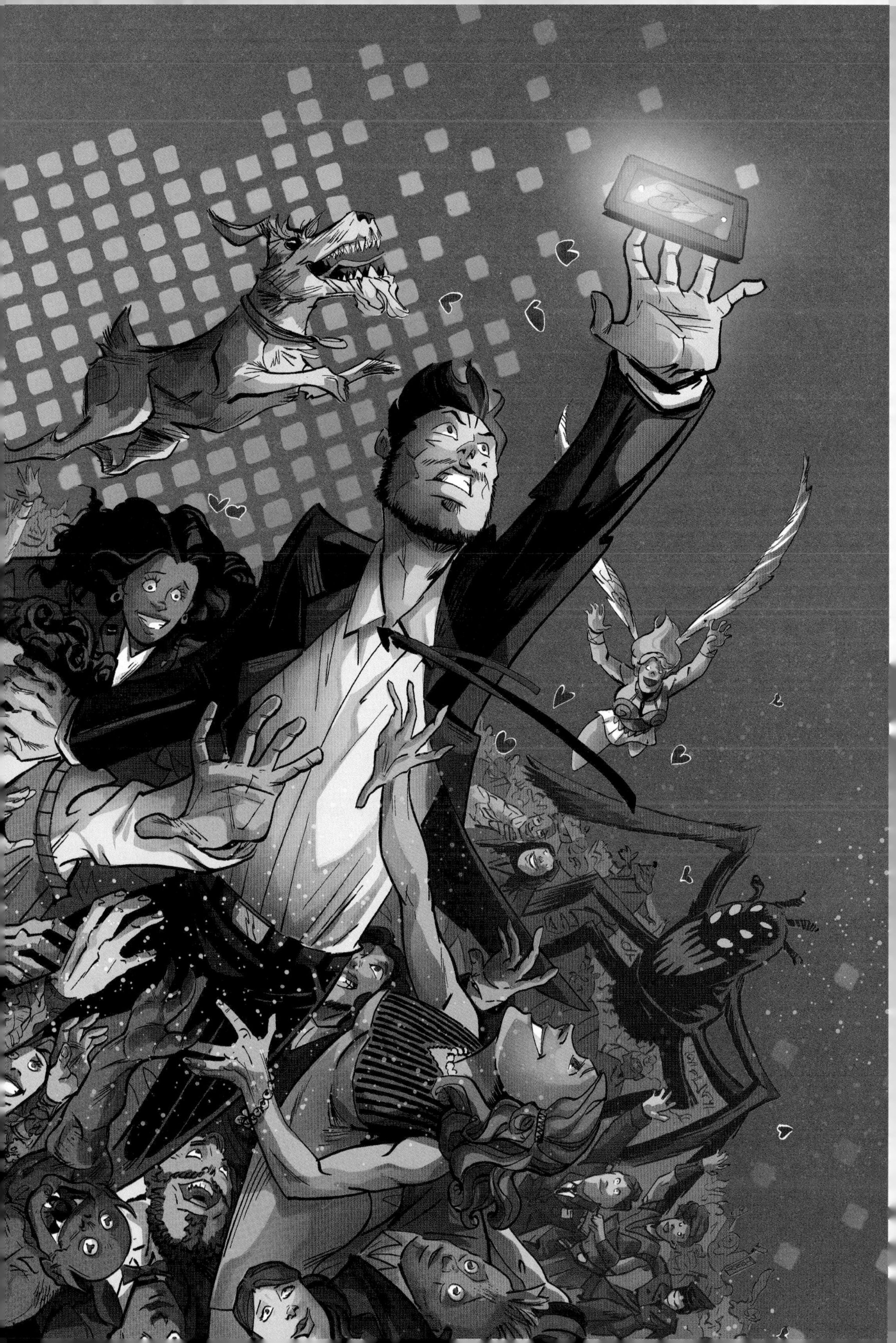

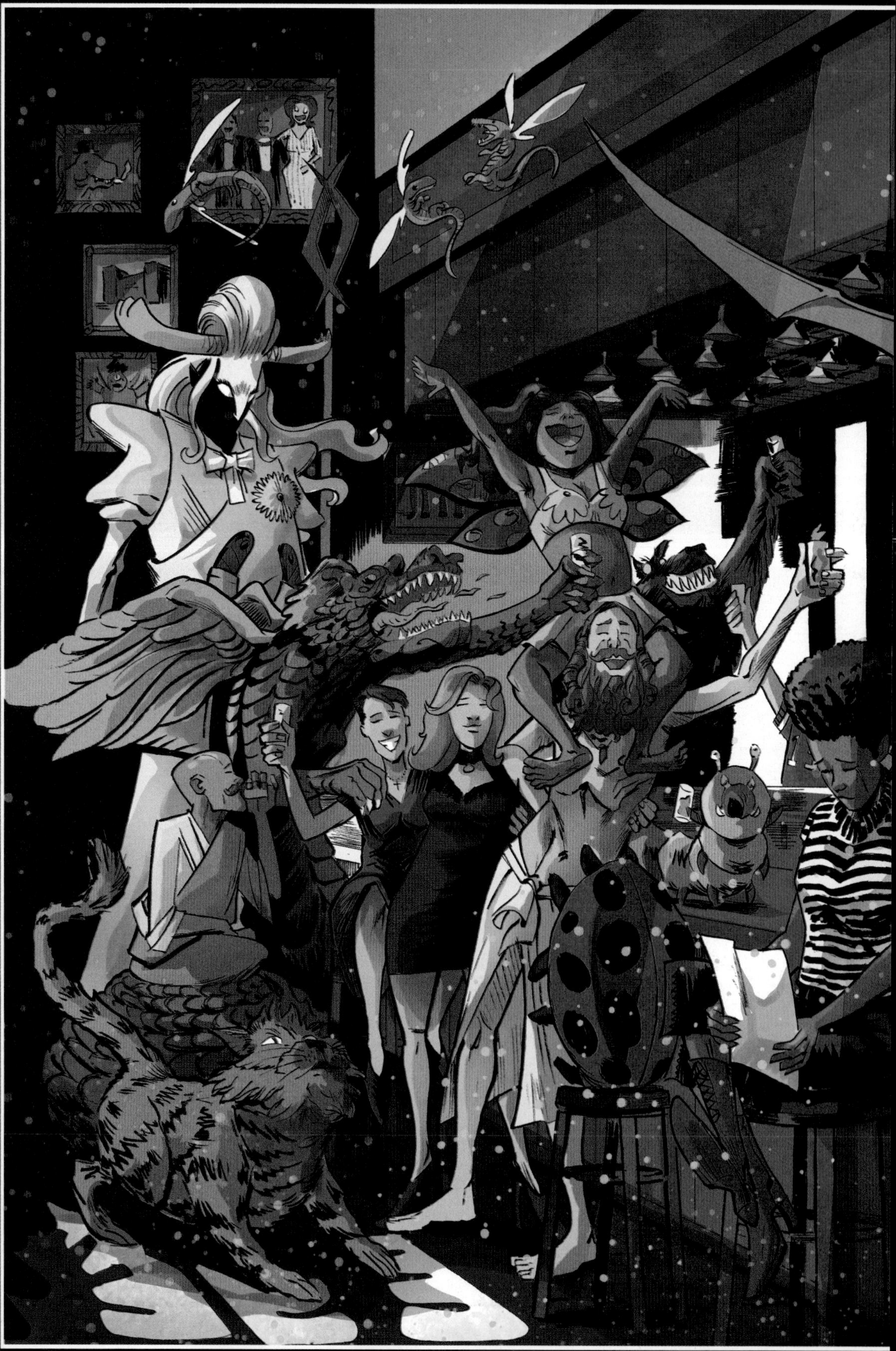

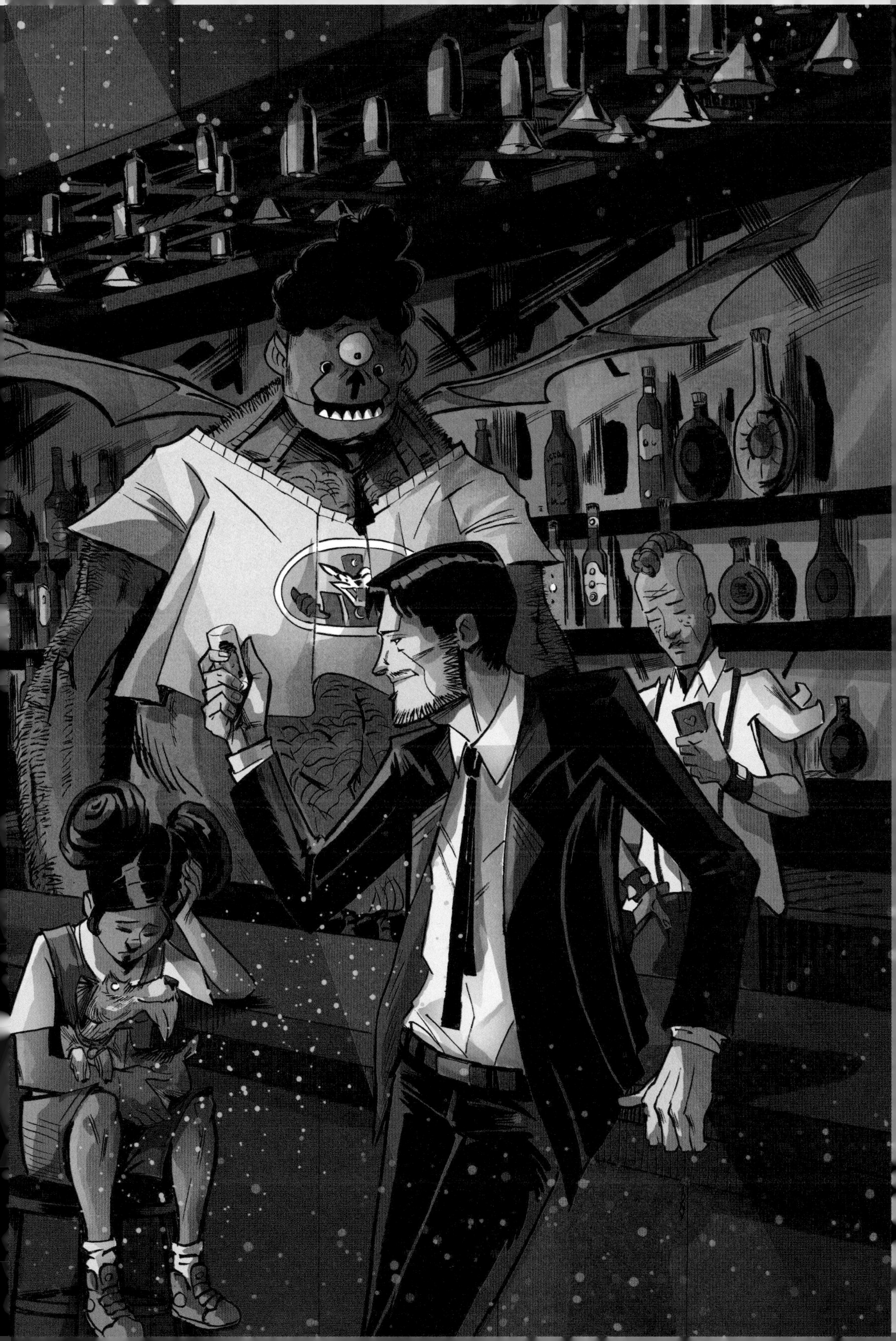

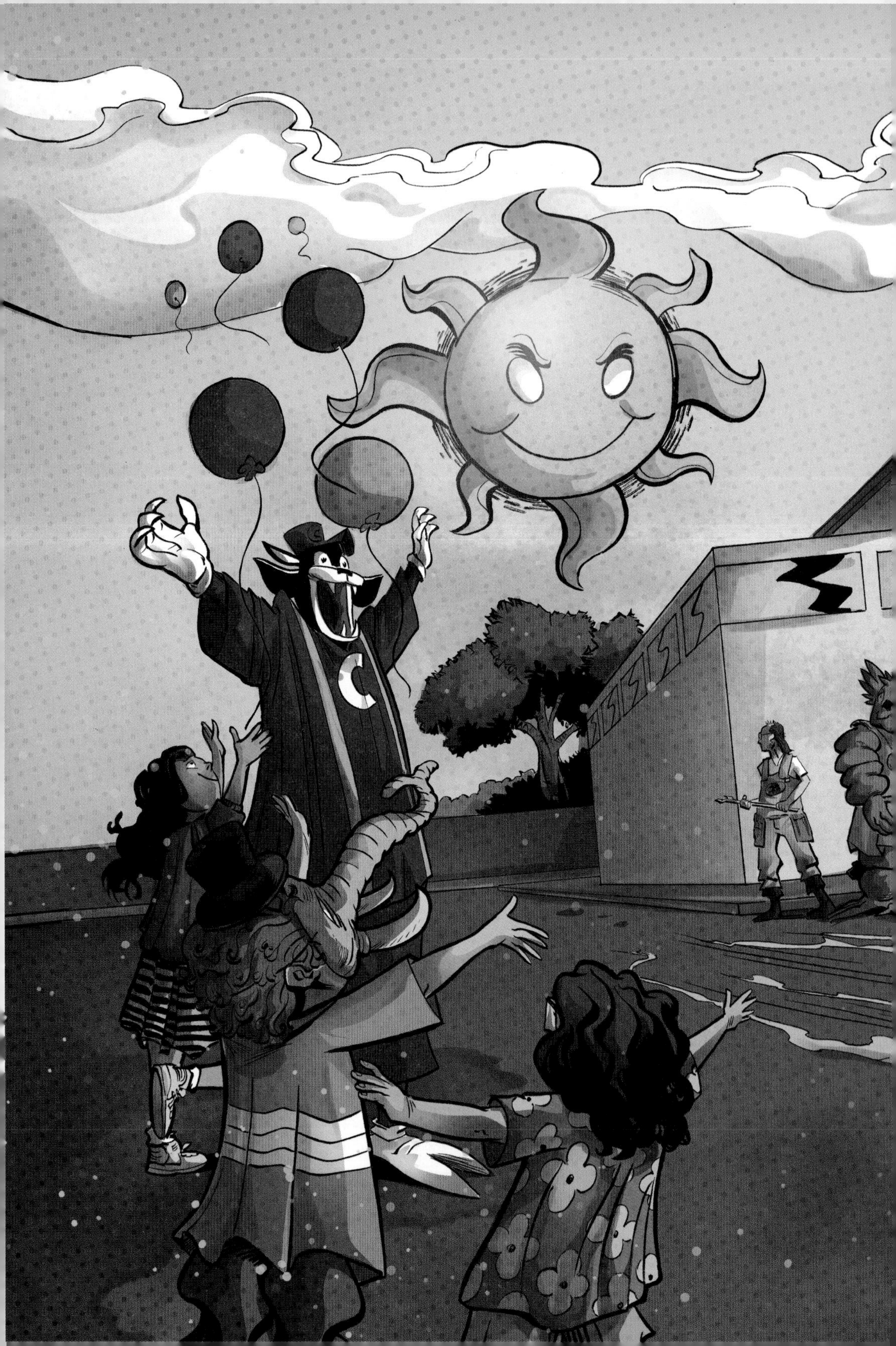

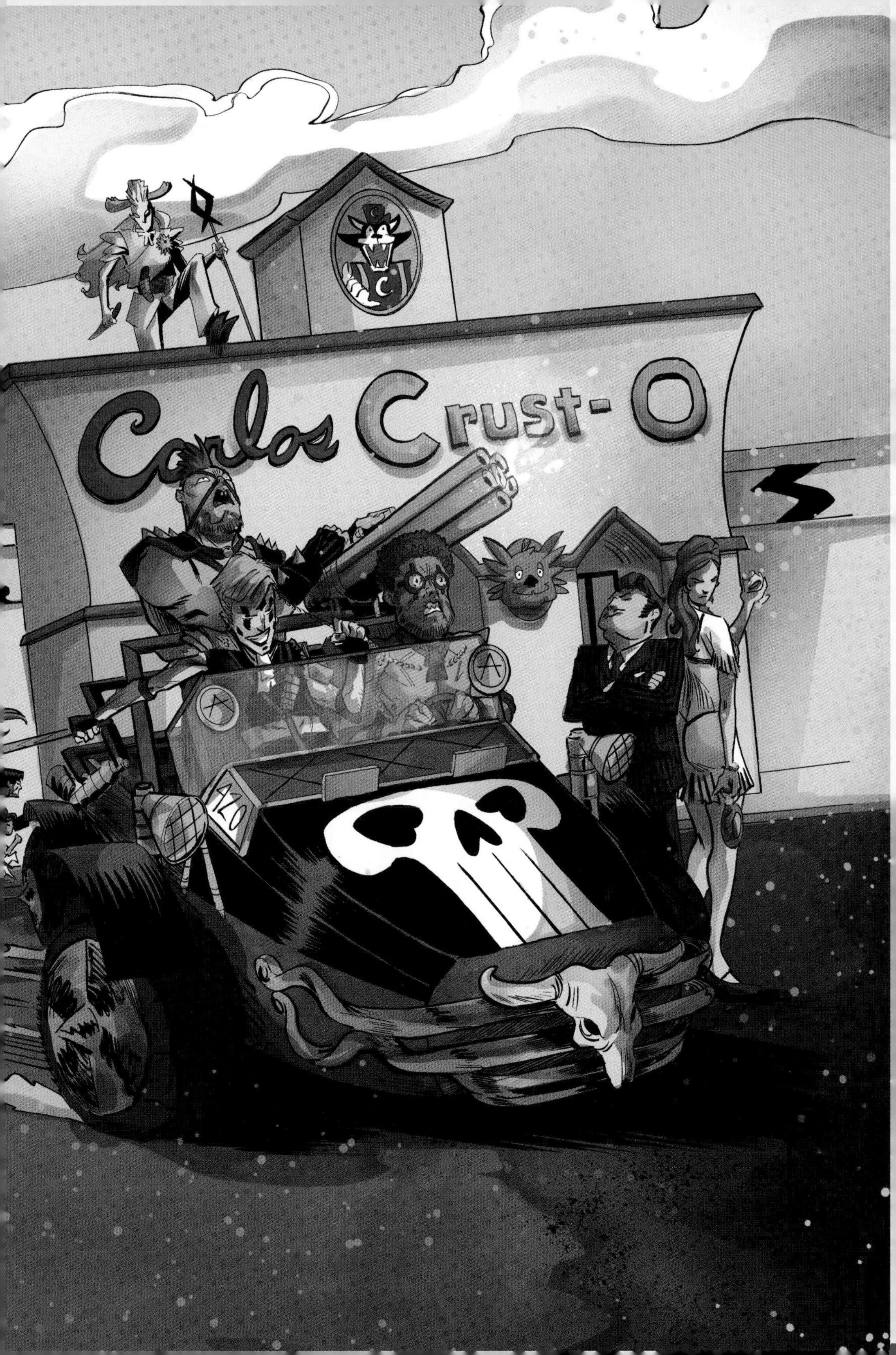
Carlos Crust-O
420

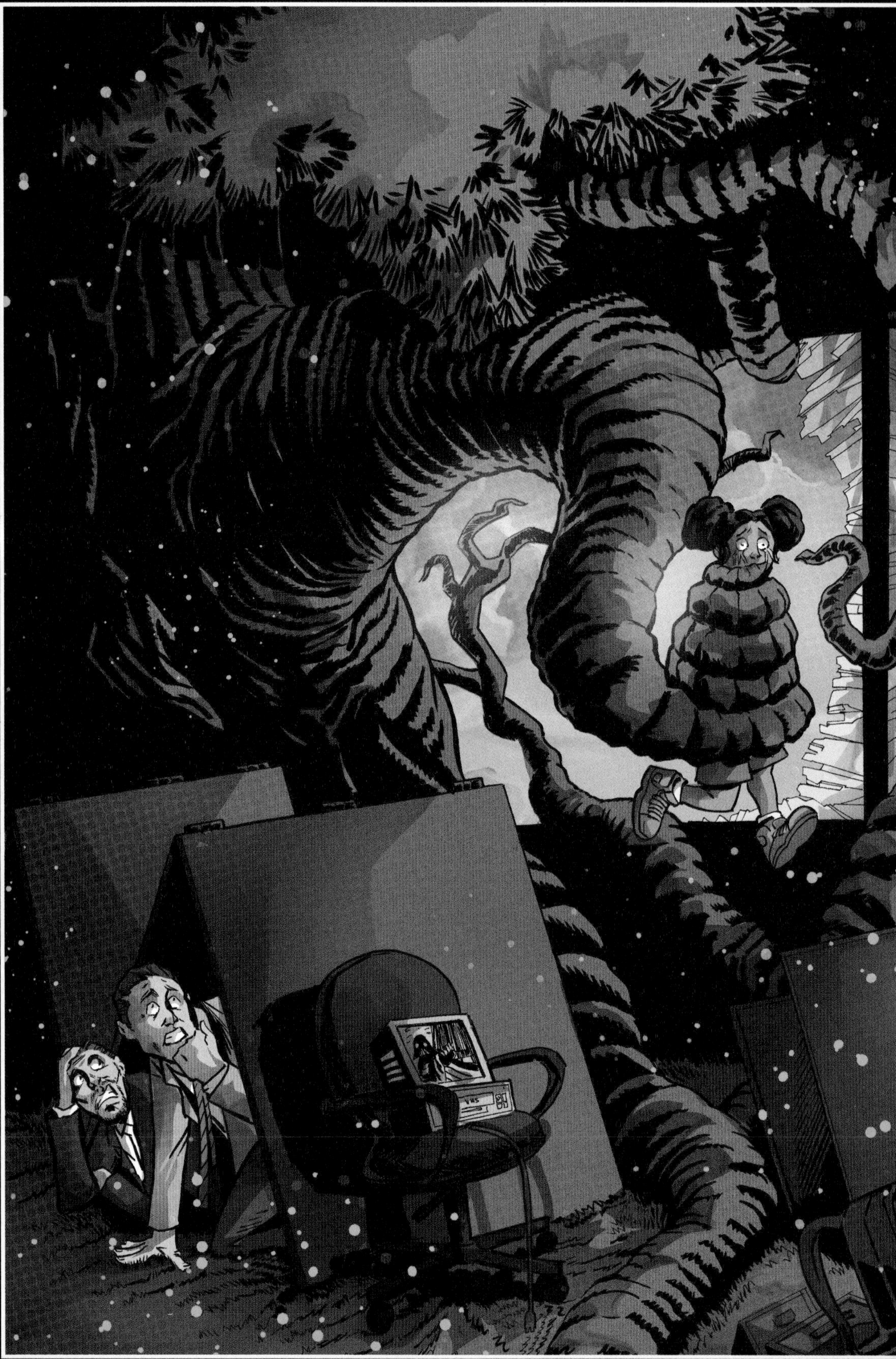

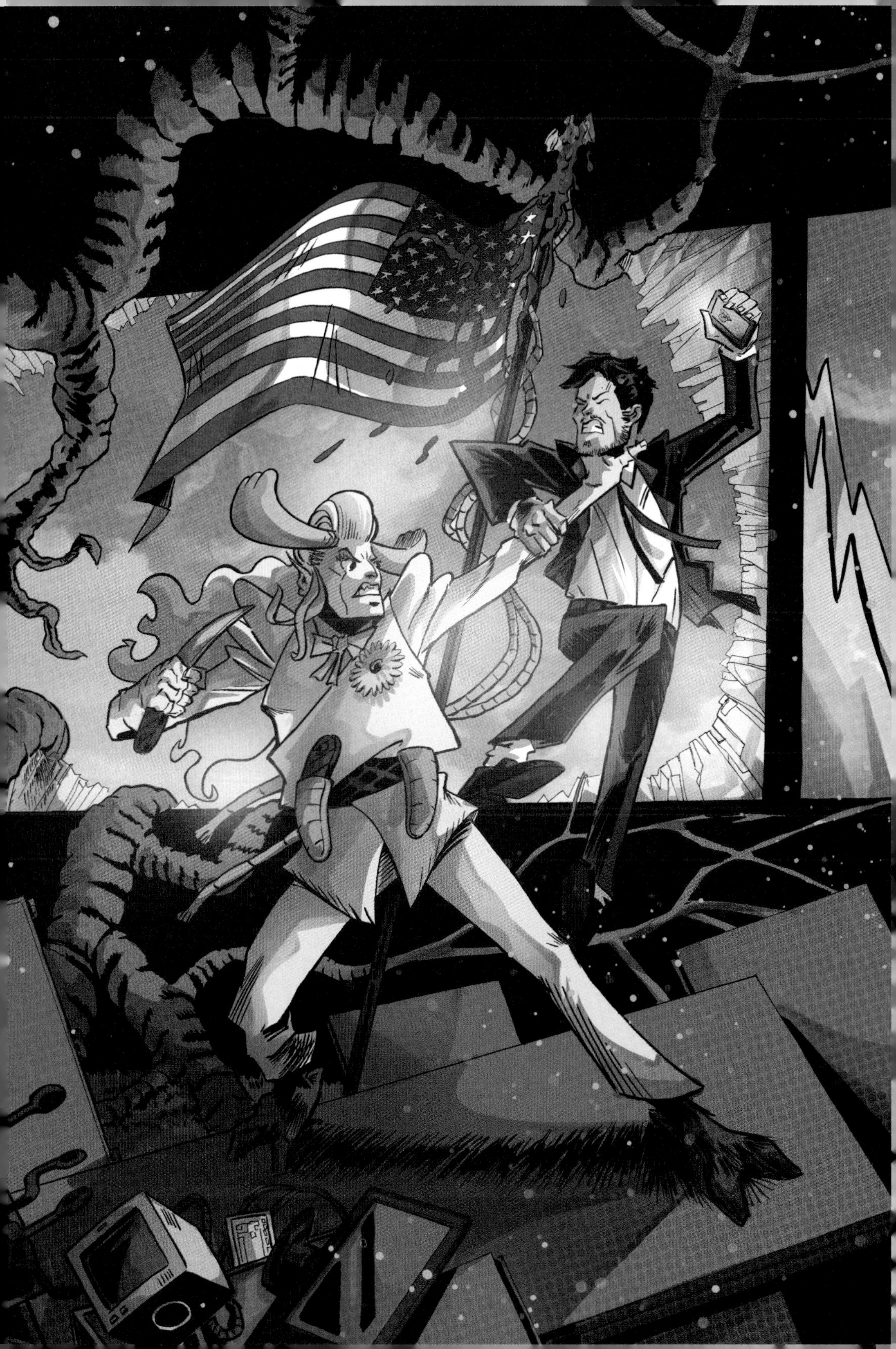

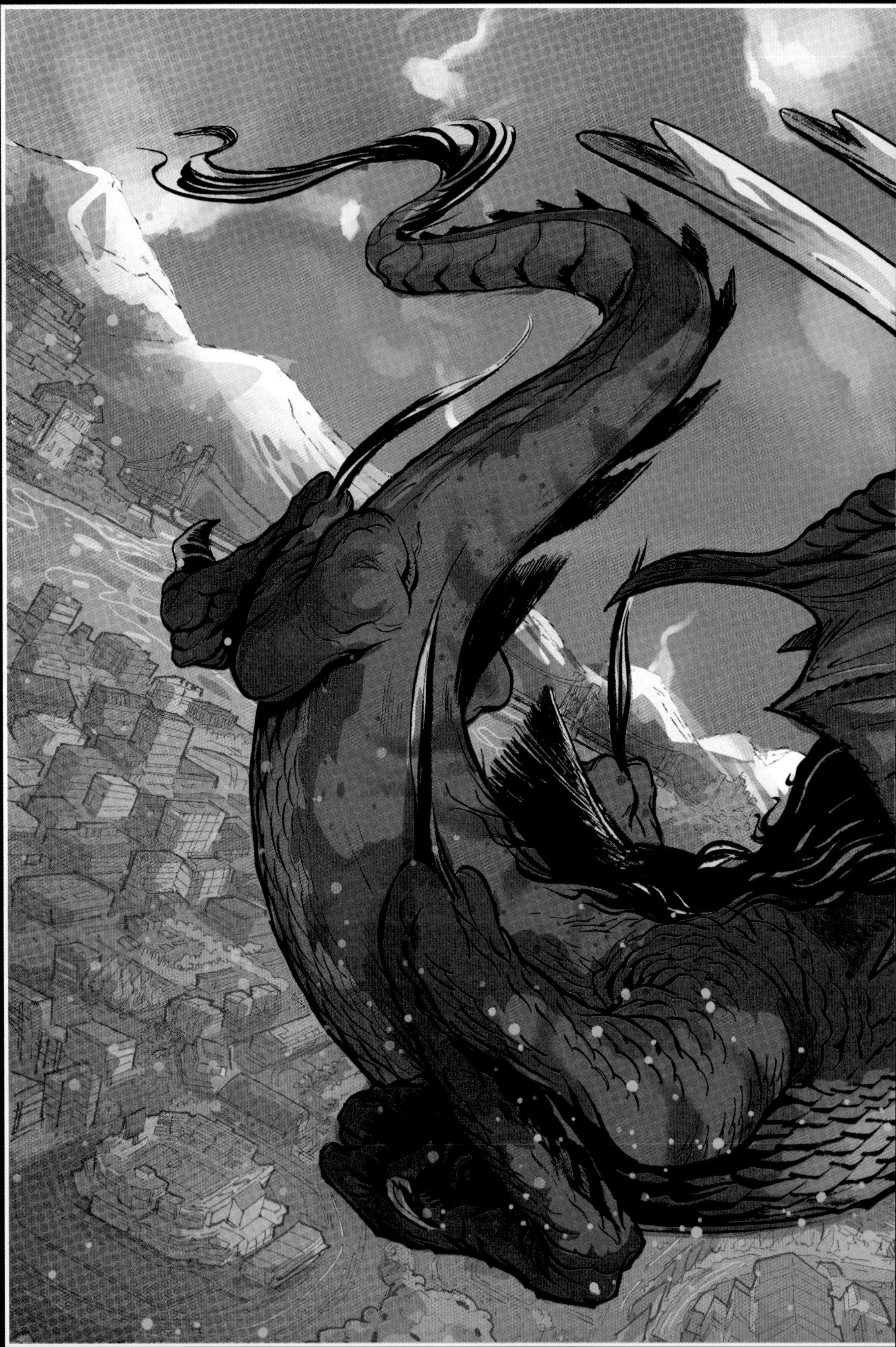

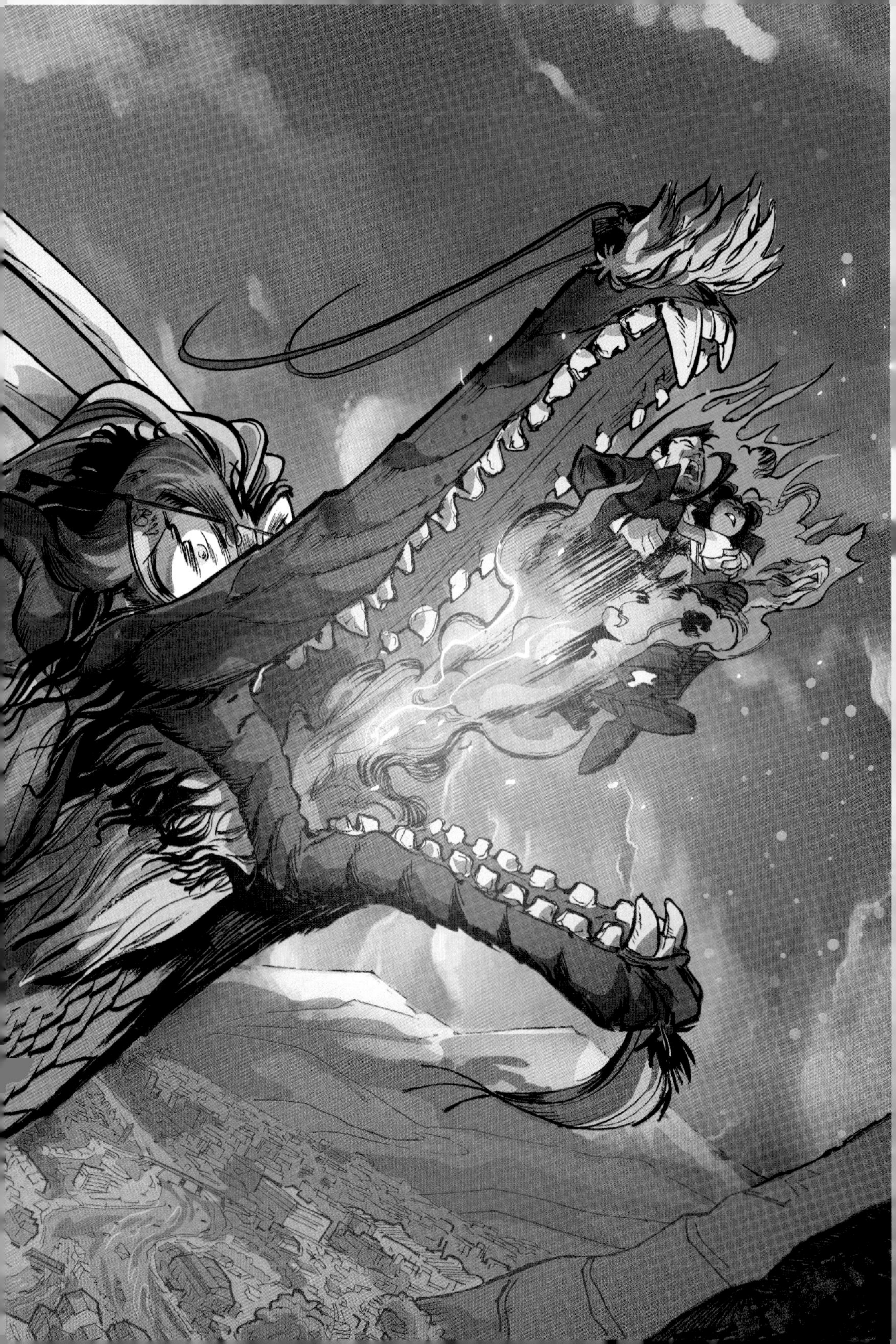

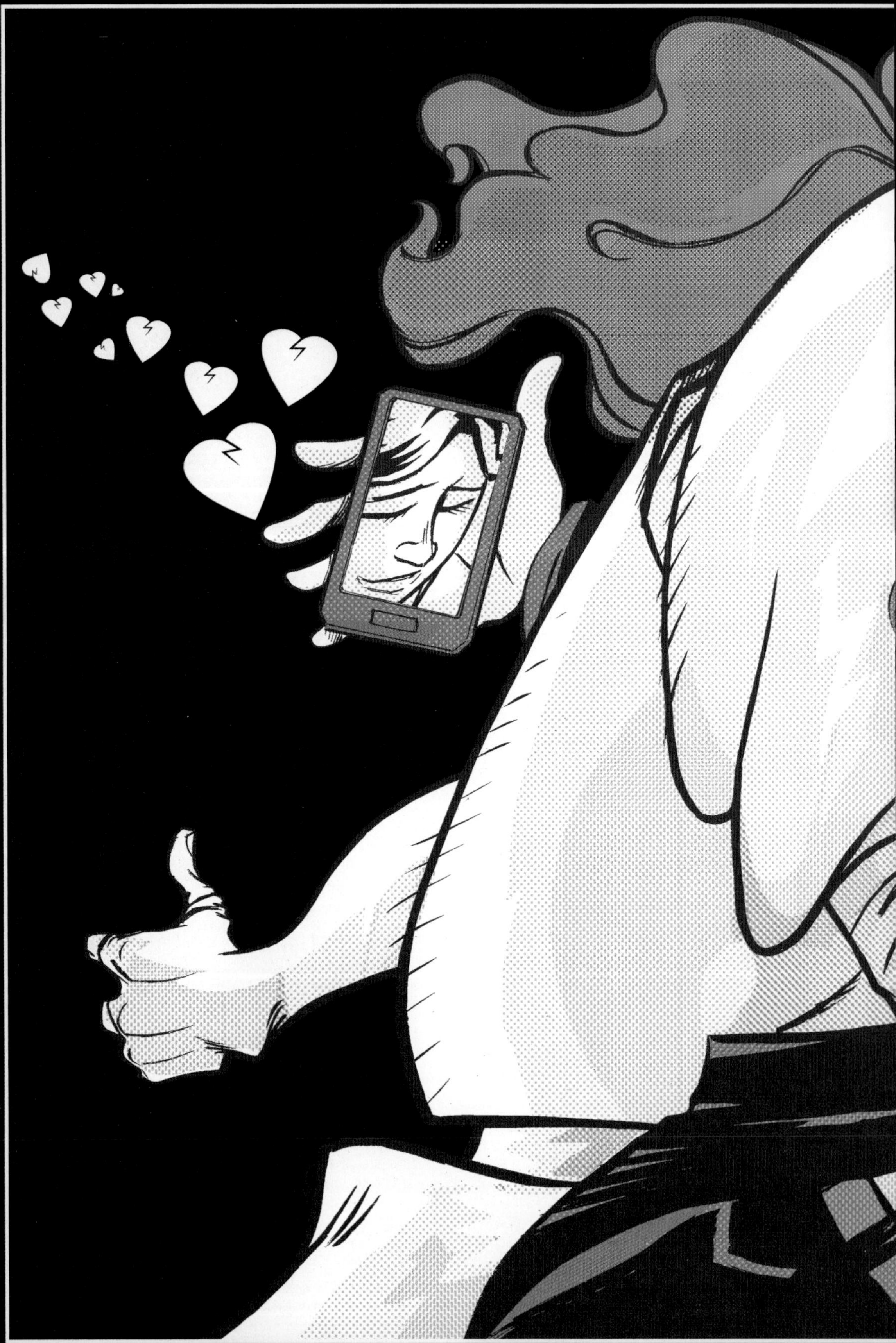

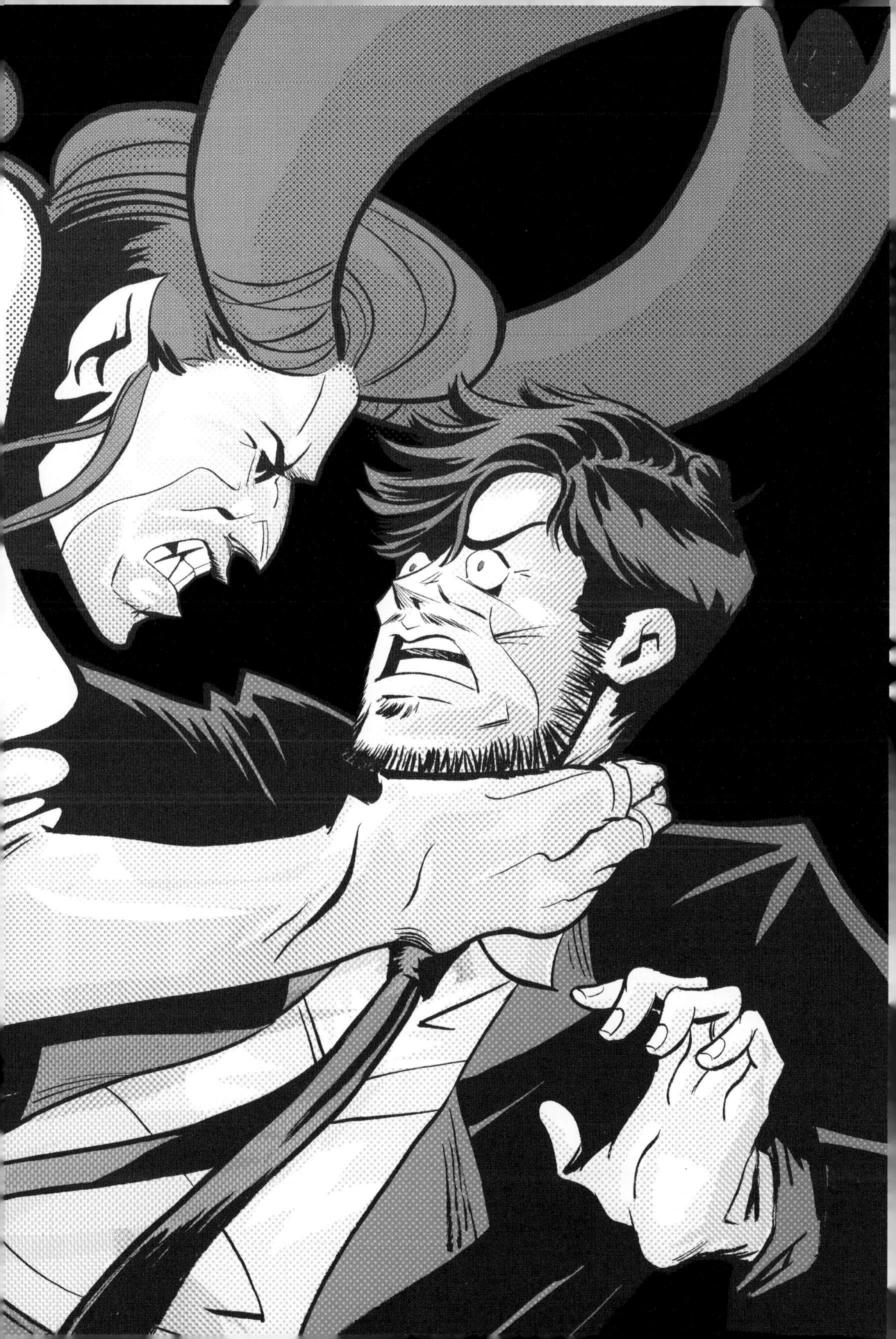

Dedicated to my mother Joni.
You cared for me more than I cared for myself, and I put you through hell for it. Through all of it we never stopped loving each other. I wish you were here now so I could hear your laugh again. I'm grateful for when you visit me in my dreams.

Also dedicated to my best friend, Shula.
I miss you, puppet. You're the best boy.

Thank you Ric, Tim, Spice, Mydu, Waggles, Crispy, Del Ducs, Orlando, C-Lew, Lo, Kim, and all the Wassels.

Love you, Pop.

Tony

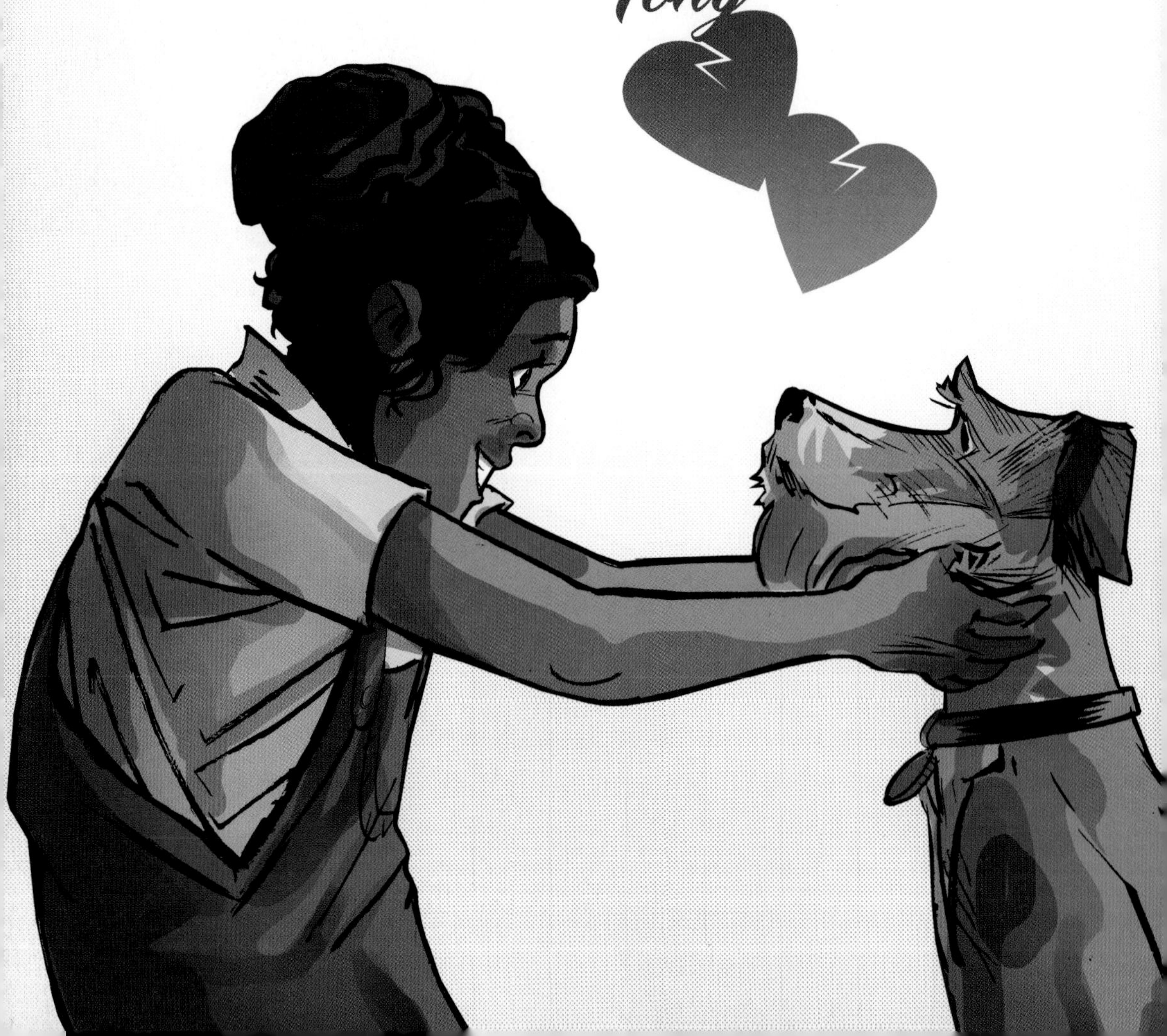